IN THE LIFE AND IN THE SPIRIT

IN THE LIFE AND IN THE SPIRIT

Homoerotic Spirituality in African American Literature

MARLON RACHQUEL MOORE

SUNY PRESS

Published by State University of New York Press, Albany

Printed in the United States of America

For information, contact State University of New York Press, Albany, NY
www.sunypress.edu

Production by Jenn Bennett
Marketing by Michael Campochiaro

Library of Congress Cataloging-in-Publication Data

Moore, Marlon Rachquel, 1971–
In the life and in the spirit : homoerotic spirituality in African American literature / Marlon Rachquel Moore.
pages cm
Based on the author's thesis (doctoral)—Univeristy of Florida.
Includes bibliographical references and index.
ISBN 978-1-4384-5408-5 (paperback : alk. paper)
ISBN 978-1-4384-5407-8 (hardcover : alk. paper) EISBN 978-1-4384-5409-2 (e-book)
1. American literature—African American authors—History and criticism. 2. American literature—20th century—History and criticism. 3. Homosexuality in literature. 4. Spirituality in literature. 5. Christianity in literature. I. Title.
PS153.N5M663 2014
810.9'896073--dc23
2014002129

10 9 8 7 6 5 4 3 2 1

My challenge to African Americans is to engage seriously and critically the relationship between Christianity and homosexuality in the same faithful way that we have typically offered a critical engagement of Christianity and race.
—Horace Griffin, "Toward a True Black Liberation Theology"

Sex is often a bodily path leading us to other dimensions of existence. It is a profound expression of wholeness [,] for spirit can be encountered in the erotic and the erotic in the spirit—they flow in and out of each other.

—Elias Farajaje-Jones, "Holy Fuck"

To be fully liberated, we have to move beyond transgression toward creativity, responsibility, sexual ownership, and sexual authority.

—Donna Weir-Soley, *Eroticism, Spirituality, and Resistance in Black Women's Writings*

Let go of your mother's God. Embrace the divine in your life as it reveals itself to you.

—Marlon Rachquel Moore, my liberation theology

Contents

Preface

Contemporary religious and political discourses still, by and large, assume a mutually exclusive binary in which "people of faith" are set apart from gay/lesbian communities. This paradigm assumes an antagonism that situates queer or non-normative sexual identities in the inferior ideological position. The discourses are diverse and deeply embedded across U.S. cultural institutions. Churches of various denominations, for example, conduct exorcisms to rid believers of the "homosexual demon" and some offer "reparative therapies" intended to alleviate desire or, at minimum, curb undesirable behaviors. Exodus International, from 1976 to 2013, for example, was the most famous and expansive Christian ministry dedicated to helping people find "freedom from homosexuality" through its religious transformation program. The following is an excerpt from the organization's "Statement on Homosexuality":[1]

> Exodus upholds heterosexuality as God's creative intent for humanity, and subsequently views homosexual expression as outside of God's will. Exodus cites homosexual tendencies as one of many disorders that beset fallen humanity. Choosing to resolve these tendencies through homosexual behavior, taking on a homosexual identity, and involvement in the homosexual lifestyle is considered destructive, as it distorts God's intent for the individual and is thus sinful.

Even when Exodus International acknowledges that a gay person can be "truly Christian" if he is a believer in the doctrine, it undermines that assertion with another: "However, if someone pursues homosexual involvement and refuses to acknowledge this as sin, it's valid to humbly question whether their commitment to Christ is genuine." Clearly, from their perspective, one cannot be both (homo)sexually active and "committed" to Christianity.

In law and politics, activists and lawmakers of various religious and political ilk invoke the religious underpinnings of their policy decisions as they assert that allowing same-sex marriage devalues and sullies the sanctity of heterosexual marriage.[2] These heterosupremacist beliefs have been codified in state and federal legislation, most notoriously in the 1996 Defense of Marriage Act and California's 2009 Proposition 8.[3] One does not have to rely on religious declarations to locate a common (though disputed) discourse on the deplorable nature of homosexuality. Homosexuality-as-destructive rhetoric figures prominently in the U.S. military's seventeen-year ban on homosexual acts, commonly called the Don't Ask, Don't Tell Policy (DADT).[4] DADT dictates, in part, that self-identified homo/bisexual servicepeople are allowed to serve as long as they do not engage in homosexual sex acts, or convey their sexual orientation through public statements or acts. Cultural critic Judith Butler has shown that DADT makes clear the mere utterance of the words "I am a homosexual" is a powerful speech act, a self-definition deemed so offensive and contagious that it constitutes homosexual conduct and a sexual propensity, which endangers the very stability of military culture (107–108). That is, to express oneself in any nonhetero manner is a violation of the law and justification for one's expulsion from membership in the military community. Like anti-gay churches, the federal law institutionalizes and normalizes homophobia and les/bi/gay/queer self-loathing.

All of this says that for a person whose sexual activity is not strictly heterosexual, or whose desires, sexual identity, and/or family structure is not heteronormative, the negative effect of being considered *evil* or *unnatural* can be profound and totalizing. Some people internalize this negative image and seek ways to escape the despised identity or stigmatized aspects of their life; others struggle against such polarizations and work to facilitate new paradigms and forge new freedoms. One way in which writers engage in this freedom struggle is through imaginative literature. Writers often negotiate their own oppression and those of others with whom they sympathize by endorsing perspectives that revise the structures and strictures by which the oppression is forged and perpetuated. In this book I set out to target responsive efforts in literature to cast off the culturally entrenched negative classifications described earlier and which aim to refigure the relationships among faith, religion, spirituality, and queer sexuality. With this motif, *In the Life and in the Spirit* converses with other relatively recent critical engagements with illustrations of the spiritual in fiction by black writers. While I was conducting this research, several important volumes of criticism and a series of essays were published, the presence of which reveals the complexity and diversity of primary sources and, simultaneously, affirms the need for more queer critical readings and for a focus on sexually queer subjects.

An important set of ideas emanate from essays by Melvin Rahming who coined the term *spirit-centered* as a way to describe stories that foreground human interaction with spiritual forces. In his 2004 essay, "Theorizing Spirit," Rahming determines that the surge in production of spirit-centered fiction necessitates a reconsideration of how critics think about this kind of work. He expresses concern that traditional critical approaches lack interrogational depth when confronted with the "non-Western concepts of reality" (2) particular to Africana fiction. What we need, he contends, is a new framework, a "critical theory of spirit" that allows us to centralize the role of spirit in the evaluation of a work of art such as this. He further clarifies this methodology in a subsequent essay, titled "Reading Spirit":

> By "spirit-centered methodology" I mean to imply a critical discussion that takes its ideological cue, ironically, from aspects of the work that subordinate ideological, even aesthetic, considerations to spiritual intent. Thus, the critical exploration of spirit-centered works anchors itself, like the work, in a paradigm of spirit—that is, in a cosmology that assumes, again like the work, the organic interrelatedness of all things in the universe. Because of the infinite nature of spirit and the inexhaustible avenues to spiritual experience, such an approach is ultimately not in the service of discrete philosophical and aesthetic constructs, although it may well call to mind these contextualized considerations. For the same reason, the spirit-centered approach cannot be prescribed: at best, it can only be described. Thus, the methodology of spirit-centered criticism is implicit in the actual attempt to explore avenues by which the text conveys its spiritual matrix and yields up the inseparability of its parts as they engage and contribute to the reader's appreciation of the work's spiritual purpose. The

> ultimate aim of spirit-centered criticism, then, is to expose some of the means by which the text engages and potentially enriches the spirit of the reader. (n. p.)

He models the theory in his readings of novels by Elizabeth Nunez, Erna Brodber, and Garfield Linton (in separate essays), but points to the abundance of such novels across the African Diaspora, including those by Toni Morrison, Earl Lovelace, Paule Marshall, Gabriel Garcia Marquez, and Nurridin Farrah, to bolster his claim.[5] I return to Rahming's ideas in my discussion of Becky Birtha's short story in Chapter Five.

Recent book-length studies further reveal the breadth and depth of these (artistic and critical) spiritual undertakings. Judylyn Ryan makes the author/director's spiritual agenda an intricate part of the discussion in *Spirituality as Ideology in Black Women's Film and Literature* whereby she highlights the African cultural retentions in poetry, autobiography, novels, short silent films and Hollywood features directed and/or authored by black women of the Americas, Caribbean nations, and continental Africa in the 1980s and 1990s. Using Peter Paris's germinal text, *The Spirituality of African Peoples*, she is able to identify the ways in which traditional African cosmologies and societal beliefs are conveyed or employed for the spiritual enrichment of black audiences. Essentially, she argues that black women authors perform, variably, as priests, conjure workers, and healers as they preach and/or enact a "life-affirming ideology" (Ryan 5) through writing and filmmaking. Of the eleven artists in Ryan's study, two feature lesbian characters in their work: Julie Dash and Ntozake Shange. James Coleman asserts, in his monograph, *Faithful Vision: Treatments of the Sacred, Spiritual, and Supernatural in Twentieth-Century African American Fiction*, that spiritual beliefs, although varied in degree and application, are fundamental and persistent in black culture. This "faithful vision," as Coleman defines it, is the spiritual agency that allows African Americans to manage their oppression and is expressed particularly through the syncretization of Voodoo/Hoodoo with Christianity. The issue of homosexuality, when it appears, is discussed only in terms of its biblical prohibition. Similarly, Tuire Valkeakari's examination of Christian-inflected signification in *Religious Idiom and the African American Novel, 1952–1998* gives a modicum of consideration to the appearance of LGBT characters. Neither Coleman nor Valkeakari completely avoid the presence of homosexuality in their primary sources, but neither is it in the design of their projects to make that desire, or the erotic more generally, a significant factor in the conclusions they draw.

Donna Weir-Soley, on the other hand, does make eroticism a central concern in her persuasive treatise on the interdependence of spiritual and sexual fulfillment in literary works across the African Diaspora. The premise of *Eroticism, Spirituality, and Resistance in Black Women's Writings* is that Western cosmology assumes a disconnect between the body and the mind, and the physical and the spiritual, and this assumption has, historically, disrupted black women's ability to properly identify with these parts of themselves. The author says that black women resist these false binaries in their art through narrative strategies that constitute a "liberating poetics of eroticism." We can find in their literature, she argues, illustrations of a restorative African spirituality: a "merger between the sexual and the spiritual [which is] a political act, an act of recovery that can potentially restore the black woman's sense of wholeness" (Weir-Soley 41). However, there is no mention of same-sex erotics or lesbian sexual fulfillment in her study. This cursory glance at current publications confirms how fertile and vast the terrain is when one contemplates the structure and function of religious rhetoric or the dramatization of spirituality in black cultural production. Yet, as I asserted earlier, LGBTQ sexuality remains, at best, marginalized in these contemplations.

Although book-length treatments of spirituality in African American literature have not been overly concerned with homoeroticism, broader-focused studies have broached the subject.[6] Particularly, *Reclaiming the Sacred: The Bible in Gay and Lesbian Culture*, an essay collection edited by a scholar of seventeenth-century British literature, Raymond-Jean Frontain, has blazed a path in its concentration on the King James Bible's influence on European and American literatures. *Reclaiming the Sacred* "illustrate[s], first, how gay writers transfigure biblical tropes to undermine what is traditionally used for homophobic purposes [and] Second, they show how biblical texts that admit or even invite the possibility of a homoerotic reading have been co-opted by orthodox tradition and how they can be reappropriated by gay writers and artists" (Frontain 1). Frontain's collection is foundational in its focus on the revisionist, appropriative, and subversive aspects of authors' engagements with religious texts in European and American lesbian and gay literatures. It does not, however, include any analysis of writing by black authors. So this book fills a critical gap and extends our view into the intellectual and artistic legacy of African

American literature that overtly engages spirituality, secular ethics, and/or theology.

I began this project with three goals: (1) to draw attention to the frequency with which black LGBT or queer-identified writers, artists, activists, and ministers critique and engage the particularly anti-homosexual rhetoric in mainstream Christian discourses; (2) to identify the ways they reclaim their access to sacredness and resist the common thematics of self-loathing; (3) and to highlight those works that most explicitly and extensively tie homoerotic energies to spiritual modalities as a site of empowerment. I endeavored, ultimately, to illuminate various ways black artists *resist the notion* that the queer and the sacred are at spiritual odds. As I began to locate African American cultural production that synthesizes salvation and homosexuality, I realized that the net I had cast was way too wide. Articulations and manifestations of queer spirituality are visible across the spectrum of cultural production: musicians, poets, filmmakers, and other performance/visual artists provide fertile soil for the growth of this research. Also, pastors, such as Tonyia Rawls and Michael Beckwith, and theologians, such as Irene Monroe, give speeches and sermons, and lead ceremonies that are important avenues into black consciousness, identity, and queer sexuality. So, by the time the manuscript was submitted as a polished dissertation, the scope was whittled down to a more manageable examination of fiction—with some backward glances to previous periods—published in the twentieth century (1963–1999).

I also quickly realized that queer spirituality in African American literature is not narrowly focused on the Judeo-Christian tradition—a state of affairs that directly reflects the diversity of African American people. While I do present an array of beliefs through my selection of texts, this book is not exhaustive or representative of the fullness of said diversity. I have scratched the surface just enough to deepen our understanding of African American subjectivity as expressed through imaginative fiction. The broader claims and purposes of this study are that African American LGBTQ literature contributes vigorously to the more general cultural debate regarding the "place" of sexuality in religious discourse and, unsurprisingly, continues to build on the appropriative and intertextual (signifying) tradition of the canon.[7] Although there are moments of crises in the narratives I selected, I intentionally avoided storylines that meditate on the burden of the closet, or whose overarching project is to narrate the coming out story and/or the physical homophobic violence that often results from the revelation.[8] The telling of those kinds of stories remains an important aspect of the struggle against the normalization of homophobia and heterosexism, but they are overrepresented in LGBTQ studies discourse. My goal is to highlight other storytelling avenues in LGBTQ literature, which produce anti-homophobic resistance and textual explorations of erotic, pleasure-based spiritual strivings. And because African American artists commonly create queer-affirming texts that depict a pro-sex, pro-erotic approach to notions of sacredness, religious rituals, and/or spiritual endeavors, I aim to begin clarifying some of the characteristic strategies and claims they make when they do so in fiction.

Acknowledgments

This book began as a dissertation project at the University of Florida. So I must first thank my dissertation advisors for their instrumental guidance in harnessing and honing my initial idea of "queering the soul": L. H. Stallings (funk-knowledgist extraordinaire), Kevin Quashie, Kim Emery, Tace Hedrick, and Stephanie Y. Evans. I also send my deepest gratitude to those who guided me in unofficial capacities: Charles Nero and Mark Reid. All of your input has shaped this work in some capacity but the final product is mine and I am as responsible for its flaws and missteps as I am in any claim to its contributions to the field. While this journey has mostly been one I've had to undertake in the quiet of my office or amid the hushed bustle of coffee shops, this work alone could never have sustained me. I am grateful for the spiritual and intellectual nest that was formed in graduate school and, if we have our way, will be cultivated for the rest of our lives: Marlo David, Darius Bost, Angelique Nixon, and Nicole Banton. Thank you for always valuing my ideas; it has taught me to do the same. I send my deepest love to the biological nest: my mother, Quintine Harrison; siblings Joyce Carol Holmes, Charlotte Moore, Tina Harrison Webber, George Harrison, Mark Davis, and Alfred Harrison; sisternieces Amanda Moore Ross and Kimberly Moore; godchild Darian Robinson; and all whose names I did not mention here. I am because we are. Jeffrey Adams, you will always be the Langston to my Zora. For the Othermothers, Valerie Brooks-Clark, Edna Adams, and Pamela Hinkle: in each your own way, you have kept me fed and protected while I loved in and out of doorways. My soul is satisfied. To my "number one fan," Sherese Hinkle, words will never be enough to capture the splendor, toil, and tenderness of the life we make together, but I hope thank you and I love you (fa real and fa life) will do for now. No matter how high I get, I'll still be looking up to all of you.

The illustration, "Orgy Under the Cross," by Richard Bruce Nugent is used with the permission of Thomas Wirth. Lyrics from "I Believe I'll Run On," written by Joe Ligon, are reprinted with the permission of Skinny Zach Music. Chapter Two is an expanded version of an essay that was published in *African American Review* under the title "Black Church, Black Patriarchy, and a 'Brilliant Queer': Competing Masculinities in Langston Hughes' Blessed Assurance" 2008 by Marlon Rachquel Moore. The evolution of some of my ideas in Chapter Four are visible in the following previously published essays: "NonMonogamous Bisexuality as the Practice of Spiritual Freedom in *The Color Purple*" 2011 by Marlon Rachquel Moore, published in *Sexuality, Religion, and the Sacred: Bisexual, Pansexual and Polysexual Perspectives*, edited by H. Sharif Williams and Lorraine Hutchinson (Routledge Press); and "God Is (a) Pussy: The Pleasure Principle and Homospirituality in Shug's Blueswoman Theology" (2008) by Marlon Rachquel Moore in *Dialogue 5: Alice Walker's The Color Purple*, edited by Kheven LaGrone (Rodopi Press).

CHAPTER ONE

Toward a Genealogy of Black Queer Spirituality

This project began as a search for James Baldwin's literary progeny. In my graduate studies of African American literature, Baldwin's name inevitably surfaced in any discussion of homosexuality because his debut novel, *Go Tell It On the Mountain* (1953), is transitional in the canon in that it places same-sex desire squarely within black religious experience, and also because of the overt depictions of (sometimes interracial) bisexual and homosexual behaviors throughout his oeuvre. According to the lore, Baldwin, the self-proclaimed "disturber of the peace," blazed a new trail when he infused religious elements into portrayals of (homo) sexual ecstasy. Well, I wondered, who followed him? Baldwin scholarship notwithstanding, critical investigations into this specific trope are scarce. So this somewhat genealogical project grew from the following questions: Who since Baldwin has written about the ways black LGBT people think of themselves in relation to notions of the sacred, God, and the afterlife? To what ends do other fiction writers attempt to disentangle (or further delineate) the knotty dilemma of the black, sexually queer, Christian-identified subject? In what ways do black writers who identify as queer, lesbian, gay, or bisexual attend to the intersection of spirituality and same-sex eros? The first answer I found was that Baldwin is not the patriarch I believed him to be.

Richard Bruce Nugent belongs at the beginning of this genealogy for two significant reasons. First, he is important to a discussion about homoeroticism in the African American literature because his lyrical, experimental narrative, "Smoke, Lilies, and Jade" (1926), is credited as the first expression of overt black male homosexuality in the canon. Second, the

1970 publication of Nugent's short story, "These Discordant Bells," in the NAACP publication, *Crisis*, connects him directly to the black queer spiritual tradition introduced by this book. The story originated within a series he called "Bible Stories," which, as a unit, appropriates the gospels of the Christian bible (narratives surrounding the birth, life, and death of Jesus) in order to imagine the homoerotic possibilities in Jesus' ministry. Because Nugent's stories briefly include a single black character, I do not analyze his work in the main chapters of this book. This makes his legacy is no less important. Thus, I take some time to expound a bit here on how he participates in the tradition.

Nugent, a painter, sketch artist, poet, short story author, dancer, and novelist, was born in 1906 into a light-skinned, or "blue-veined," socially elite African American family in Washington D.C. Although he was not secretive about his sexual affinity for men in his private life or in his writing, Nugent published poetry, artwork, and short stories under the pseudonym "Richard Bruce" to protect his family's reputation within their social circle. "Smoke, Lilies, and Jade," his best known work, was published as part of an artistic rebellion undertaken with his closest friends and collaborators at the time, which included Langston Hughes, Aaron Douglas, Zora Neale Hurston, and Wallace Thurman. They were the self-named "Niggerati," the young, emergent intellectual and creative voices of the 1920s who were avowedly determined to resist the conservative politics of representation, called the New Negro ideology, espoused by the well-connected older generation of intellectuals, namely W.E.B. Du Bois, James Weldon Johnson, and Alain Locke.[1] Although he was among like-minded artists in the Niggerati, according to his contemporaries, Nugent stood out as the "most colorful and sensational member" (Perry, qtd in Nugent 19) of the cohort. His effeminate mannerisms and openness about same-sex attractions in his work made him a problematic representative of the race. Additionally, the themes of multiracial identity, nudity, and erotic sexuality figure prominently in his visual art and writing. These artistic choices placed him outside the New Negro ideology's narrowly defined blackness—well, these choices plus his affinity for certain European aesthetics[2]—and cost him publication opportunities and, for a while, his rightful place in history.[3] Eventually, Thomas Wirth, Nugent's literary executor, would recuperate Nugent's legacy in published essays, and by creating a website dedicated to his life and work, and through the 2002 publication of Nugent's "lost" manuscript, *Gentleman Jigger*, a *roman á clef* based on his experiences during the Harlem Renaissance. Nugent's novel provides an alternative narrative to Wallace Thurman's *Infants of the Spring* (1932) and Langston Hughes' memoir, *The Big Sea* (1940), in its depiction of upper class Harlemites who "live sexually on the sharply transgressive edge of their culture" (Rampersad,"Foreword" ix). Wirth also edited *Gay Rebel of the Harlem Renaissance: The Collected Works of Richard Bruce Nugent*, which was published in 2005. The sketch "Orgy Under the Cross" (Figure 1) and the remaining extant "Bible Stories" are published for the first time in it.

The short story that establishes Nugent as a contributor to the literary epistemology of black queer spirituality is the first story in the series, "Beyond Where the Star Stood Still," which provides the premise and context for subsequent stories. In it, Nugent infuses homoerotic attraction into the biblical tale of the magi, alternately known as the "three wise men" and the "three kings," which travel to bestow on the newborn Jesus gifts of gold, frankincense, and myrrh. One of the magi, King Casper, an Ethiopian, is the sole black character in the series. He absconds with King Herod's "most beautiful and most beloved" catamite, Carus, after the boy reveals Herod's murderous intent toward the newborn Jesus. Their relationship is the focus of the second story in the series, "The Now Discordant Song of Bells," in which King Caspar attempts to instruct the young boy in theological matters. Carus seizes the opportunity to express his homoerotic attraction and romantic desire through philosophical wordplay. When King Caspar asserts, "God is love," Carus signifies by inverting the words and thus expanding the axiom's meaning to include his desires:

> [Carus:] "Ah, true. Love is God."
>
> Caspar turned his head to view the boy before saying, "Thou hast not heard me."
>
> And Carus, desiring to see the full lips move more and reveal the great blunt teeth, argued, "but thou thyself hath said, Love is God."
>
> And Caspar answered, "No, Carus. That God is love."
>
> "And yet, Caspar, I can only understand that it is as I have said. *If one is the other, is not the other the one?*
>
> "[...] Thou art allowing thy words to use thee, Carus."
>
> And Carus had desire to note the contrast his [white] hand would offer on Caspar's ebony one, but, sitting still and childly, continued saying, "But only that thou mayest know, Caspar, that *thou awakes God in me.*"

> "I awaken God in thee?" Caspar raised himself to his elbow and gazed at the lad, for there was that in Carus' voice that he did not understand. He questioned, "Thou meanest, I awaken love?"
>
> Carus concealed his excitement at the unconscious awakening in Caspar's voice, shown in its tone rather than in the question. And Carus replied as simply as before, "Is it not as thou art teaching me, Caspar?"
>
> And Caspar answered, "Thou must not make little of my sayings, Carus, when I speak with seriousness to thee." Carus was pleased with the look in Caspar's eye and the unknowing entreaty in his voice. For Carus had seen like signs before and did not know that Caspar was in truth a simple man. So he was bold beneath his childly innocence as he asked, "Is it light speech to say I love thee?" And Caspar, in his earnest zeal, placed a hand over Carus' hand where it lay on the sand, and his speech was impetuous, "But see thou, Carus, the love of which thou speakest is an active thing, and that of which I teach thee is a name." (127–128, italics added)

Carus is not a passive student; his insistence that he "can only understand that it is as I have said" is an outright refusal to limit the interpretive possibilities of the meanings of love and God. Essentially, Carus argues for a spiritual principle, which means *the feeling of love is a supreme state of being* or that *love is the reigning emotion.* He filters the teacher's message through the lens of his lived truth and offers it back to the king as a testimony: "Where there is love, there is God." Thusly, he transforms a cornerstone theological principle into a romantic confession and an interpretation of the divine energies that connect and draw humans to each other. His irreverent inversion, "Love is God," subverts the conformist limitations of the dominant paradigm; yet, it neither rejects Casper's God nor refuses Carus's own sense of self.[4] In this way, the exchange is a blueprint for homoerotic spirituality. Nugent's contributions to black queer spirituality can also be seen in his drawings; artifacts that are featured in *Gay Rebel* but are beyond the scope of this book.[5]

Although what I have produced in this book is, ultimately, a claim to a thematic kinship instead of an historical or genealogical analysis proper, the main chapters serve as the answers to the research questions I posed regarding LGBTQ spirituality in literature (the reasons for a limited focus on novels and short stories are stated in the Preface). Also, in the concluding chapter, I list additional texts that fit into this classification. So at this

Figure 1. Sketch, "Orgy Under the Cross," by Richard Bruce Nugent, date unknown. Used with permission of the Nugent estate.

point I must shift the emphasis from the artistic production of homoerotic spirituality to the interrogatory and interventionist discourses which constitute the critical community that presages and facilitates the work I do here. Let us now look toward a genealogy of black queer studies in religion and spirituality.

Before the appearance of *Gay Rebel*, Nugent's historic contributions were acknowledged in a brief overview of his life by Charles Michael

Smith, titled "Bruce Nugent: Bohemian of the Harlem Renaissance," in the groundbreaking collection, edited by Joseph Beam, *In the Life: A Black Gay Anthology. In the Life* appeared in 1986 and is now a time capsule of artistic and critical voices of black men-loving men in the era of AIDS.[6] Many of its contributors were not only responding to the absence of black representation in what was becoming a renaissance of gay male literature; some also used the opportunity to give voice to the emotional pain inflicted by black institutional ambivalence and, in many cases, those institutions' outright refusal to engage in compassionate outreach during the crucial, deadly height of the 1980s AIDS crisis. As the decade progressed, dominant discourses about the transmission of HIV became increasingly hysterical and condemning of those people who contracted AIDS, the so-called gay disease.[7] Beam's *In the Life* provides testimony of the alienation many were experiencing as black gay people in a white supremacist homophobic society.

It also delivers an important intervention into African American religious discourses in a compelling essay by Pastor James Tinney, entitled "Why a Black Gay Church?" Tinney forged a black gay-inclusive church movement when he was excommunicated from the Church of God in Christ denomination after hosting a revival for gays and lesbians that was endorsing in its tone. That experience, while painful, catapulted him onto a path of restoration, not of his individual faith to his sexuality, but one that aimed to restore his idea of the role of church to its gay believers. He founded the Faith Temple, a nondenominational fundamentalist church, in Washington D.C. Faith Temple defined itself as a culturally black sanctuary for homosexual Christians based on the following separatist principles laid out by Tinney in the essay (I consider this approach a type of restorative separatism, in the vein of Alice Walker):[8]

> The development of Black gay churches will make it possible for Black gay Christians, for the first time, to hear the gospel in their own language of the Spirit, respond to the gospel in their own ways, *and reinterpret the gospel in their own cultural context*—taking into account both race and sexual orientation at every step in this process. In a socio-political sense, this is called contextualization; in a psychological and existential sense, this is called authenticity; and in a biblical sense, this is called conversion. Whatever it is called, however, it refers to the full liberation of the total Black Gay Christian. (76, my italics)

Tinney argues that full liberation is made possible through reinterpretation and, throughout the essay, emphasizes the need to remain "truly and unquestionably Christian" through adherence to the essence of doctrine (77). In response to the mainstream forces that seek to silence or convert gay people into sexual conformists, Tinney advocates for a queer(ed) space in which a black+homosexual+Christian theology can be enacted "every step." Through this process, he imagines that the gays and straights of his denomination could reunite as equals under God. Reverend Tinney embodies what it can mean to be in the life and in the spirit and, although he died from AIDS-related health complications in 1988, his gay-affirming convictions continue to take shape in many communities.[9]

In the follow-up to *In the Life*, an anthology titled *Brother to Brother: New Writing by Black Gay Men* (1991) features the classic essay by Charles Nero, "Toward a Black Gay Aesthetic: Signifying in Contemporary Black Gay Literature." Nero assesses the heterosexism and homophobia in the most celebrated works of the African American literary canon (notably, Toni Morrison's *Beloved, Tar Baby*, and *The Bluest Eye*), and reveals how gay writers produce fictional works that revise, critique, or otherwise respond to normative representations of the black experience, including family life, marriage, slavery, and religion. In the section titled "Signifying on the Church," he points out ways Larry Duplechan's novel, *Blackbird*, signifies on Reverend Tinney's revelation that he had undergone an exorcism before being excommunicated. Nero finds that by imaginatively expanding Tinney's narrative, "Duplechan exposes an unholy alliance … [in which] the church is willing to oppress its gay people to prove its worth to the middle classes" (306). Significantly, Nero's essay and, generally, the series of black gay anthologies announce the existence of a black gay aesthetic propelled by *visibility politics*; that is, a belief in the power of literature to "render their lives visible and, therefore, valid" (290)—a politics, which, historically, has propelled much of African American cultural production.

The critical framework of this book is a fusion of theoretical and cultural perspectives and sexual discourses, namely those wrought by feminism/womanism, African American literary theory, queer theory, and lesbian/gay studies (individual texts are cited in the relevant chapters).[10] However, as a study that makes a case for understanding African American religious thought and spiritual expression as part of the ongoing struggle for sociopolitical freedom and, specifically, when I assert that a certain text constructs a "liberation theology," the arguments I make rely on a theoretical paradigm wrought from, and which is inherently conversant with, rhetorics of Black Theology. This is an important connection to make because Black Theology is a discrete subsection of the religious studies field and one that, until recently, has not been overtly connected to discourses in lesbian/gay studies or fiction studies. It has been, however, always connected to African American literature. The earliest work in this field was guided by a political investment in proving that black American Christian religions were relevant to the struggle for racial justice in the 1960s. Its emergence represents the rejection of mainstream Civil Rights–era integration politics of the contemporary moment, an intellectual posture that sought to abandon white Christian norms as they related to biblical interpretation, the role of religion in social change, and worship practices.[11] Eventually, theologians and practitioners would add sexual freedom and an interrogation into the role of pleasure to the liberation agenda as well.

As part of the cultural shift to Black Power politics in the 1960s and 1970s, seminary students and religious scholars began to affirm African American folk traditions and explore the African origins of black worship services. These scholars also searched their religious history for a tradition of political commitment to freedom. They found much historical support in literary culture, such as: Bishop Richard Allen, founder of the first independent black denomination in the United States (African Methodist Episcopal) distributed abolitionist messages in his church's pamphlet; David Walker's 1829 *Appeal to the Colored Citizens of the World* distinguishes between the pseudo-Christianity of American slavery and true Christology, which promises liberty to all believers; the claims made in the authorized biography written during her lifetime, *Harriet Tubman: Moses of Her People* (1886), that visions and prophetic messages from God were key to Tubman's success on the Underground Railroad; and the words attributed to Nat Turner in his "confession" that God led him to slay his enemies "with their own weapons" when he led the bloody uprising against white slave owners and their families. Ultimately, the proponents of Black Theology found that the struggle for political freedom has always been located in black religious expression.

Fictional literature became more relevant as the late 1970s and early 1980s marked the rising influence of the feminist movement. Black women entered seminary school in larger numbers than ever before and from them emerged Womanist Theology, an adaptation of Alice Walker's extensive definition of womanist consciousness. Their work defines a womanist liberation agenda over and against the Eurocentric, middle class focus of white feminism, as well as the male supremacist myopia of the first generation of Black Theology. Prominent voices include Renita Weems, Kelly Brown Douglas, Cheryl Sanders, Delores Williams, and Katie Canon. Womanist theologians introduced three important strategies to black religious studies: the use of women's roles in the bible to challenge conventional views of women in ministry; the advocacy of holistic theology with an emphasis on folk culture; and the use of black women's novels as primary sources for locating theological concepts (Hopkins 156). Canon, the first ordained black female Presbyterian minister (in the United States), explains the usefulness of fictional literature for religious studies: "As creators of literature [,] black women are not formally historians, sociologists, or theologians, but the patterns and themes in their writings are reflective of historical facts, sociological realities and religious convictions that lie behind the ethos and ethics of the black community" (57). Although my goal in this book is not to pinpoint specific denominational beliefs or "realities" in literature, I do ultimately work from the premise that fiction is an important resource for locating overt and implied rhetoric regarding theological and ethical matters. My research is concerned with how these arguments are constructed around black LGBTQ humanity to challenge or critique conservative religious attitudes.

Since the 1990s, religious studies discourse has moved toward radical integrations of spirituality and sexuality and, thus, has provided useful frameworks for interpreting fiction. James Cone and Gayraud Wilmore published articles in *Black Theology: A Documentary Anthology* (1993), which reject the occlusion of sexual variability, and encourage church leadership and scholars to consider the damaging effects restrictive interpretations of human sexuality have on individuals, families, and communities.[12] Michael Eric Dyson makes the case for a "theology of eroticism" (*Race Rules* 91), which, he believes, would provide a more realistic framework for people of faith. Horace L. Griffin published *Their Own Received Them Not: African American Gays and Lesbians in Black Churches* (2007) to provide, among other insights, an historical analysis of the role stigmatized black sexuality plays in the homophobic attitudes found in contemporary congregations. Working along similar lines of thought, Kelly Brown Douglas asserts in *Sexuality and the Black Church: A Womanist Perspective* (1999) that an anti-homophobic sexual discourse of resistance must come from church leadership. As if in response, Anthony Pinn and Dwight Hopkins, as co-editors, put forward essays in *Loving the Body: Black Religious Studies and the Erotic* (2004), which steer the conversation away from identitarian notions of sexuality so that the concern is with the role of pleasure in spiritual endeavors. They assert that to truly free the body, "a black liberation agenda must not only involve the restructuring of socioeconomic, political, and cultural space, it must also involve an appreciation of the body and the pleasuring of the body" (Pinn and Hopkins 6). Contributors to *Loving the Body* consider issues of (Christian) faith, desire, fantasy, and sensuality through the lenses of literary studies, biblical and pastoral studies, cultural criticism, and ethics—including an essay that begins with a meditation on the ethical concerns raised by *Say Jesus and Come to Me*, the Ann Allen Shockley novel I analyze in the fourth chapter of this book.[13]

A NOTE ON TERMINOLOGY

This is not a study of religious belief. I define *religion* as a set of beliefs regarding the existence and nature of a single or pluralistic god/creator (theology), and the perceived relationship, between that/those god(s), humanity, and the cosmos. Religion often involves traditions and narratives that delineate morality and the meaning of life for its followers. By extension, a *religious person* is one who is committed to the claims and rituals of a particular tradition. Although religion and spirituality can crisscross and conflate in the life of an individual, one as belief and the other as practice, the two can be distinguished. Using Akasha Gloria Hull's wording, I employ the term *spirituality* to refer to beliefs in and responsiveness to ethereal, permeating, ultimately positive, divine energies that connect all that exists (2). A *spiritual person*, then, is one who believes that he or she can access these divine energies through conscious engagement—physical, sensual, psychic, and ritual acts. Spirituality can be an individualized, malleable, and evolutionary relationship with one's own intuition and sense of self, the cosmos, and humanity; for spiritual engagement requires faith but is not necessarily contingent on a firm understanding of a god/creator. (That is, one can be an agnostic who believes that the precise definition and knowledge of a creator is unattainable and still maintain a spiritual practice that conveys faith in divine forces.)

So, for the purposes of this study, any characters, narrators, and plots are spiritual or, as the subtitle indicates, "in the spirit" when their thoughts, actions and outcomes reveal a reliance on the power of a spiritual realm, or the supernatural. I do not use religion and spirituality interchangeably, but spiritual beliefs and organized religions function similarly for people as lenses through which one views the self and others, life and death, the physical and metaphysical, supernaturality, sacredness, and morality. So religious themes emerge, at times, because this study is concerned with how these concepts intersect with lesbian, gay, bisexual, and transgender experiences, and identities in African American literature.

Christian belief is overrepresented in African American fiction, relative to the diversity of religious memberships across the culture; so its presence is marked in ways other organized religions are not. Readers who seek definitive connections between indigenous African or Native American religions, for example, will not find them. However, when Ann Allen Shockley's lesbian character imagines herself a Hausa queen doing a holy dance around a campfire, for example, I investigate the ways that cultural reference enacts a queering of African heritage. In other words, I do not overlook the significance when a text overtly identifies with a particular belief system. Otherwise, my main endeavor is to describe how queer spiritualities are constructed in each individual text and identify how that construction fits into the larger literary tradition. The objectives of a religious study or theological analysis are different from what I aim to achieve in this book.

I should also take some time here to briefly address the use of "queer" and "in the life" synonymously throughout this book. There are three related but somewhat divergent iterations of "queer" in the U.S. context with genealogies and connotations that intersect: queer politics, queer theory, and queer studies. The advent of queer politics is located in late 1980s lesbian and gay activist organizations, namely ACT UP and its derivatives, such as Fed Up Queers, and Queer Nation. The goals of the early queer power movement were to draw attention to the AIDS crisis and to agitate medical, government, and social institutions to work to end the disease and to care for its victims through direct action.[14] Activists committed "vigilant acts of political and cultural provocation" ("ACT UP New York") whereby they disrupted cultural institutions with acts of civil disobedience. Places such as a post office, a Catholic church service, the New York Stock Exchange, Food and Drug Administration, and the National Institutes of Health were targeted for demonstrations, which brought attention to the AIDS crisis and, often, accused the institutions of hindering progress. These activist groups represent a collective anti-normative ethos, an insurgent politics, and liberatory discourse that reclaims *queer* as a term of empowerment and collective identity that includes kink communities (such as bondage/discipline), bisexual, transgender, and intersexed populations.

For its detractors, this collectivity is its most insidious danger; despite all its positive intent, queer as a political identity can become a totalizing gesture, an effacement of the radical politics and specific concerns of the sexual minorities and marginalized communities it claims to include.[15] Nonetheless, for those invested in defamiliarizing "normal" and problematizing the status quo, queer ignites "a strident reminder of difference, perversity, and a willingness to position oneself outside of the norm" (Goldman 84). Importantly, queer politics is distinguished from the comparably more conservative, assimilationist, "we are just like you, so treat us the same as you under the law," gay rights strategies that seek acceptance from and integration into government and social institutions through marriage rights and military service, such as those embraced by Log Cabin Republicans and the Human Rights Campaign. A queer politics insists that "we are *not* like you and we *still* deserve equal human rights and equal treatment under the law."

After queer politics, queer theory has developed, despite pleas from some its earliest framers,[16] as an academic endeavor. It has emerged as an analytics with its own (intellectual) guerilla tactics: Judith Butler, Eve Sedgwick, Teresa de Lauretis, and Michael Warner are among those credited with producing queer theory's first canonical texts.[17] Each of these writers generated ideas that stand "in direct contrast to the normalizing tendencies of hegemonic sexuality [which are] rooted in ideas of static, stable sexual identities and behaviors" (Cohen, "Punks, Bulldaggers, and Welfare Queens" 23). In other words, queer theory constructs itself against the overdetermination of neatly packed sexual identities and is an approach that aims to deconstruct even the norms of "straight" and "gay" because that binary, too, participates in a taxonomy that obscures the existence of a broad spectrum of human sexual behavior. Its key assumption, arguably, is that all sexuality is socially constructed and should be examined for essentialist, unnuanced or otherwise prescriptive understandings. Such a premise facilitates discourses of desire, pleasure, and sexual practice without prioritizing a concern for qualifying markers, such as "gay" and "straight." Ultimately, then, the application of queer theory is to assume an intellectual posture that rejects or interrogates the presupposed "natural" development of established norms regarding morality and sexuality, and which works to illuminate the cultural machinations which police the boundaries of "normal."

A third iteration, also in academia, is queer studies, which is alternately called LGBTQ studies, lesbian/gay studies, or sexuality studies. Lesbian/gay studies concerns itself with the lives, histories, and cultural production of marginalized sexual behaviors, identities, and populations, and work in this field often involves the application of the other articulations of queer thought and praxis. Scholars in the field also analyze the ways cultural institutions are organized around the maintenance of heterosupremacy and homophobia. Historian Jonathan Katz's *The Invention of Heterosexuality* is an example of a text that denaturalizes "heterosexual" by tracing the changing attitudes and influences that transposed it from a descriptive medical term into a discrete identity, which now operates in everyday language as a signifier of gender and sexual norms. As Katz has shown, discursive structures aid and abet material structures. Such as in the way discursive boundaries around *hetero* were enforced with anti-vice laws, police raids, and cross-dressing fines. Meanwhile, desires and expressions not considered hetero were pushed further into the margins so that they would appear to be unusual or negligible aberrations. Also, Judith Butler's *Excitable Speech* explores racist, sexist, and homophobic language in institutions, such as the U.S. military's ban on verbalizing or otherwise expressing a lesbian, bisexual, or gay identity. She demonstrates that such policies promote the (il)logic of homophobia as a reasonable and "normal" perspective.

My use of "in the life" to discuss sexuality reflects my participation in and engagement with black queer studies, a critical formation in academia that bridges theorizations wrought from black studies and queer studies.[18] The phrase became popular in 1970s African American vernacular which functions, semantically, similarly to the (neo)colloquial "queer." It is an umbrella term that has always been used, by participating members, to refer to a life outside of respectable employment or respectable sexuality; that is, it points to extralegal economies, such as sex work and gambling houses, or underground social activities such as gay bars and drag queen culture.[19] It is the "street life" that singer Randy Crawford cautions against in her best known recording. To state, "I am in the life," in reference to sexual behavior is to say, "my gender performance, sex acts and/or desires are considered transgressive in straight culture."

While expressions of homoeroticism are my particular focus within queer- and in-the-life discourses, the phrase does not always translate to a lesbian or gay identity. Being in the life is more about *what one feels and does* and can also refer to gender nonconformity, particularly as it relates to female masculinity and male femininity.[20] To say that one is in the life is not necessarily a claim to a sexual identity; it is a claim to a community.

As a lesbian who came of age in the 1980s, *in the life* is a naming that is particularly close to my heart, as it was *the* circulating lesbian/gay signifier in my social networks at that time. Use of this phrase is part of what seems to be a universal tradition among oppressed communities that erect linguistic fences through code switching as a way to speak the unspeakable within earshot of their oppressors. It is the way folks "in the know" can ask each other if someone is potentially sexually available or to simply find out if someone is "one of us" without exposing their own or the other person's privacy to the gaze of the gender police among us. Its common usage among black people across the nation was illustrated by the emergence of *In the Life: A Black Gay Anthology* discussed earlier. Inspired by black lesbian feminist writing and activism, particularly the accomplishments of Audre Lorde and Barbara Smith, Joseph Beam, editor and contributor to the anthology, insisted that black gay literature could play an equally important political and cultural role—just by existing and being accessible to those who needed to see affirming reflections of themselves.[21] He knew that the expression "in the life" would resonate with a particularly underserved audience. Ultimately, my use of it in the title of this book is intended to invoke Beam's cultural politics and indicate my respect for his (assemblage of) groundbreaking critical and creative perspectives; to show reverence for the waymaking writer-activists and everyday theologians whose names I may never know; and to pay nostalgic homage to my lovers and friends, long lost or long found, who abide with me in life and spirit.

OVERVIEW

I make no claims to a singular or definitive black queer spiritual perspective. Rather, I propose that individual writers present their own theory of an integrated spiritual and sexual expression or experience, the prevalence of which constitutes an identifiable lineage, in the canon, of sexually inclusive and queer spiritual articulations that connect writers across generations and genres. As a literary community, these writers offer the possibility of possibilities (à la Samuel Delany). Overall, this project highlights and chronicles how their strategies of anti-homophobic resistance overlap and diverge in their depictions of blackness in the spiritual realm and, when relevant, how those depictions dovetail into broader literary concerns.

In the first two chapters, I introduce my formulation of the Gay Christian Narrative. For its congregation, the church serves as a buffer against various shades of violence members experience as racial minorities. They are reminded that God is on the side of the oppressed and that the suffering and eventual deliverance of the Israelites is a metaphor for black strivings in the United States. Church is also a space in which cultural specificities are reinforced, valued, and celebrated. Nonetheless, it is not a romantic oasis of sameness. As Cathy Cohen persuasively argues in *The Boundaries of Blackness*, rhetorical boundaries of respectability are placed around "The Black Community," which has led to institutional policies and baseline assumptions that alienate or suppress certain behaviors, identities, beliefs—and people. Gender and sexual nonconformists often experience this cultural gatekeeping as religious hate speech. For them, the church is a contradictory home space that half-affirms and half-indicts, as God is on the side of the racially oppressed but "hates the sin" of black gay/les/bi/trans people. Gay Christian Narratives reject and revise this hate speech and reclaim the sacredness of black queer bodies through biblical allusion, the revision of same-sex biblical narratives through a homoerotic lens, and the use of sacred songs to endorse and underwrite homoerotic encounters.

I launch the discussion in Chapter Two with a close reading of "Blessed Assurance," Langston Hughes' recovered tale of an effeminate teenage boy who sings a duet with his church's minister of music who is also male. It is my contention that, as the men vocalize the poetic oath from the *Book of Ruth*, a sacred text in Jewish and Christian canons, they subvert heteronormative restrictions on gender performance by, in effect, producing a lyrical drag show.

I argue in Chapter Three that James Baldwin employs many of these strategies in *Go Tell It on the Mountain*, *Just Above My Head* and in the short story, "The Outing." So, together, Chapters Two and Three make the larger argument that Gay Christian Narratives challenge the presumption that people of religious faith are inherently in tension with gay/lesbian communities. The characters, plots, dialogue, and other narrative strategies suggest that people of religious faith are *part* of gay and lesbian communities.

While Hughes and Baldwin represent the revisionist and appropriative aspects of the Gay Christian Narrative, the women writers in subsequent chapters provide a different take on the relationship between the queer subject and African American church traditions. That is not to say that these are completely separate "women's traditions," because there are Christian-identified characters in some of these stories, too. What writers in the Philosophies of the Spirit section do, overall, that is distinct, is prioritize individual truths, intuition, and folk/alternative traditions. That is, Christian doctrines and black church traditions are visible but decentralized in the larger scheme of the narratives. I begin the discussion in Chapter Four with an analysis of the iterations of *soul talk*, a term coined by Akasha Gloria Hull, and acts of sermonic seduction in Shockley's *Say Jesus and Come to Me*, and Walker's *The Color Purple*. Though they are widely divergent aesthetically, they share the perspective that the erotic, intimate sensual pleasure shared between the black women characters *is* the substance of their spiritual connection with each other, and with the planet, and with the cosmos.

In Chapter Five, I argue that Birtha crafts a neo-spirit narrative in the tradition of the ex-slave spiritual autobiography, namely that of Rebecca Cox Jackson. As she relates her human-to-spirit sexual encounters, Birtha's narrator displaces the black church's authority and position as the locus of healing and spirituality with depictions of the domestic space as the intersection of life and afterlife. By the story's end, the butch/femme romance is taking place outside of the physical body. Birtha's magical realism segues into my discussion in Chapter Six of queer spirituality in other fantasy genres.

In the third section, fantasy genres provide nontheist cosmologies that deliver new possibilities for constructing, challenging, and revising previous theological arguments and spiritual aesthetics. Octavia Butler's dystopic Earthseed series, *Parable of the Sower* and *Parable of the Talents*, follows the life and mythology of a black female preacher whose life is affected by a confluence of oppressive religious, commercial, and political regimes. Butler's protagonist is a gender-passing, gun-toting survivalist with a seductive aura reminiscent of Walker and Shockley's female minister characters. Significantly, this preacher's sermonic seduction involves butch masculinity and masochistic suffering. I find that the God-talk in her ministry is precarious under scrutiny and submit evidence that the Earthseed doctrine is actually Humanism cloaked in religious language.

Chapter Seven concludes the study as it highlights further the ways sci-fi perspectives can expand current applications of the term *spirituality*. In *The Gilda Stories*, Jewelle Gomez writes counter-hegemonic scriptures in which a lesbian vampire operates as a spirit worker among humans and who is guided by an ethos of emotional reciprocity. Gomez avoids overt theological arguments; rather, she uses fantasy/futurism to generate a spiritual aesthetic based on a love ethic between humans and vampires, and between all beings and the ecological environment.

PART I

Gay Christianity

CHAPTER TWO

Gay Christian Narrative

Langston Hughes's "Blessed Assurance"

> What gay people do, in part, when they demand that the church view them as whole persons and gay members of the body of Christ is to call attention to the bodies that gather when souls commune.
>
> —Dawn Moone, *God, Sex, and Politics: Homosexuality and Everyday Theologies*

The black church has never been a space used solely for religious worship.[1] For generations, it has also served as a cultural incubator where oppositional discourses to anti-black racism are nurtured and sustained. Scholarship in Black Theology teaches us that, from the earliest days of North American slavery, often hidden deep in the woods or in the slave quarters, enslaved people toiled in spiritual labor—through dance, song, sermon, prayer, and expressed belief—against the religion-based normalization of their bondage.[2] Believers "sifted out the essence of true liberation" (Hopkins 21) in biblical passages, which resulted in the rejection of mainstream interpretations of religion-based passivity and often facilitated a critical reinterpretation of the bible that justified duplicity, murder, uprisings, and escape in the name of liberation.[3] That is, black Christian discourses emphasize those parts of the bible that speak to the believers' material circumstances. Through the work of free communities of color, the black church would became a prominent black hub of educational, humanitarian, and political organizing in the North, especially in response to the governmental abandonment signified by the end of the

Reconstruction period. Probably nothing signifies its importance to black liberation than the fact that, during the modern Civil Rights Movement, black churches were the predominant target of terrorists' burnings and bombings. And, as the publicized sermons of (and the eruption of white outrage in response to) President Barack Obama's pastor, Reverend Jeremiah Wright demonstrate, black religious discourses still produce critical perspectives that do not align with mainstream narratives.[4]

Manifestations of this approach to Christianity are evident in the lyrics of spirituals, the sacred songs into which singers could tuck their desires for freedom and justice. When taken together as a religious text, the collective message of the spirituals communicates a faith that "allowed for the fullness of liberation," which means spiritual liberation (from sin and immorality) and also includes one's material life (Spencer 32). As a genre, spirituals communicated this liberation theology through religious lyrics that were infused with subversive, duplicitous meanings. For example, during slavery, lyrical yearnings for Canaan, Heaven and New Jerusalem also articulated a desire to reach Canada, a free state in the United States, or the state of being outside of physical bondage.[5] Jon Michael Spencer attests that spirituals wear a mask behind which lie "confrontation and conflict" (13). And over time, as black people endured the dehumanizing realities of slavery, black codes, the international popularity of minstrelsy, and Jim Crowism, these sacred songs continued to serve as a reservoir of counter consciousness. Mary Ellison observes that,

> Spirituals were far more revolutionary than most people, until recently, have imagined. Close examination shows just how subversive they were, and it is not surprising that so many were used as "freedom songs" by the civil rights movement of the 1950s and 60s. Songs like "Go Tell It on The Mountain" [and] "We'll Never Turn Back . . ." were all spirituals being used a second time to stir up a spirit of resistance. (qtd in Scott 166)

Freedom songs adapted lyrics and melodies of spirituals and gospel songs to reflect the contemporary struggle against institutional racism. Yet, in doing so, the singers unmasked the spiritual. That is, the freedom song was not designed to perform religious double-speak; its approach is direct and clear. For example, the line, "woke up this morning with my mind stead on Jesus" was sung as, "woke up this morning with my mind stead on freedom"; and "if you want to get to Heaven, do what Jesus says" was changed to "if you want to get your freedom, register and vote." An inherited theology of liberation provided the subtext of the freedom song, but this song openly engaged in ideological conflict and confrontation.[6] This was not a shift in the politics of religious tradition; adaptation of strategy to one's circumstances *is* the tradition.[7] The construction of a liberation theology and oppositional consciousness is the black church tradition.[8]

This chapter begins with an illumination of the oppositional politics of the black church and black sacred music tradition because these cultural elements are crucial to understanding literary representations, such as those in the Langston Hughes short story discussed in the following section and the James Baldwin texts discussed in the next chapter, in which writers "do" liberation theology in their depictions of black male characters who are members of Christian congregations. The *Gay Christian Narrative*, as I have chosen to call it, involves male characters ensconced in black church traditions and for whom religious expressions are fused with their homoerotic desires. In this and the next chapter, I aim to show some of the ways the African American Gay Christian Narrative provides overt and affirming reflections on the divine nature of homosexual experiences, as well as homoerotic appropriation of biblical narratives. My underlying argument is that the resistance tactics embedded in the oral tradition are also deployed in African American LGBTQ literature in ways that further expand black theological claims to liberty, spiritual freedom, and salvation.

PUNKS AND PRAISESONGS: LANGSTON HUGHES' "BLESSED ASSURANCE"

Langston Hughes (1902–1967) was a prolific writer and composer. He authored sixteen books of poems; two novels; three collections of short stories; four volumes of "editorial" and "documentary" fiction; twenty plays; children's poetry, musicals and operas; three autobiographies; several radio and television scripts, and magazine articles. In addition, he edited seven anthologies, many that promoted emerging black writers in the 1960s. He was born in Joplin, Missouri but was well traveled, domestically and internationally, by his late twenties. His writing was always focused on the lives and experiences of black Americans. For example, his drama about so-called miscegenation and the U.S. South, "Mulatto," became the longest running Broadway play written by an African American (October

1935 to September 1936) until Lorraine Hansberry's "A Raisin in the Sun" took the designation—a feat that also honors Hughes because the title and central concern of the drama is taken from a line in his poem, "Harlem." In addition to the songs he composed for his musical dramas, music played a central role in his writing. In his autobiographical reflections, he cites the influences of spirituals, jazz, blues, all considered "low culture" forms, and African rhythms as musical elements that resonate deeply in the poetry that launched and maintained his career. He claimed to have often found inspiration and penned lines of poetry while sitting in nightclubs; and he would eventually recite the polished versions of these poems to music, a formula now called spoken word performance and is credited as a precursor to rap music.

This love for black folk culture, as expressed in his poems, and his depictions of working class Harlem in fiction were derided by black critics who were the gatekeepers of the New Negro ideology, a politicized approach to art that took root in the post–WWI era, when Jim Crow segregation was still the law in the South and the practice everywhere else in the country. Publications by black authors had continually diminished after emancipation and, in response to this lapse in output, many black intelligentsia and established elites, including James Weldon Johnson, W.E.B. Du Bois, and Alaine Locke, were determined to identify and foster a new generation of artists and intellectuals who would be a "credit to the race" and affect social change. They prescribed to the logic that, in addition to the social elevation of African traditions and histories, respectable representations of black American life were a way to prove black cultural contributions to American society (and Africa's to the world) and, subsequently, would earn the respect of white Americans and soften their racist attitudes. This, they believed, would then lead to equal treatment under the law and equal access to public facilities and resources.[9] As I discussed in the introduction, Hughes and other young artists, including Bruce Nugent, Zora Neale Hurston, and Wallace Thurman, found this approach too artistically and intellectually constraining. And they chose to depict the "low down" folk, as Hughes writes in "The Negro Artist and the Racial Mountain," whose "joy runs bang! into ecstasy . . . [and whose] religion soars to a shout." The gatekeepers were not pleased. In his autobiography, *The Big Sea*, Hughes remembers the public scolding he took from reviewers:

> *Fine Clothes to the Jew* [his second book of poems, published in 1927] was well received by the literary magazines and the white press, but the Negro critics did not like it at all. The Pittsburgh *Courier* ran a big headline across the top of the page, *LANGSTON HUGHES' BOOK OF POEMS TRASH.* The headline in the New York *Amsterdam News* was *LANGSTON HUGHES—THE SEWER DWELLER.* The Chicago *Whip* characterized me as "the poet low-rate of Harlem." Others called the book a disgrace to the race, a return to the dialect tradition, and a parading of all our racial defects before the public. . . . The Negro critics and many of the intellectuals were very sensitive about their race in books. (And still are.) In anything that white people were likely to read, they wanted to put their best foot forward, their politely polished and cultural foot—and only that foot. (265–267)

Instead of conforming to the bourgeois standards with which he was being bludgeoned, Hughes responded by depicting these cultural tensions in his work. He also continued to affirm black musical styles that were not yet appreciated by mainstream audiences.

Hughes often uses these musical expressions to convey a racial, political, or spiritual consciousness. He explores double consciousness and African American intra-cultural tensions through portrayals of music performance in his short stories, such as the artist's physical decline when he chooses the "high art" of the symphony over the jazz that made him famous in "Home" (1934); and in the conflicts pianist Oceola encounters in "The Blues I'm Playing" (1933) between her patron's preference for European classical styles and the African musical inflections of the jazz-inflected Blues that Oceola loves. The artist in "Home" represents the inevitable decline in the spirit and distinction of African American culture that would result were it to ever completely detach itself from its African roots. In "The Blues I'm Playing," Oceola takes a stand for the Blues and accepts that the music that sustains her soul does not have to be embraced by the white woman who listens to it with condescending disdain. In regard to his use of jazz forms, Felicia Miyakawa indicates that Hughes shows us the transformative nature of jazz in his poetry and fiction, and from him we learn that jazz offers redemption from the decadence of western civilization; and that it also gives access to the immediate, the sensual, and the intuitive as it overcomes the intellectual, mechanical, and puritanical (275). The "transformative nature" of music also includes religious songs.

According to Leslie Sanders, editor of *The Collected Works of Langston Hughes Vol. 6: Gospel Plays, Operas, and Later Dramatics*, virtually all of Hughes's stage writing after 1942 incorporates music in some form. She documents that he wrote five complete operas and several cantatas, as well as the musicals and gospel plays, and hundreds of song lyrics, "all of which demonstrate his strong determination to inject an African American presence into a range of cultural forms" (Sanders 1). His most famous religious plays are *Tambourines to Glory* (1956, which was developed into a novel), and *Black Nativity* (1961), the former of which is credited as the origination of the gospel play genre. Also included in *The Collected Works* are *The Gospel Glow* (1962), *The Master of Miracles* (1962), and *The Prodigal Son* (1965). Significantly, between the publication of his last two gospel plays, in 1963, Hughes issued *Something in Common and Other Stories* in which the short story "Blessed Assurance" appears. The short story deals with black church culture and involves the affirmation of black religious traditions. It also involves a critique of the very culture it celebrates: An effeminate male character appropriates heroic bible characters and employs sacred songs to subvert the policing of gender in his family of origin and in the Baptist church in which he is a member.

The appearance of "Blessed Assurance" might seem significant simply because it could offer insight into the rumors that Hughes had maintained inconspicuous homosexual relationships with the domestic partners and travel companions who were often seen accompanying him after he bought a townhome in Harlem in 1948.[10] But, even in the rebellious, revolutionary spirit of the 1960s, the politics of the day were such that the Harlem poet laureate would risk his standing as literary royalty were he to make such an acknowledgment. By then he was an elder of the arts, highly esteemed around the world and able to use his stature to usher in new talents. He was very much a respectable representative of the race. So much so that his respectability, and therefore his sexuality, has become an important point of contention for his legacy-keepers, namely his literary executor, George Bass, and biographer Arnold Rampersad. Tellingly, as recently as 1988, Rampersad, who had worked closely with Bass, remained invested in countering any perception of Hughes as a closeted "gay poet" (a moniker that emerged during the Gay Rights Movement) when he suggests in the second volume of *The Life of Langston Hughes* that the author's body of work "is virtually devoid of pieces that even hint at an interest in homosexuality" (334) and, further, proposes that Hughes found the theme appealing so late in his career because of James Baldwin's success with the interracial and bisexually themed novel *Another Country* in 1962. Perhaps the contention lies in how "interest" is defined: recent literary scholarship makes it clear that there is no shortage of sexual and gender dissidents in Hughes' oeuvre.[11] "Manly" women and "soft" men regularly populate his narratives, albeit for comedic effect, and even appear in his memoir, *The Big Sea*, in stereotypically negative terms.

But let us for a moment consider the life and writing of Hughes in a different context. Hughes arrived in Harlem during the 1920s, when the borough was considered the "sexual pleasure center of Manhattan."[12] George Chauncey excavates the history of the vibrant queer Harlem social scene in the 1920s and 1930s in *Gay New York: The Making of a Gay World*:

> If the Village was considered the city's most infamous gay neighborhood by outsiders, many gay men themselves regarded Harlem as the most exciting center of gay life. In a segregated city, it was the only place where black gay men could congregate in commercial establishments, and they were centrally involved in many of the currents of Harlem culture, from the creative literary circles that constituted the Harlem Renaissance to the blues clubs and basement speakeasies where the poorest of Harlem's residents gathered. African-Americans organized the largest annual communal event of New York's gay society, the Hamilton Lodge Ball, which attracted thousands of white as well as black participants and spectators. (227–228)

Hughes was familiar with these queer social spaces and befriended many people who are known to have engaged in non-normative sexual behaviors. Hughes recalls the Hamilton Lodge Ball as the place "where men dress as women and women dress as men" and they all assemble in a "queerly assorted throng on the dancing floor" (273) in his memoir, *The Big Sea*. During this period, Hughes also socialized with Alberta Hunter, a popular jazz and blues recording artist who was regularly featured in the *Chicago Defender*'s New York Society column with her female romantic partner, Lottie Tyler. In 1929, Hunter and Tyler attended a Paul Robeson concert with Hughes and his close friend and multitalented artist, Carl

Van Vechten (De La Croix 106). Van Vechten and his wife, Fania Marinoff, were known for their sexually flamboyant and "exotic" parties (Berry 79). Hughes describes these parties, too, in *The Big Sea*, along with the notoriously queer-friendly salons hosted by millionaire heiress, A'Lelia Walker (244–245).

As a resident of Harlem, and close friend to Renaissance writers who are known to have regularly slept with men (Thurman and Nugent; plus, according to Nugent, Hurston also engaged in homosexual behavior),[13] he was also witness to the increased surveillance of "deviants" by the New York's anti-vice movements and sodomy laws.[14]

Hughes depicts this increasingly oppressive environment in "Café 3 a.m.," a 1951 poem that sympathizes with the effeminate men who were subjected to state scrutiny and violence. The collection in which it appears, *Montage of a Dream Deferred*, is intended to be read as a single poem, a series of lyrical snapshots of contemporary life in Harlem taken at different times of the day.[15] In the poet's snapshot of the city at 3 a.m., vice squad members are described as having "weary, sadistic eyes" as they watch the "fairies" socialize in the café. The poem's narrator objects to the surveillance by asserting "God, Nature, or somebody made them that way" (*Collected Poems* 406), an objection that also articulates a queer-affirming theology. The timing of the poem is significant because the Gay Rights Era inaugurates in the United States in 1950 with the establishment of Mattachine Society, followed by the Daughters of Billitis in 1955, two groups that were dedicated to transforming society.[16]

Though they were preceded by a short-lived human rights group in 1924 in Chicago, Mattachine and Daughters of Billitis are credited as the first successful ("success" being broadly defined) activist organizations dedicated to changing laws that criminalized consensual homosexual acts between adults. They also assisted defendants in anti-sodomy cases and made it part of their institutional mission to improve the self-esteem and self-image of "homophiles." It was also their articulated mission to influence the ways in which homosexuality was understood in the mainstream through the production of homosexual-affirming media. They held meetings that were draped in secrecy and anonymity to protect participants from law enforcement, distributed leaflets in public spaces, and provided financial and legal support for members who had been fired from their jobs or arrested. Membership in California swelled and they were able to institute chapters in other major cities, including Washington D.C. and New York City, two metropolises where Hughes is known to have spent considerable time. Though it is only a supposition, Hughes could have easily read their leaflets or heard about their consciousness-raising activism from those folks in the life who surrounded him; most notably, Van Vechten stayed abreast of the goings-on in lesbian and gay culture through the 1950s.[17] What we are left with, alas, is the potential for such knowledge and access to the activism, and the fact that his defense and representation of the "low-down folk" included effeminate black men—many of whom he had to have encountered in his theater work.

The real importance of "Blessed Assurance," though, is that in it Hughes does not deploy gender transgression solely for comedic purposes (as he does in his plays). At the age of sixty-one, he created a space for addressing effeminate masculinity in a church community by offering a tale of an aging father, John, struggling to accept his son's homosexuality. Rampersad characterizes John as a "sophisticated voyeur [that] neither criticizes nor endorses the son or his organist-admirer" (334), but it is clear that the gender politics conveyed through black fatherhood and black worship are anything but neutral. With humor, sarcasm, and the poet's keen ability to capture truth in tiny snippets, "Blessed Assurance" illustrates how, in E. Patrick Johnson's words, the body is the one organizing site of multiple and competing signifiers within the black church service ("Feeling the Spirit" 92). John's queer son, Delmar, is one such body. He stands at the center of the story as a site of triangulated and competing signifiers of black masculinity: the patriarch, the preacher, and the "punk."

The first point on the masculinity triangle is John, who represents black patriarchy. The third-person narrator seems sympathetic to John's homophobic resignation that "to [his] distrust of God [,] it seemed his son was turning out to be a queer" (58). The story's first few passages supply a catalog of Delmar's apparently feminine characteristics: he performs his chores without complaint, washes dishes too easily, does not antagonize his younger sister, played with dolls in his childhood and wears "exaggerated ornamental glasses." His preferred sport is tennis, not his father's game of football, and he is a member of the glee, French, and drama clubs. The narrator generates this list, ostensibly, as proof of Delmar's failed masculinity, and of John's rightful parental embarrassment. But we soon learn that these passages are not really about Delmar; they are about John's failure as patriarch.

John has fathered an intelligent, talented, and likeable son. He is described as a "brilliant queer" because as his social resume reveals, he is well rounded and excels in his high school studies. He is ranked highly in his class and has avoided the allure of the street life. Or as John laments, "No juvenile delinquency, no stealing cars, no smoking reefers, ever" (58). However, Delmar's brilliant queerness is also testimony of John's inability to transmit a socially acceptable masculinity to the next generation. Delmar is also a brilliant queer in terms of his physical appearance and mannerisms. As is expected of him by society, John has attempted to guide his son to what he considers more appropriately gendered behavior.

> That Spring he asked, "Delmar, do you have to wear *white* Bermuda shorts to school? Most of the other boys wear Levi's or just plain pants, don't they? And why wash them out yourself every night, all that ironing? I want you to be clean, son, but not *that* clean." . . . Another time, "Delmar, those school togs of yours don't have to match so perfectly, do they? Colors *blended*, as you say. . . . The boys'll think you're sissy." . . . Once again desperately, "If you're going to smoke, Delmar, hold your cigarette between your *first* two fingers, not between your thumb and finger like a woman." (59)

Here his brilliance is physical; his is a shiny masculinity, marked by its flawed motion among other black male bodies. Delmar's brilliant queerness highlights his nonconformance to working class masculinity: his bourgeois sensibility, a level of cleanliness usually associated with women's domesticity, a keen sense of fashion, and the cigarette reference suggests he imitates movie starlets. In other words, Delmar lacks a cool pose, a mask of tough posturing defined, in part, by restrained and aloof masculinity associated with African American men, constructed to hide sensitivity and express power (Majors and Billson 5).[18] John's explanations for his criticism tie into his desire for Delmar to be read as cool by other men. He wants Delmar to meet a particular standard set by him; by his male peers at school; and by societal norms so he routinely reinforces the expectations of a traditional, physically dominant heterosexual masculinity. These corrective efforts reassert the superiority of the "manly" man over other genders by demeaning both women and "soft" men.

As I said earlier, Hughes knew what it was like to experience cultural pressure to "properly" represent the race; and the effeminate man, presumed to be homosexual, has always been positioned rhetorically outside the bounds of proper and respectable black representation. As Essex Hemphill reminds us, black sexuality is considered politically, morally, and spiritually correct only if it expresses itself in patriarchal, religious-based constructions of family, politics, art and culture, and any variance or transgression can cause one to be burdened with shame (182). E. Patrick Johnson coined the term *hegemonic blackness* to describe this constant shaming and imposition of normative pressure. In *Appropriating Blackness: The Performance and Politics of Authenticity*, he uses the phrase to explain that maleness, strength, and overall leadership ability are qualities equated with a hetero-butch masculinity, which means that women and "soft" men are the least desirable racial representatives. He writes:

> The representation of effeminate homosexuality as disempowering is at the heart of the politics of hegemonic Blackness. For to be ineffectual is the most damaging thing one can be in the fight against oppression. Insofar as *ineffectiveness is* problematically *sutured to femininity and homosexuality* within a black cultural politic that privileges race over other categories of oppression, it follows that the subjects accorded these attributes would be marginalized and excluded from the boundaries of Blackness. (Johnson, *Appropriating* 51; emphases added)

Male femininity is generally an unacceptable representative of black leadership and, in a father-son relationship, is generally not a source of patriarchal pride. Hegemonic blackness leaves little room for gender and sexual transgression, as is evidenced by Hughes' own sexual ambiguity.[19]

In "Blessed Assurance," John's attempts to "correct" his son's behavior represent hegemonic blackness and, from his perspective, he is doing what is best for his son. He is concerned about his son's transition into adulthood because "the boy is colored [and] Negroes have enough crosses to bear" (58). In other words, John is aware that the obstacles of systemic racism are varied and nebulous enough to thwart black men's dreams without the additional fallout from the homophobic surveillance of sexuality in and outside of black communities. To be black and identifiably queer is to be marked for social (and sometimes physical) crucifixion. So, John is concerned about the weight of the homosexual stigma for Delmar and, more crucially, for himself because Delmar's improper performance of masculinity reflects directly on John as the patriarch. As the story continues, it becomes clear that John competes with other influences, other representations of manhood in Delmar's life. In spite of his efforts to dull it with normative correctives, Delmar's queerness remains radiant.

John is also a failed husband. He lost his wife to "another man who made more money than any Negro in their church. . . . Owned a Cadillac. Racket connections—politely called *politics*" (59; original emphasis). That John is unable to maintain a cohesive family unit is another mark against his manhood. The mention of the other man's political and financial clout suggests that John may have lacked in his role as breadwinner or simply that the new man's income dwarfs John's. He also calls his wife's new lover "burly," revealing that he is also physically larger than John. In patriarchal symbology, these features combine to construct the new lover as the alpha-male and John as the weaker, and therefore less desirable version of manhood. In this way, John's issue with Delmar's masculinity is intertwined with his own sense of displacement and deficiency. And, because he cannot "fix" his son, perhaps John finds some relief in Delmar's wish to attend Sorbonne, a university in Paris, France.

Like many parents, he had hoped his son would attend his alma mater, a predominately black university, but that, too, has changed with the realization that Delmar was "turning out to be queer." Black colleges and fraternities are enclaves of hegemonic blackness that will not easily accept Delmar's nonconformity.[20] John ponders: "[I]s the Sorbonne like Morgan [State University]? Does it have dormitories, a campus?" (60). He considers Delly's future and well-being, but the admission of his probable homosexuality never firmly settles in his mind. For John to acknowledge to himself the motivation behind his own sudden advocacy of the Sorbonne would be an acknowledgment of the other possible truths as well. As John meditates on this, the narration tumbles into garbled stream-of-consciousness, which demonstrates his ambivalence: "In Paris he had heard they didn't care about such things. Care about such what things didn't care about what?" (60). Time and again John struggles with denial. In the most provocative passage, as he seems to come to terms with Delmar's sexual orientation, his mental process begins to break down:

> "God, don't let him put an earring in his ear like some," John prayed. He wondered vaguely with a sick feeling in his stomach should he think it through then then[sic] think it through right then through should he try then and think it through should

> without Blacking through think Blacking out then and there think it through? John didn't. (59–60)

The repetition of the phrase "think it through" is significant. What will happen if John can think this situation through to its logical conclusion? Can Delmar be queer *and* a legitimate extension of John's manhood? As the symbol of black patriarchy, John clings to a self-destructive macho ideology that insists he expel Delmar from the community. The other embedded question is, can he (and we) think this through without blacking out?

I am not qualified to give a medical explanation of "blacking out," but the way in which John's speech gets hung up on itself just at the moment of possible admission (and acceptance?) of what Delmar's soft masculinity could mean for Delmar's sexuality suggests that such an admission is literally outside of John's cognitive reach. Instead, his internal monologue gets stuck like a needle on a scratched record, jumping back to its starting point or skipping so that the same word is repeated without progression: "with a sick feeling in his stomach should he think it through then then think it through right then through should he try then." His attempt to think it through launches him into intellectual and physical vertigo; and, perhaps, John's unsteadiness represents the old guard politics as it confronts the shifting landscape of black representation that emerges in Delmar's post–gay rights generation. He must choose whether to think it through or black out. More important to the story's classification as a Gay Christian Narrative is Delmar's unwillingness to exercise caution in the face of this cultural pressure to deny or suppress his difference. On the contrary, Delmar, with the aid of his church's minister of music, acts out his queerness in a particularly Christian spotlight. It is important to note here that the minister of music, an important figure in the story, is a character ubiquitously rendered as effeminate in modern representations of black gospel choir culture.[21] These depictions exist partly because *he* exists as such in many communities, and because the gay subculture within black churches has become a topic of discussion since the onset of AIDS; and, more recently, because some black church leaders have made their opposition to the gay marriage movement a public decree.[22]

If the pew is the established woman's place in the church, as C. Eric Lincoln argues, and the pulpit the man's, perhaps the choir is best understood as a queered space of gender nonconformity and other acts of resistance.[23] Bishop Yvette Flunder of Oakland, California, is founder of the Fellowship, an organization of black pastors and churches openly welcoming of lesbian, gay, bisexual, and transgender members. According to Bishop Flunder, gospel choirs have always have been havens for LGBT people (qtd in Webster n. p.). E. Patrick Johnson uses a personal anecdote to attest to the negotiated space of the black gospel choir:

> The choir in the Black church has always been a place where gay men could show off their virtuosity while exploring their sexuality. I was one of the church sissies who, because of my high vocal range, held the reign of choir diva until I was about 17 years old. For me and so many others like me, it was a place where we could safely express our queerness in covert ways while taking pleasure in pushing the gender limits. (qtd in McNeir n. p.)

As I alluded to in Chapter One, these internal conflicts have led to various responses from the gays and lesbians within these institutions. Some leave for more welcoming denominations. Some repudiate their inherited religion altogether and seek other interpretations of God or spiritual transcendence. But some people are able to negotiate the queered space of musical performance, which affirmed Johnson's reign as a choir diva, even as it also ingrained in him the condemnation of the identities and sexual behaviors commonly associated with his diva mannerisms. Johnson explains that those for whom the church is a large part of their identity and for whom religion is a central force in their life will remain "in a place that is often very inhospitable [to them] . . . finding ways to exist within it" (qtd in McNeir n. p.). Arguably, the visible presence of gays and lesbians in this space is not just a negotiation, but is its own form of resistance.

Michael Eric Dyson also attests to this notion of structural opposition through visibility, but from the perspective of an ordained Baptist minister. He reflects on the phenomena of the church's open secret as a painful kind of "erotic dishonesty":

> One of the most painful scenarios of black church life is repeated Sunday after Sunday with little notice or collective outrage. A black minister will preach a sermon railing against sexual ills, especially homosexuality. At the close of the sermon, *a soloist, who everybody knows is gay, will rise to perform a moving number*, as the

> preacher extends an invitation to visitors to join the church. The soloist is, in effect being asked to sing, and to sign, his theological death sentence. His presence at the end of such a sermon symbolizes a silent endorsement of the preacher's message. Ironically, the presence of his gay Christian body at the highest moment of worship also negates the preacher's attempt to censure his presence, to erase his body, to deny his legitimacy as a child of God. (*Race Rules* 105; my emphasis)

Dyson observes the counter narrative that the gospel soloist embodies and performs, which challenges the "theological death sentence" of the sermon. Religion professor Johari Jabir further expounds on this dynamic in "Preachers and Punks, Sissies and Saints: Constructions of Black Religious Masculinity in the Climactic Moment of Black Worship." Jabir argues that in the theater of traditional black churches, the performances of the male preacher and the male musician who is perceived as homosexual can construct a hierarchical preacher/punk binary, which privileges the preacher by placing him in the masculine space. Although it has multiple meanings, the term *punk* originated in U.S. prisons to mean the passive homosexual partner, a usage that maintains the privileging of dominant sexuality.[24] Jabir's interpretation of the climactic moment of worship (that Dyson speaks of also), is that,

> In the context of black worship, these two masculinities cooperate and collaborate to construct each other's masculinity through two of the most essential material aspects of black worship—the pulpit and the Hammond B3 organ. The communication between the two is simultaneously cooperative, collaborative, and contesting. Both cooperate to produce the moment of ritual—the sermonic climax. Both collaborate in the production of the other's masculinity. And, at times, both contest the other's masculinity in ways that find them disagreeing, not about the goodness of God but about the meaning of what it means to be a man. (4)

Dyson's reflections and Jabir's argument queer the ideological tensions that can exist between sermon/song and preacher/minister of music, which sets an interpretive stage for Hughes' short story and the ways in which central characters Delmar and Minister Jaxon resist the proscriptions of hegemonic blackness regarding what it means to be a man in church.

The minister of music can comprise as many roles as choir director, lead musician, or songwriter. The title *minister* in a church conveys, first, that it is a leadership role and, second, that production of music or song in the service of God can be considered a type of evangelism. He who surrenders to the spirit and serves as its vessel makes his talent an instrument of God in the same way that oratory skills used in the pulpit establishes a preacher's voice as "God's trombone."[25] Still, in the greater scheme of the church program, he is the subminister, or passive partner to the preacher. Manley is positioned, among the competing representations of masculinity for Delmar, as a man who is perceived as gay, or the "punk." As a subminister, Manley competes with John (and later, the preacher, Pastor Greene) in the shaping of Delmar's manhood. Thus, it is meaningful that as part of his masculine instruction he composed a song based on the Christian Bible's *Book of Ruth*, dedicated it to Delmar and, "without respect for gender" (Hughes, "Blessed Assurance" 60), assigned Delmar to sing lead. The decision to have Delmar sing Ruth's words provides the first ruptural and critical act because the performance will disrupt the religious reinforcement of proper gender binaries.

The *Book of Ruth* establishes Ruth as Jesus' ancestor through her celebrated relationship with her mother-in-law Naomi. Ruth and Naomi simultaneously lose their husbands and, according to Hebrew law and custom, are expected to separate and find new husbands to support them. However, instead of moving back into her father's house until she can remarry, Ruth defies tradition by moving with Naomi to Bethlehem and supporting her "better than seven sons" (Ruth 4:15). Her loyalty is exemplary because she chose to leave the family, culture, and religion of her birth for Naomi. In *Lethal Love: Feminist Biblical Readings of Biblical Love Stories*, Mieke Bal attests that the verb used to describe Ruth's attachment, "to cleave," is the same one used to refer to the matrimonial bond in *Genesis* (72). Ruth pleads, "Entreat me not to leave thee . . . for where you go, I will go . . . your people will be my people, and your God will be my God." This moment is heralded in religious studies as the greatest proof of Ruth's love and devotion to Naomi and, in a larger sense, to the Hebrew God.

With this in mind, consider that when Manley assigns Delmar to quote these words as lead vocalist, he asks Delmar to perform as Ruth in the musical (imagine a man singing of Eve's experience with the serpent or as the narrative voice of the Virgin Mary). The affect of having him do so transforms the church into a queer space in which two men can vocalize their devotion to each other. Meanwhile, "As the organ wept and Delmar's voice soared above the choir with all the sweetness of Sam Cooke's tessitura" (61), Manley fainted. When the music stops unexpectedly, "Amens and Hallelujahs drowned in the throats of various elderly sisters who were on the verge of shouting [and] swooning teenage maidens suddenly sat up in their pews" (61). By fainting, the musician interrupts the women's pleasure, the "sisters" and "maidens," as he succumbs to his own physical and spiritual response to the religious performance. The sweetness of Delmar's voice creates a male-on-male connection that supersedes the implied heteronormativity in his role as musical foreplay to the preacher's soulful penetration.[26]

In regard to traditional literary representations of black church worship service, Hughes' portrayal revises the heteronormative scene into a spectacle of queer disruption and connects to Johnson's suggestion that when the spirit "touches" heterosexual male parishioners, it penetrates their bodies and creates in them a sense of powerlessness and aura that is akin to orgasm. Maurice Wallace presents a similar queer theory of the sermonic climax: "To submit fully to the self-shattering in religion and/or sex is to sacrifice the aura of fucking or being fucked" (5). Manley succumbs to the self-shattering ecstasy when he collapses; and their duet (the "sweet voice" accompanied by the "weeping organ") becomes Delmar/Ruth's serenade:

> When the organ went silent, the choir died, too—but Delmar never stopped singing. Over the limp figure of Dr. Jaxon lying on the rostrum, the "Entreat me not to leave thee" of his solo flooded the church as if it were on hi-fi. . . . Finally, two ushers led [Manley] off to an anteroom while Delmar's voice soared to a high C such as Tried Stone Baptist Church had never heard. (61)

Delmar's lyrical drag show as the voice of Ruth is the first transgression in the conservative church space. The second is that they display a homoerotic spirituality. They are able to express an unsanctioned version of same-sex love through their holy worship.

The narrative plants seeds that facilitate these interpretive possibilities: in addition to the song dedication, there is mention that the couple broke away from the choir group during a visit to New York to visit Greenwich Village, a well-known cultural site of sexual dissidence.[27] John narrates this story as a flashback and it is he who is connecting the chronological dots in his attempt to come to terms with his son "turning out to be a queer" (58). His worries are compounded by the fact that Delmar has begun growing a beard "like the beatniks" (59). With this kernel of information, one can infer that Manley and Delmar are either romantically involved, or Manley is guiding Delmar's entry into "the life" as a mentor (by affirming his nonconforming gender expression through vocal performance and introducing him to a major cultural landmark of nonconformists) or both. As a representation of queer spirituality, the song is an expression of same-sex loyalty, dedication, and desire.

In the African American tradition of dual coding, their song is duplicitous for it as much a spiritual as it is a love song. Delmar as the singer is the soul's mouthpiece, the passageway through which the soul's desire is manifested as breath, tongue, and vocal chords. Manley, in his role as the organ(ist), is a natural accompaniment to the lyrics. When the mouth moves, the organ surrenders or, as Delmar's sister explains to John: "Some of the girls say that when Delmar sings, they want to scream, they're so overcome, but Dr. Jaxon didn't scream. He just fainted" (Hughes 61). They utilize the space in religious rhetoric for queer transgression and subversion.

First, when he sings over Jaxon, the lyrics declare his emotional loyalty. In light of his possible departure for France, Delmar may be using the song—already understood as a same-gender sentiment—to express his desire to remain close to Jaxon. Second, in his role as soloist he is also the vessel through which the Word as lyric is projected into the world. His song refers to family loyalty as analogous to the Christian devotion to God. A traditional reading might assert that the gender of the lead singer should be overlooked and the moment understood only in terms of his role as a Christian singer, but the narrative makes clear that this exhibition, for John at least, is "perverse." Together they raise a praisesong to the heavens and to each other. They expand the traditional interpretation to vocalize that if Ruth and Naomi's cleaving is a worthy, holy celebration, so, too, is theirs. The preacher's reaction is to assume control of the service, at which time the triangle of competing masculinities comes sharply into focus. The pulpit masculinity is at odds with the singer's masculinity, whose performance, in turn, scandalizes the patriarch.

The preacher, Pastor Greene, emerges to calm the startled church audience. "Dr. Jaxon has only fainted, friends," he assures them. "We will continue our services by taking up collection directly after the anthem"

(61). It is unclear if he is directing the choir to finish the song without Jaxon or announcing the end of the anthem. But John believes it is a signal for his son to continue his indecent lyrical drag show and tries to intervene. Five times, he orders Delmar to "shut up." For a moment, there is silence and the next voice is Reverend Greene's. "We will now lift the offering," he commands. "Deacons, raise a hymn. Bear us up, sisters, bear us up!" (62). The pastor wants to put the derailed program back on its heteronormative track so he enlists other, more traditional men to take control and the women to assist in their long-established secondary function. In this way, the preacher corroborates with John; still he competes with John as a role model of religious masculinity. While "Christianity is not the sole source of Western gender-role ideologies for black Americans, it is a major one . . . [it] is certainly the case that patriarchy is a protected modus operandi, a visible if unacknowledged tradition, and one of the most cherished and tenacious values in the black church" (Cole 160). The choice of language is telling, for it is couched in terms of physical labor. Hegemonic blackness toils to veil or close the fissures through which non-normative formations emerge. Deacons are told to "raise" a hymn, to lift a song over any remaining echoes of Delmar's high C, while the women are instructed to "bear up," carry, endure, and hold the men. Even the change in the musical genre from the improvisational spiritual to the contained compositions of the hymnbook suggests an effort to control the environment. It is not enough.

The next voice is not that of a deacon or the churchwomen. It is Delmar's. His voice booms through the cultural pressure to return to the group's idea of natural order. He changes to the hymn, "Blessed Assurance," from which the title of the story is taken, but it is in the spirit of resistance. He refuses to be silenced by the voices of normative masculinity. The song further demonstrates the space in religious rhetoric for dual coding and double-consciousness. Delmar sings the first two lines alone: *Blessed assurance, Jesus is mine! Oh, what a foretaste of glory divine!* Following his lead, the congregation "swung gently into song" with *heir of salvation, purchase of God, Born of the Spirit*. This scene reflects a kind of performance that Dyson associates with the legibly gay singer in traditional churches, which, by his visibility and vocal ability, negates Christianity's attempt to censure his presence, to erase his body, to deny his legitimacy as a child of God (Dyson 235). "Blessed Assurance" is a Gay Christian Narrative that successfully transforms gender transgression into a critique of heterosexism and hegemonic blackness through its blend of sacred music and gender nonconformity, as well as the characters' appropriation of the *Book of Ruth* for their same-sex romance.

In this chapter I argue that the Gay Christian Narrative inscribes queer possibility into biblical morality tales and, at times, black religious communities. When Hughes places the celebrated oath of loyalty from the *Book of Ruth* into the mouth of the "sweet" choirboy, he illuminates the queer erotics that often surge through the homosocial bonds in gospel choirs. The story also facilitates queer feminist reconsiderations of Ruth's long-term companionship and financial support of her former mother-in-law. I continue this line of argument in the following chapter as I analyze James Baldwin's expansion of black theological claims to liberty, spiritual freedom, and salvation in his fiction.

CHAPTER THREE

Sacred Sensuality

Just Above My Head

This chapter continues the discussion of the Gay Christian Narrative with a look at some of the ways in which James Baldwin participates in the genre. After a brief biographical introduction, I build on Michael Cobb's study of the religious rhetoric in some of Baldwin's early work, and following David Field's assertion that Baldwin "develops more a *corrective to* than a repudiation of Christian theology" (444; italics added), I add my observations of such corrective theology in his final novel, *Just Above My Head* (1979). My goal in this chapter is to show that Baldwin's illustrations of (hetero and homo) erotic spirituality and his appropriation of religious words construct conversion narratives in which sexual intimacy and dynamic love acts—what I call *sacred sensuality*—are central to his corrective approach and to his brand of queer spirituality.

Baldwin was born in 1924 in Harlem, New York. He has contributed to nearly every literary genre, including the novel, personal essay, short story, poetry, literary criticism, screenwriting, and playwriting. A prodigy with a thirst for fiction, he read works by Charles Dickens, Fyodor Dostoevsky, and Harriet Beecher Stowe before his teen years. In 1948, at age 24, Baldwin left for Paris, where he was able to find enough distance from the American society he grew up in to write about it: these years would be his most productive creative period. In Paris, he published literary criticism and "Sonny's Blues" (1951), his most anthologized short story to date. After ten years of working on it, the publication of his autobiographical debut novel *Go Tell It on the Mountain* in 1953 firmly established

Baldwin's standing in elite U.S. and European literary circles. It is about his relationship to his father and the church, which, according to Baldwin, are the same thing (Standley and Pratt 240). Over the next decade, Baldwin moved from Paris to New York to Istanbul, and wrote two books of essays and two novels, *Giovanni's Room* (1956) and *Another Country* (1962). Pulled by the call of the black liberation struggle across America, Baldwin returned to the United States in the 1960s to use his fame as a platform to communicate and clarify the historical context and demands of the Civil Rights Movement. During this period, *The Fire Next Time* (1963), his most famous nonfiction work, was published. After the turbulent, assassination-filled decade of the 1960s, he returned to France, where he pushed through paranoia, depression, and writer's block to complete *Tell Me How Long the Train's Been Gone* (1968) and *If Beale Street Could Talk* (1974). In 1979, he published his final novel, *Just Above My Head*, a work some critics consider his return to the brilliance of his debut novel. He continued to publish nonfiction until 1985.

Baldwin's upbringing in a Holiness/Pentecostal church culture deeply influenced his novels *Go Tell It on the Mountain* and *Just Above My Head*, where Baldwin's characters navigate the crossroads of Christian identity and homoerotic yearning. Each of these narratives features the emotional, sexual, and spiritual maturation of a young boy in a context in which religion plays a large role in his family life or career. The cohesion of religious disillusionment and coming-of-age are not simply coincidental themes—they merged similarly in Baldwin's early life. Particularly, his ideas about masculinity are often filtered through the Oedipal struggle that existed between him and his stepfather, David Baldwin, a Louisiana-born, itinerant Pentecostal preacher who, according to Baldwin, was "righteous in the pulpit, and a monster in the house" (Standley and Pratt 78). A primary source of their tension, Baldwin believed, was that he was the "outside" child, the oldest and only offspring (in the brood of nine) from his mother's previous relationship. His stepfather's unsubtle contempt led to competition and hatred between them. Eventually, Baldwin found solace in another home, a different church than that of his family, which was led by a woman pastor, Mother Horn. At Fireside Pentecostal Church, under the tutelage of Mother Horn, the young man developed into a popular, fiery child preacher at age fourteen. For this reason, the age of fourteen becomes *the* symbol of transition in many of his stories, including those discussed in this chapter. Meanwhile, instead of bringing the Baldwin men closer, "all those sermons and tears and all that repentance and rejoicing had changed nothing" between them (*Fire Next Time* 54). On the contrary, this only fueled their competition. According to Baldwin, the local demand for his father's preaching was dwindling at the time that the young boy's reputation was growing (Campbell 9).

Even though it is apparent that he was still seeking approval from his stepfather when he joined the ministry, it was also the fear of his burgeoning "sinful" desires that drove him to the pulpit. Evangelism was a means of hiding from himself. "I rushed home from school," Baldwin recounts, "to the church, to the altar, to be alone there, to commune with Jesus, my dearest Friend, who would never fail me, who knew all the secrets of my heart. Perhaps He did, but I didn't, and the bargain we struck, actually, down there at the foot of the cross, was that He would never let me find out" (*Fire* 34). But he eventually did find out:

> I knew how I worked myself up into my own visions, and how frequently—indeed, incessantly—the visions God granted me differed from the visions He granted to my father. I did not understand the dreams I had at night, but I knew that they were not holy. For that matter, I knew that my waking hours were far from holy. I spent most of my time in a state of repentance for things I had vividly desired to do but had not done. (*Fire* 35)

This passage hints at the synthesis of the sacred and profane (presented here as states of consciousness/unconsciousness and wake/sleep) that blossom in Baldwin's novels. His desires, as they were revealed to him in his dreams, were not holy according to his religious paradigm. Ultimately, he realizes, his conflict was not with God, but with his religion; with the differences between his beliefs and his reality; and with what he had been taught and what were his self-discovered truths. Over time, his hatred for David Baldwin settled into indifference, and his inner conflict with self-knowledge and doctrinal teachings developed into full-blown disillusion with the Christian religion. He describes an overwhelming struggle that ends in his casting off the cloak of the ministry and, eventually, organized religion altogether. In an articulation that suggests secular humanist leanings, Baldwin proclaims:

> [W]hoever wishes to become a truly moral human being . . . must divorce himself from all the prohibitions, crimes and hypocrisies of the Christian church. If the concept of God has any validity or

> any use, it can only be to make us larger, freer, and more loving. If God cannot do this, then it is time we got rid of Him. (*Fire* 47)

I cannot assert with any confidence that Baldwin ever "got rid" of God for himself, but his Christian characters engage in behaviors that demonstrate alternative understandings of a "larger, freer, and more loving" engagement with spirituality.

I focus on passages from three of Baldwin's gay Christian narratives (in order of discussion): "The Outing," *Go Tell It on the Mountain*, and *Just Above My Head* were published in very different phases of his career. Each of these stories is relevant to this discussion because, as I said earlier, they feature the emotional, sexual, and spiritual maturation (or engagement) of a young boy in a context in which religion plays a large role in his family life or career. In the first two texts, a short story that appeared in a 1965 collection *Going to Meet the Man*, and his debut novel, which appeared more than a decade earlier, Baldwin pays particular attention to the conversion experience and, as Michael Cobb has demonstrated, employs violent language that replicates the pain of denial, rejection, or the suppression of the homosexual self required by the characters' religious community. I also demonstrate that Baldwin suggests, alternatively, in *Just Above My Head*, that redemption and healing can be found in a salvific, sacred sensuality which bonds bodies, souls, and hearts to each other.

"PAGAN LUST" AND SPIRITUAL RESISTANCE

Baldwin analogizes the relationship between the biblical characters David and Jonathan in *Go Tell It on the Mountain* and the short story "The Outing." In the bible, David slays the towering Philistine giant, Goliath, with a stone and a slingshot. He would eventually become King David, ruler of Israel for forty years and, according to the gospels authored by Mark and Luke, is the great-grandson of Ruth (mentioned in the Hughes short story), and an ancestor of Jesus. He is depicted, variably, as a righteous king, fearless warrior, selfish and licentious man, skilled harpist and poet, and is credited with composing the *Book of Psalms*. Most relevant to us is the bible's documentation of the intense bond and devotion between David and his friend Jonathan, the son of a king. The men are often cited in LGBT discourse as an example of queer validation in the bible and are widely depicted in white-authored gay literature.

In the bible, the books of Samuel 1 and 2 narrate how the boys' mutual devotion subverts social norms when Jonathan defies his father's wishes (on multiple occasions) to the extent that David is able to inherit the kingdom of Israel illegitimately. After the killing of Goliath, the reigning king of Israel, Saul, rewards David by appointing him a commander over his armies and gifting him a bride—the king's daughter, Michal. Since David is known to be a talented harpist, he also bestows on him the title of the king's personal musician. Apparently, all of Israel is grateful and in awe of David's feat over the menacing giant, even Jonathan, the son of Saul and heir apparent to the throne of Israel. As a gesture of goodwill and respect, he hands over his uniform to David and, as the following passage reports, both the king and his son adopt him into the family immediately:

> And it came to pass, when he had made an end of speaking unto Saul, that the soul of *Jonathan was knit with the soul of David*, and Jonathan loved him as his own soul. And Saul took him that day, and would let [David] go no more home to his [own] father's house. Then *Jonathan and David made a covenant, because he loved him* as his own soul. And Jonathan stripped himself of the robe that was upon him, and gave it to David, and his garments, even to his sword, and to his bow, and to his girdle. (1 Sam. 18:1–4, KJV; my italics)

Although traditional interpretations insist that the men were not exhibiting a sexual or erotic bond, bible scholars disagree about the possible meanings of the "knitting of souls" and the constant reaffirming of the "covenant" of love, which binds the men from the moment they met.

Continuing with the summary: Things soon change after the initial generous reception into the family. David becomes successful in many battles and, consequently, his popularity arouses the insecurity of King Saul. By various stratagems, the jealous king seeks his death, but the plots only endear David the more to the people, and especially Jonathan, who eventually aids and abets David's escape from the assassins. Throughout this epic tale of (Saul's) subterfuge and (and the boys') vigilance, the bible describes, in glowing terms, Jonathan and David's closeness: they are constantly embracing and kissing, and openly weep together. They seek each other out and make time to be alone together and, when alone, profess their mutual commitment. Jonathan goes against his father, his family, and his own inheritance of the kingdom, in favor of supporting

David. Years later, Saul and Jonathan will die in battle together; and David exclaims sorrowfully, "I am distressed for thee, my brother Jonathan: very pleasant hast thou been unto me: thy love to me was wonderful, passing the love of women" (2 Samuel 1:26 KJV). For the anti-homophobic reader, the relationship is, at best, ambiguous; for advocates of same-sex love, it is the biblically sanctioned model for their own relationships (Frontain 1). In Baldwin's application of this narrative blueprint, there is an unmistakable erotic undercurrent.

Briefly, it must be noted that in his appropriation of the Jonathan/David saga, Baldwin also gestures to another biblical character, Elisha, a master prophet from a different historical period. As the bible story goes, Elisha was the protégé of the great prophet and highly beloved Elijah. So adored by God was he, that Elijah was taken up in a chariot of fire instead of having to experience physical death. Elisha, ever the devoted companion and apprentice, witnessed the death-miracle. In an unprecedented move, Elisha asks God for, "a double portion" (2 Kings 2:9) of his mentor's spiritual anointing as an inheritance. This is important because it was the law of the land that the first-born son inherit a double portion of his father's property (Deuteronomy 21:17)—and Elisha was not in the elder prophet's bloodline. What his prayer does, then, is make a claim to an inheritance through spiritual kinship. For some bible scholars, this signifies that relationship between Elijah and his near-doppelganger, Elisha, "involves a refraction of the fierce fidelity of David and Jonathan" (Brodie 55). Apparently, God approves the request; Elisha's prayer is answered and his ministry prefigures that of Jesus. His miracles include: parting the Jordan River, feeding a large group of people with a supernatural increase in the amount of food, water and food purification, healing of a leper, and the resurrection of a dead child. There is also a posthumous miracle whereby a dead body was hidden in Elisha's burial chamber and "when the man was let down, and touched the bones of Elisha, he revived, and stood up on his feet" (2 Kings 13:20–21). In two of his gay Christian narratives, Baldwin combines the legacies of Jonathan, the son of a king; and David, the warrior-poet; with that of Elisha, the master prophet.

Baldwin first summons the legacies of Jonathan, David, and Elisha in "The Outing," which was published three years before *Go Tell It on the Mountain* and is considered an early sketch of the novel. The story is set in the summer, during an annual Fourth of July church day-trip across New York's Hudson River by ferry. The protagonist is Johnnie, the son of the pious Deacon Grimes, a formerly itinerant preacher from the South who is awaiting his promotion within their church's hierarchy. Deacon Grimes wants the opportunity to preach but must settle for being a deacon, a powerful but mostly administrative position, until the pastor deems him suitable for the pulpit. Johnnie, as the son of a preacher, correlates to Jonathan in that he is expected to eventually join the ministry (access to the church's throne); and Deacon Grimes's mounting dislike toward his son's friend, David, corresponds to Saul's resentment of the brother-outsider of biblical lore. Between Johnnie and his father lies a palpable "unnamed and deadly tension" (776),[1] which stems from Johnnie's refusal to join the church, an act of teenage rebellion that embarrasses and infuriates the deacon. The deacon's other two children, including his nine-year-old daughter, have already fallen in line as members. This is related to why David is looked on with suspicion by Deacon Grimes and the rest of the church. He is not from a family that attends this church and he has befriended the rebellious child, Johnnie. Meanwhile, the father-son tension is on display in every interaction. At one point, Johnnie "knew that his father would then and there have knocked him down if they had not been in the presence of saints and strangers" (777). Instead of physical violence, the deacon hurls a threat: "Don't you get grown too fast. We get home, I'll pull down those long pants and we'll see who's the man, you hear me?" (777). The threat to strip the boy down to nakedness is an infantilizing gesture, as it suggests physical domination and punishment, and contains a subtle reference to the size of Johnnie's penis, which is, presumably, still smaller than his father's. We are reminded of this in a subsequent passage when, immediately following the deacon's threat, Johnnie is teased by his older brother, Roy, for his sexual innocence. The scene ends with Roy's braggadocios claim that he knows he "aint no baby [because] I got everything Daddy got" (777). So David's surfacing manhood is being challenged and critiqued in his relationships with his brother, friends, and father.

So Johnnie is navigating conflicting social messages and pressures. On one hand, there is the social expectation that, as a teenager, he will "be a man" and show romantic interest in girls. On the other, he is being pressured by the church community to become "saved" from such desires through commitment to a religious masculinity that espouses chastity and other conservative tenets regarding sexuality. It is significant that the characters are teens on the precipice of adulthood. Their bodies are yet uncorrupted—as far as the church members know—and this is the challenge facing the congregation. The saints want to "bring [the boys'] souls to safety in order . . . to steal a march on the flesh while the flesh still slept" (787). But the flesh is wide awake in each of them, evidenced by their boasts of pubic hairs, changing bodies, and talk of girlfriends. But Johnnie is not interested in either of the options posed by his father and brother. His emotional focus is on David as the following passage describes.

> They faced the water, their arms around each other.
>
> "Your old man was kind of rough this morning," David said carefully, watching the mountains pass.
>
> "Yes," Johnnie said. He looked at David's face against the sky. He shivered suddenly in the sharp, cold air and buried his face in David's shoulder. David looked down at him and tightened his hold.
>
> "Who do you love?" he whispered. "Who's your boy?"
>
> "You," he muttered fiercely, "I love you." (783)

So they love each other, but does it surpass the love of women? For Johnnie, their bond is an abiding "presence," which "seemed to reach out to him" and which "held him with such power" (790). In the bible, David loved Jonathan resolutely, but David was also a flawed character who disappointed God by allowing his sexual desires and greed to lead him astray at times.[2] Keeping in mind that "The Outing" is not an allegory, we can see a hint that David's affection and attention will stray from Johnnie.

The pressure to perform an assertively hetero masculinity plays out in the larger group of boys, which includes the older brother, Roy. The boys collaborated on a gift for a teen girl in the church, Sylvia, for her birthday. At the first opportunity, David is to hand over the gift in the presence of all the boys. But Sylvia is well guarded by her mother and Elisha, the highly esteemed church musician who is possessive of the young lady's company. So, in this early sketch, Elisha appears only as a competitor and an obstruction for the band of brothers. The boys surreptitiously sneer at Elisha because he is the image of religious masculinity to which they are compared and found wanting. When David is finally able makes his move, he is out of the view of everyone. His conversation with Sylvia is flirtatious and she hints that if he joins church at the next revival, she will spend more time with him. So it is to the dismay (and displacement) of Elisha, and the quiet disapproval of her mother, that Sylvia allows the unsaved David to walk with her back to the boat at the end of the picnic. The return trip reveals David's divided desires and that Johnnie, so assured earlier, is clearly threatened by David's apparent submission to the heterosexual rite of passage.

Like the novel it gave birth to, the short story raises questions about the affect of religious rhetoric on the queer subject. Is David's interest in Sylvia the threat Johnnie believes it is? Is David's attraction to a "sanctified" girl fueled by a desire to be less alienated by the church folk? What kind of people will Johnnie and David become if they succumb to the pressure to accept religion and also continue to experience homoerotic desire? Will they "remain, finding ways to exist within it"? (Johnson qtd in McNeir n.p.). Johnnie seems to intuit the demise of the relationship, that it will not be allowed to surpass gender norms. Baldwin further develops this interrogation in the characters' depictions in Book One of the tripartite novel, *Go Tell It on the Mountain.*

In the first section of *Go Tell It,* Baldwin pays particular attention to the conversion experience and, as Michael Cobb successfully argues in *God Hates Fags: The Rhetorics of Religious Violence*, he employs violent language that replicates the pain of denial, rejection, or the suppression of the homosexual self that is required by traditional Christian dogma. This is important because it functions as the critique that precedes the "corrective" spiritual practice that is offered in Baldwin's later fiction. "Johnnie" is changed to the more mature "John," and the birth order has changed so that he is the firstborn. The novel opens with the announcement of his fourteenth birthday, a signal that he is on the precipice of manhood. On this occasion, he is both afraid and rebellious. For, as in the short story, a central issue is the question of John's salvation. "Everyone had always said that John would be a preacher when he grew up, just like his father" (9). Yet John rejects his birthright to the pulpit. He has a different idea about what kind of man he wants to be. The narrator describes it as "hardheartedness" against the "holy life," which would deny him the secular pleasures: "He would not be like his father or his father's fathers" (17). First, his fear of becoming like his "father's fathers" is symbolized by his fear of what being "saved" looks like in worship service. "Catching the spirit," or succumbing to possession by the Holy Ghost, is highly prized evidence of one's salvation in the Pentecostal denomination and he finds the idea of the loss of control, the gesticulating bodies, and primal sounds frightening. So it is a meaningful moment in the novel when he suddenly finds himself on the floor of the church, "astonished beneath the power of the Lord" (183). As Cobb points out, the language evinces a wounding of the self. As the saints prayed, John

> [W]as invaded, set at naught, possessed. This power had *struck* John, in the head or in the heart; and, in a moment, wholly *filling him with anguish* that he could never in his life have imagined, that he surely could not endure, that even now he could not believe, had opened him up; had *cracked him open*, as wood beneath the axe . . . as rocks break up; had *ripped him* and felled him in a moment, so that John had not felt the wound, but only the *agony*, had not felt the fall, but only the *fear*; and lay here, now, *helpless, screaming*, at the very bottom of darkness. (187; emphasis added)

The italicized words illuminate the torturous descent into darkness, which is not at all akin to the traditional renditions of religious ecstasy of finding the light of salvation. It is a metaphor for the internal struggle against forces so powerful as to seem to rip the self into slivers.

John is also afraid of his attraction to boys and the pleasures he finds in homoerotic fantasy and masturbation. Mainly, these energies are projected onto Elisha's "powerful frame," as it was called in "The Outing," a figure that maintains a large presence in John's consciousness. When we encounter the same group of characters from the short story, Elisha retains his role as symbol of a nearly unattainable (and, consequently, resented) youthful piety. Elisha, a seventeen-year-old preacher from Georgia, is the pastor's nephew, and described as "tall and handsome . . . played basketball and . . . had been saved at the age of eleven" (15). He is the minister of music and a teacher at the Temple of the Fire Baptized in Harlem. At the beginning of the story, John watches Elisha intently as he teaches; intermittently ashamed and confused when their eyes meet. John's eyes caress the preacher's body as he admires "the leanness, and grace, and strength, and darkness of Elisha in his Sunday suit" (11). He sees in Elisha the son Gabriel probably yearns for, because "no one really expected of [the younger brother] Roy what was expected of John" (11). Elisha represents his failings as a son, a heterosexual, and as a Christian. So John's state of mind is affected by overlapping and conflicting desires. His resistance to becoming saved and joining the path to ministry is as much about his secrets as it is about his well-known strained relationship with the Deacon.

His struggle is dramatized as he lays on the floor of the church, literally captured by the Spirit, physically and emotionally situated between Elisha and his father, staring up at a large cross displayed on the wall of the sanctuary. His yearnings fluctuate as he lies there; alternately he wants to escape, and also to "confound" his father with a display of spiritual endowment on the level of Elisha's:

> And the Holy Ghost was speaking—seeming to say, as John spelled out the so abruptly present and gigantic legend adorning the cross: *Jesus Saves*. He had stared at this, an awful bitterness in his heart, wanting to curse—and the Spirit spoke, and spoke in him. Yes: there was Elisha, speaking from the floor, and his father, silent, at his back. In his heart there was *a sudden yearning tenderness* for holy Elisha; *desire, sharp and awful as a reflecting knife*, to usurp the body of Elisha, and lie where Elisha lay; to speak in tongues, as Elisha spoke, and with that authority, to confound his father. (188; my italics)

Notice that John hears the Spirit speak twice: it speaks to him and then *inside* him. The first fact is that the Spirit speaks a simple confirmatory "yes"; the second fact seems to be that it is Elisha—or John's attraction to Elisha—that is being affirmed. Significantly, the second voice is distinguished as internal because its effect is emotional and visceral. John's emotional environment changes immediately: bitterness is transformed into yearning tenderness. Part of his fixation with Elisha is a desire to embody the beauty, certainty, and overall ministerial masculinity Elisha so easily exudes. These emotions are tied to a wish to "confound his father" with a display of spirit possession—holiness—that "would conquer the great division between his father and himself" (201). Does not every boy want his father's approval and love? Still, it is also struggle against succumbing to his father's desires for his life, a capitulation that would, presumably, involve a denial of the erotic experience he is having as he lays near Elisha.

The rhetoric of this entire chapter conveys a soul-piercing crisis in which puberty, Oedipal impulses, and coming out to oneself (realizing homosexual inclination) converge in John's consciousness. That is to say, Baldwin portrays John's experience on the threshing floor as a battle of wills; and it is not so much a battle with the will of God, but with interpretations of manhood.[3] Even before he is sucked into the mystical whirlwind that moves through the church, John is terrified by the idea of a spiritual wrestling match by which, once subdued, he would be tied to a life in the pulpit. The first voice he hears as he lay on the floor is his own "malicious, ironic" (187) interior self that aims to be free of the constraints of church life. His inability to obey this desire triggers "bewildered terror" and more screaming. The coming out is signified in the double entendre in which "sudden yearning tenderness" for Elisha is felt as "sharp and awful as a reflecting knife," which is to say the longing cut into his consciousness quickly and deeply. This turn of phrase follows the "tightening in his loin-strings" that occurs in the beginning of the spiritual wrestling match. Perhaps, in the frenzy of holy dancing, crying, praying, and ecstatic utterance, John's desire for the beautiful Elisha also manifests as an erection as sharp as a reflecting knife. Overall, the scene generates circulating energies—the overwhelming Holy Spirit that holds him hostage on the floor, the lust for Elisha that is projected as ministerial envy, and the unspoken plea for his father's love. Rather than a blissful release and relief through possession by and submission to the Spirit, John's conversion experience is wrought with psychological violence, fear, and confusion.

In the broad view of Baldwin's work regarding religious conversion and/or the meaning of salvation, we can see a shift in the focus of his rhetorical project in the later fiction. These early narratives do not offer theological correctives concerning same-sex erotics. Instead, Baldwin appropriates biblical themes and invokes these particular legends to tell a modern story about religious masculinity and patriarchal legacy—an identical subtext to Hughes' short story in the previous chapter. *Go Tell It* and "The Outing" raise questions about the roles families and church communities have scripted for the boys in their care. What is lost when we insist on a single narrative of sexuality? And a single narrative of masculine expression? Or a single path to righteous living? These Gay Christian Narratives implicate the church and religious doctrine as sites of spiritual bondage and wounding.[4] They also identify the fundamentalist evangelical church as a space in which homoerotic dynamics can emerge and surge, even (or especially) during passionate or climactic moments. The way Baldwin takes up some of these questions in his final novel, *Just Above My Head*, is to supplement the struggle against submission with an alternative paradigm.

SUBMISSION TO SACRED SENSUALITY

Kenneth Burke, in *The Rhetoric of Religion*, argues that the use of sacred words in a secular context effectively raises that word or phrase to the level of the sacred. According to Burke, religious expressions are imbued with a sacred aura because they represent a holy and otherworldly realm in the imagination of the speech community, and then are used among secular terminologies to apply that sacredness to the secular experience:

> For whereas the words for the supernatural realm are necessarily borrowed from the realm of our everyday experiences, out of which our familiarity with language arises, *once a terminology has been developed for special theological purposes the order can become reversed*. We can borrow back the terms from the borrower, again secularizing to varying degrees the originally secular terms that had been given "supernatural" connotations. (7)

So the paradox is that a word that conveys a sacred notion is set aside—borrowed—in the consciousness as metaphysical or supernatural and then, for effect, is moved back into the realm of the natural, even though it is always the language of the physical world. These words inherently represent the physical because this is the limit of human experience. Still, the psychosocial weight of its "supernatural" status is real. In semiotic terms, a sign that represents the heavenly or godly sphere can bestow its sanctity or supernaturality on other signs in its discursive system. Once they are considered holy or sacred words, they are borrowed back into secular speech for an intensifying affect.[5]

One of the shifts in *Just Above My Head* from an illustration of what Cobb calls the use of religious rhetoric as hate speech, are the ways in which Baldwin employs this borrowing back technique. In candid sexual scenes, particularly, he interposes descriptions of eroticized bodies with lyrics from spirituals and hymns; and also, in one passage, demonstrates how the act of sacred music performance can create an aura of sacredness around that which is otherwise deemed abominable and unholy. Instead of a character traumatized by religious hate speech, the reader witnesses a paradigm shift in which a moment of "sinful" behavior is used to illustrate transcendent carnality. The transformative experience is not restricted to church buildings or worship service, the novel argues, it also occurs in bedrooms, and between lovers' thighs and lips. This is a Gay Christian Narrative because homoeroticism and spirituality merge in Baldwin's romantic use of sacred songs and religious terminology. In her important study of Baldwin's later fiction, Lynn Orilla Scott attests that "Gospel music is represented as a coded expression of an oppressed community, but—most important—in Baldwin's work it is also represented as a coded expression of sexual desire" (144). Trudier Harris further observes that, in this novel "awash with sexual baptisms," Baldwin portrays the connection to the divine as an erotic connection between men of faith (169). But we see in the analysis that Baldwin does not limit his portrayal of the sacred erotic to men's relationships with each other. The core message is more inclusive: consensual sex acts, and the pleasure garnered therein, can be ceremonies that save and heal the soul. This is the salvific principle of sacred sensuality.

Just Above My Head follows thirty years in the lives of a group of friends who are either members of or otherwise associated with the all-male Trumpets of Zion gospel quartet through their Harlem church community. By the end, they variously survive incest, the Korean war, urban poverty, and the Civil Rights Movement—and some do not survive. Arthur, who over the course of the novel becomes a world-acclaimed soul music artist, shares the narrative's center with Julia, at first a fiery child preacher who later emerges as a world-traveled fashion model. The salvific principle of sacred sensuality is demonstrated most vividly in the descriptive passages that feature two major characters, Arthur, age sixteen, and Crunch, his nineteen-year-old friend, during their years in the quartet. The first passages we examine between Arthur and Crunch reveal the ways in which music is the metaphor and central expression of their erotic journey.

For example, when he and Crunch kiss for the first time, "something like terror leaps in Arthur: something in him sings" (190). Also, importantly, to capture the ambivalence and self-consciousness of each moment of gender and sexual transgression, Baldwin often triangulates fear, joy, and (the problem of) voice in his narration. So, when Arthur yearns for Crunch from across a table in a church cafeteria, the spiritual, "Deep River," is invoked to communicate the immensity of his feelings, and is combined with the sensory experience of smell. The narrator explains: "Crunch's smell was in his nostrils, the overwhelming image of the hair in his armpits, the basketball player's thighs and ankles, *deep like a river*, Arthur thought, insanely, his arms, his arms; then suddenly, silence dropped on him like a heavy cloud" (193; original italics). The allusion to the spiritual articulates a liberation theology; it expresses a belief that God hears the pleas of those in bondage. To reach freedom, one must cross the river Jordan "into campground," which research suggests was an allegory for crossing the Mississippi River into free territory during the slavery period.[6] The lyrics are:

Deep river.
My home is over Jordan.
Deep river, Lord.
I want to cross over into campground.
Oh, don't you want to go,
to the Gospel feast?
That Promised Land,
where all is peace?
Oh, deep River, Lord.
I want to cross over into campground.

Simultaneously, the song retains its religious meaning of a desire to be with God in the afterlife. Baldwin attaches these spatial and spiritual meanings to black male erotic desire.

The phrasing in the passage also reminds readers of Langston Hughes' 1922 poem, "The Negro Speaks of Rivers." The poem challenges the then-widely held racist notion that black people have no remarkable history. It does so by tracing the African presence from the earliest Nile cultures to the banks of the largest and longest river in North America, the Mississippi River. I've known "ancient dusky rivers" the speaker concludes, and "my soul has grown deep like the rivers." The poem expands black creativity, freedom, and cultures to a time "older than the flow of human blood" while emphasizing a present-day black interiority. To have this famous political assertion emerge in the middle of a homoerotic fantasy enacts a blanket queering of black history: Crunch's long, black body represents ancient same-sex desires and ancient masculinity. Arthur thinks the phrase, *deep like a river*, as his mind's eye caresses Crunch's legs and arms. Therefore, "deep" in this case indicates a physical presence. Crunch's body and its sexual potential is a space into which Arthur imagines sinking. From an emotional perspective, Arthur's "overwhelming" craving is likened to drowning, for the desire rises so quickly and so "insanely" as to feel bottomless.

Another passage builds on these meanings as the boys moan, sweat, and sway through their performance of a sacred song. It retains the water metaphor but utilizes the sense of sound as their vocal performance functions as foreplay and foreshadowing. That is, before they consummate their relationship physically, they achieve it melodically in a church performance with the Trumpets of Zion. Baldwin describes it thusly:

> Crunch's guitar began, as Arthur's voice began,
>
> *Take me to the water*
>
> Crunch moaned,
>
> *yes! Take me to the water!*
>
> He heard [another's singer's] witnessing falsetto, but he answered Crunch's echo,
>
> *take me to the water/ to be baptized.*
>
> He paused, and closed his eyes, sweat gathered in his hair; he listened to Crunch, then he started again. [Repeats refrain with call-and-response between group members].
>
> He paused again . . . trusting every second of this unprecedented darkness, knowing Crunch and he were moving together, here, now, in the song, to some new place; they had never sung together like this before, his voice in Crunch's sound, Crunch's sound filling his voice,
>
> *So*
> *I know*
> *None*
> *don't tell me, I know, I know, I know!*
>
> as though Crunch were laughing and crying at the same time
>
> *but the righteous*
> *so true!*
> *none*
> *don't you leave me now!*
> *but the righteous*
> *[. . .]*
> *yea, little fellow, come on in!*
> *shall see God.*
>
> Crunch and he ending together, as though on a single drum. (199)

Overtly, the song refers to baptism, the religious ritual whereby a believer demonstrates his or her spiritual renewal through full immersion in a body of water; it is a symbolic "washing" away of the old way of being. So the singer directs the audience to take him to the river to act on his faith, a requirement, as the song says, to prove himself before his God.

Further, the river symbolism, which emerged in the previous scene and is threaded through this one, allows Arthur to verbalize his erotic attraction to his fellow vocalist (earlier, he simply sank into silence) in the African American oral tradition of dual coding. Through this performance, Arthur articulates a desire to fully submerge into Crunch's "deepness." The narration indicates that Arthur is completely in tandem with Crunch's musical strides as they moved toward "some new place," which is their mutually recognized spiritual-emotional bond. Crunch's understanding of the subliminal significance is evidenced in his responses. "Don't tell me. I know! I know! I know" he exclaims, sounding as if he were "laughing and crying at the same time." The unprecedented merging in which Arthur's experiences "his voice in Crunch's sound, [and] Crunch's sound filling his voice" foreshadows their sex acts. The musical performance, particularly the way in which "Crunch's [guitar] sound fill[s] his voice," and Crunch's ad lib, "yeah, little fellow, come on in," foreshadows the subsequent fellatio scene.

In the succeeding passage, Arthur and Crunch express themselves through physical affection, including oral sex and intercourse. This time Baldwin incorporates lyrics from the spiritual "You Must Come in at the Door" to communicate the confluence of their sexuality and spirituality. Significantly, the meaning of the water imagery changes so that it now symbolizes uncontrollable and overwhelming emotions:

> Crunch moaned again, surrendering, surrendering, as Arthur's tongue descended Crunch's long black self, down to the raging penis. He licked the underside of the penis, feeling it leap, and he licked the balls. He was setting Crunch free—he was giving Crunch what he, somehow, knew that Crunch longed and feared to give *him.* Arthur understood Crunch's terror—the terror of someone in the water, being carried away from the shore—and this terror, which was his own terror, soon caused him to gasp. . . . A moment came when he felt Crunch pass from a kind of terrified bewilderment into joy. A friendly, a joyful movement, began. *So high, you can't get over him.* Sweat from Arthur's forehead fell onto Crunch's belly. *So low*—and Crunch gasped as Arthur's mouth left his prick standing in the cold, cold air, as Arthur's tongue licked his sacred balls—*you can't get under him.* Arthur rose, again, to Crunch's lips. *So Wide. You can't get around it.* It was as though, with this kiss, they were forever bound together. Crunch moaned, in absolute agony, and Arthur went down again. Little fellow. Baby. Love. *You must come in at the door.* (208)

The lyrics in the song "My God Is So High" construct the Creator as an omnipresent and inescapable force. Baldwin appropriates this worldview to illustrate homoerotic energy, love, and, perhaps, as a way to say that one cannot escape one's own truth. Even as Arthur knows he is "setting Crunch free" or in religious terms, saving him, the reasons for the underlying terror cannot be ignored: these boys are deeply entrenched in a religious doctrine that teaches that this behavior offends God.[7] Together in spirit and ecstasy they struggle against the homophobic ideologies of hegemonic blackness. They face the terror of community judgment and, in narration that relies on "the eros inhabiting the language of religious surrender and redemption," the text links salvation, sex, and Spirit (Edelman 69). As they move closer to a climax, the narrative interjects testimonial lyrics to broaden the reader's understanding of what is happening spiritually. Baldwin uses the normalizing authority of sacred words to stake a claim for homoerotic sacredness and to make vibrant what is not supposed to be part of normalcy; that is, the queer (Cobb, "Pulpitic Publicity" 287.)

The appropriation of religious song to express human desire for freedom, dignity, and love in this world as well as the next, conflates sacred and secular meaning in a manner consistent with a long African American tradition of representation (Scott 169). But according to ethnographer Glenn Hinson, sacred song is much more than religious expression in black Holiness/Pentecostal tradition, which is the denomination represented in this novel. In his research Hinson discovered that, among this sect of Christians, song stands apart in worship services.

> For the saints, pleasuring the Lord is the frame within which all sacred song falls. Whenever one joins the choruses of a congregation, sings as a performer before a church audience, hums melodic praises in a moment of privacy, or simply listens to sacred songs on the radio, *one enters a sphere imbued with associations of celestial agency and godly delight*. Engaging with song thus entails more than just engaging in praise. It also entails . . . partaking of the holy. (110–111 italics added)

Herein, Burke's and Hinson's ideas connect so that the intersecting of erotic ecstasy with a sacred song elevates Arthur and Crunch's lovemaking to the very pinnacle of "pleasuring the Lord." It is a sanctification of the homosexual act. As they move together in sacred sensuality, the narrative follows their emotional movement from terror to joy and finally to love. Sexual ecstasy, sealed with a kiss and the affirmation, "you must come in at the door," is imbued with associations of celestial agency and godly delight. It is worship, praise, and baptism, as Arthur and Crunch are dipped in body waters—sweat, spit, and eventually semen—in a moment that marks the sensual initiation into their love affair. This narrative strategy creates a metaphysical, theological space for romantic/sexual love between black Christian men.

In the following passage, lyrics from the spiritual "My Soul's Been Satisfied" are used to describe the boys' feelings during and postcoitus. This is a song about being rescued by the companionship of the gospel of Jesus Christ and may be an iteration of 2 Corinthians 5:17, in which Paul writes, "Therefore if any man be in Christ, he is a new creature: old things are passed away; behold, all things are become new." Some of the lyrics include:

> Said He would be my comfort
> Said He would be my guide
> Well, I looked at my hands, my hands looked new
> I looked at my feet and they did too
> And ever since that wonderful day
> My soul's been satisfied.
> Well, it was way down yonder in the valley
> I was wandering all alone.
> And it was there I met my Jesus, where
> He claimed me for His own.
> And then He put His arms all around me there
> And then He drew me up to His side.
> Oh yes, I'm satisfied.

With these scriptures and lyrics in mind, observe the way Baldwin entwines the notion of spiritual renewal and contentment with romantic emotional involvement:

> They were beginning to know each other; the biblical phrase unlocked itself and held them together in a joy as sharp as terror. Crunch lay on his belly for Arthur and pulled Arthur into him, and Arthur lay on his belly for Crunch, and Crunch entered

> Arthur—it was incredible that it hurt so much, and yet, hurt so little, that so profound an anguish, thrusting so hard, so deep, accomplished such a transformation, *I looked at my hands and they looked new, I looked at my feet and they did, too!* But that is how they sang, really, something like fifteen minutes later, out of joy of their surrender and deliverance, out of their secret knowledge that each contained the other. (213; original emphasis)

Baldwin's narration of the transformative experience of anal penetration inverts Maurice Wallace's analogy above in which he asserts, "To submit fully to the self-shattering [moment] in religion and/or sex is to sacrifice the aura of fucking or being fucked" (*Souls A'fire* 5). Baldwin's narration demonstrates that the aura of being fucked is akin to the submission to the spirit at the climax of ecstatic worship. (If any man enters another, is he also a new creature?) Crunch and Arthur alternately surrender their bodies to each other and it is this private performance, "their secret knowledge," which transforms and brings deliverance to both the giver and receiver. They then transpose that joy onto the sacred act of pleasuring the Lord through song.

To clarify that his theological premise is not about being fully inclusive of every potential version of sexual coupling but, rather, is that humanity must save itself through deeper and truer intimacy and self-knowledge, Baldwin contrasts damaging forms of sexual interaction with those that allow the self to heal and flourish in healthy ways. This is especially apparent in the depiction of Julia's emotionally tumultuous life as a child preacher; the character is obviously informed by Baldwin's own flight from the pulpit. Julia was a (regionally) renowned child preacher from Arthur's church community who grew up to become a sex worker; then worked a stint as an international fashion model; and finally ends up in Yonkers, New York. The spiritual rupture in her life is precipitated by two equally devastating events: Julia is fourteen when her father rapes her, and this violation, coupled with the death of her mother—after much feverous prayer and attempts at faith healing—was the final traumatic push in her fast-paced journey toward religious disillusion. Actually, those events occur in the opposite order: after the disastrous outcome of relying on the power of religion, instead of conventional medicine, to heal her mother, Julia is raped by her father, Joel. Joel justifies his behavior to his daughter as a natural desire that is suppressed by societal taboo but which is not unusual:

> What happens between you and me happens, happens all the time—this ain't the last time or the first time or the only time. I just ain't being a hypocrite about it—that's all. . . . *All* little girls wants their daddy—everybody knows that. I didn't do a damn thing but give you what you wanted. . . . We love each other, well, let's just love each other. We doing any harm to anybody? (235)

This version of love is depicted as a debilitating and exacting force on the spirit. As the incestuous relationship continues, Julia exists in a state of stunned and confused loyalty, and so continues to preach for some time; meanwhile, her father sinks into alcoholism. To answer Joel's question, the narrator describes the rape as attempted soul murder: "Every thrust of her father's penis seemed to take away the life that it had given, thrust anguish deeper into her, into a place too deep for the sex of any man to reach, into a place it would take her many years to find, a place deeper than the miracle of the womb, deeper, almost, than the love which is salvation" (172). *Almost* deeper than love.

Then, this depiction of a traumatized black woman whose vision is clouded by madness, despair, and suicidal thoughts is contrasted with sexual love between friends as the path to redemption, healing, and reclamation of the self. At the insistence of Arthur's mother, Arthur and Crunch visit Julia to subtly investigate rumors that she had left the ministry. Without them having to inquire, she explains that she has become completely disillusioned: "I don't know how to save nobody's soul. I don't know how to save *my* soul" (227). When Crunch and Julia eventually engage in sexual intercourse, the form of salvation proffered by the tenets of Julia's religion is displaced by the "love which is salvation." Or, to use Clarence Hardy's perspective in *James Baldwin's God*: "In God's place we find the sweaty bodies that always seem to take center stage in Baldwin's imagination (58). Indeed, the heterosexual encounter is as juicy with emotion and bodily fluids as the earlier encounter between the men. Without exception, bodily pleasure is always in concert with spiritual enhancement in this novel. So after assuring the much older Crunch of her consent, Julia undresses him and actively pursues her salvation:

> He felt at once helpless and helplessly powerful: he could not refuse her. She unbuckled his belt, he let his pants fall to the floor. Her body, now, again as though she were blind, strained

> against his body, discovering it. He let her have her way, tremendously excited, but frightened, too. He wondered if she really knew what she wanted, he was afraid he would hurt her; but she put her hand on him and looked up at him with eyes which held neither fear nor pain. She pulled him down with her to the floor and, very, very, slowly, he entered her—she holding him close, sweating, straining to take it all, as he grew larger and larger, and though still trying be gentle, thrust harder and harder. She thrust to meet him, with astonishing strength, smiling and calling his name over and over. . . . [S]he laughing and crying and calling his name and pulling him always deeper into her—almost as though his lunging body would touch and open and drench and heal her soul. He, as it were, prayed with her, longing to give her all that she needed. (240)

Although the description would be improved with more detail about female arousal and orgasm, the presence of sweat, tears, and semen convey well the bodily theology at work in the novel. It is made immediately clear that Julia has been baptized and given herself back to herself anew. Importantly, though, the finding of the sexual-spiritual self is not associated with lost innocence; that is, Julia does not become a woman in this scene. Instead, the affect of redemptive intimacy is the re-membering of the body and the return of equilibrium. If the incest was a near-death experience, consensual intimacy is the resurrection of the will to live: "What her father had stolen from her, Crunch had given back. She was fourteen [again]: suddenly, she was only fourteen" (241). Julia realizes that she is not destined to be her mother's replacement and the bond she builds with Crunch, who would depart for the Korean War within a week, is the first step she takes away from her tomblike existence in her father's house and onto a path of healing.

In another context, L. H. Stallings makes the eloquent observation, "Sexual desire is a song; the body, its lyrics; the spirit, its music; and the mind, its arranger. It can be remade, sampled, and remixed for the needs of the performer and the audience" (*Mutha Is Half a Word* 221). Baldwin's work demonstrates such musicality as it samples religious terminology and remixes baptism, conversion, and ecstasy to compose a melody of black eros that endorses queer sexuality. For the needs of his audience, Baldwin lyricizes sensuality, an engagement with the body, as the gateway to (and indivisible from) the spiritual realm. This construction of spirituality rejects widespread religious practices that require the sacrifice of bodily desires to gain spiritual access to God or in which deprivation is often equated with holiness. By this I mean premarital chastity (the delay of pleasure), or lifelong chastity (the sacrificing of pleasure) as religious or spiritual practice. This kind of splitting of the self, as Audre Lorde once commented, has "reduced the spiritual to a world of flattened affect, a world of the ascetic who aspires to feel nothing" (56). The ascetic lifestyle is not the height of spirituality, she argues, but is the height of "self-abnegation." Baldwin's characters and narration in his last published novel resist such self-abnegation by equating the erotic bond with spiritual engagement through the language of sacred music and other religious terminology, all of which elevates the bond into the realm of the sacred.

PART II

Philosophies of the Spirit

CHAPTER FOUR

Soul Talk and Sermonic Seduction

The Color Purple

Say Jesus and Come to Me

While Hughes and Baldwin represent the revisionist and appropriative aspects of the Gay Christian Narrative, the women writers in this chapter provide a slightly different take on the relationship between the queer subject and African American church traditions. Admittedly, the distinction is somewhat specious because, on first glance, it is clear that the novels in this chapter by Ann Allen Shockley and Alice Walker are as much influenced by the bible and Afro-Christian traditions as the writers in the previous chapters. And inversely, Baldwin's bodily theology shares some elements of the "soul talk" (explained later) featured here. Where they mainly diverge is in the ways each narrative critiques and revises the limitations presented by the religious conservatism that characters encounter in their respective contexts. For Delmar in Chapter Two and the lovers, Arthur and Crunch, in Chapter Three, it was the limitations placed on black masculinity that they pushed against, and it was within the space of musical performance that they were able to find room for possibility and public transgression. We find in the upcoming discussion that the gender-based boundaries faced by women require woman-centered alternatives.

This and the following chapter constitute my study of philosophies of the spirit that foreground individual truths, intuition, and folk knowledge. The authors are part of a larger cultural shift that occurred among

African American women fiction writers and poets in the 1980s away from an emphasis on feminist rhetoric and toward illustrations of social justice work(ers) attuned to the spiritual profundity of the everyday environment. In a collection of interviews considering the reasons for the shift, *Soul Talk: The New Spirituality of African American Women*, Akasha Gloria Hull explains that the energy and activity that was highly visible in the 1970s, appeared to be declining and "politicos and various cultural observers were declaring that social activism was dead" (6). Actually, Hull realized, such "transformative energy" was not diminishing but "expanding to encompass an enlarged spirituality" (6), one that produces a feminist discourse that operates in three dimensions simultaneously: progressive politics, spiritual consciousness, and creativity.[1] I take up Hull's term for this particular synthesis, *soul talk*, to discuss three narratives that foreground supernatural material, or that involve characters in a conscious relationship with the realm of spirit, and maintain a feminist sensibility (Hull 2). I show that soul talk intersects with same-sex eroticism to reveal a black lesbian or bisexual liberation theology; a belief system in which the sensual pleasure shared between the women characters *is* the substance of their spiritual connection with each other, with the planet, and with the cosmos.

RELIGIOUS AROUSAL AND SERMONIC SEDUCTION: *SAY JESUS AND COME TO ME*

The reclusive writer Ann Allen Shockley has worn many hats in the literary field but is most celebrated for her pioneering work as an archivist, librarian, and fiction writer. In her early years as a librarian, she co-authored *Living Black American Authors: A Biographical Directory* (1973), which was the first compendium of contemporary African American writers. She was commissioned to write the groundbreaking *Handbook of Black Librarianship*, which, among other topics, includes descriptions/locations of established African American collections, provides guidance for how to select and establish a black-authored collection, and includes some historical background of library organizations. She is also credited with filling an important void when she edited *Afro-American Women Writers 1746–1933: An Anthology and Critical Guide*, which was the definitive source when it appeared. Her most recent novel is *Celebrating Hotchclaw* (2005), a story that situates a transgender person's experience on the campus of a historically black university.

Although her early fiction has been mostly ignored by critics, Shockley's focus on gender politics in African American communities and the creation of the first black lesbian protagonist in the novel *Loving Her* (1974) garnered her the most critical attention her work has received to date, most of it negative.[2] The protagonist in *Loving Her*, Renay, provides a lesbian feminist response to the homophobic and heterosexist myopia of black nationalist discourses as it "problematizes illusive notions of a fixed or unitary black heteronormativity" (Melancon 644). In a subsequent project, *The Black and White of It* (1980), Shockley continued to stimulate new discourse by publishing the first collection of lesbian-themed short stories by an African American. *Black and White* portrays successful professional women who negotiate their oppression as lesbians in different ways, and provides a representation that "disrupts the constructs of racialized sexuality and the heterosexualization of desire" (Stallings, "Re-Reading" 69). Shockley often uses the context of traditional black institutions, such as marriage and the historically black college, as a launching pad for non-traditional ideas (Gomez, "Celebrating" 10). Such is the case in her 1982 novel, *Say Jesus and Come to Me*, wherein she uses the context of a black church service to construct a homoerotic spirituality that disrupts traditional notions of black religiosity. As I mentioned earlier, *Say Jesus* could easily fit into the Gay Christian Narrative category because it involves a Christian woman who negotiates her oppression as a lesbian *within* her faith community instead of separating herself from it. Yet Shockley's narrative is more syncretic in its depictions (than Baldwin or Hughes' are) in that it also draws on and emphasizes the African roots of her character's spirituality. The novel also executes a particularly feminist politics at a "higher, more spiritualized frequency" (Hull 6) than her earlier anti-racist work.

In *Say Jesus*, Reverend Myrtle Black is a controversial character who embodies the intersection of sexual desire and religious enjoyment: audiences experience her sermonic performance as magnetic lesbian energy. A traveling minister from an acclaimed and respected family of evangelists, her preaching was in steady demand and she was always able to draw large crowds. Her routine was to preach a fiery sermon, connect with a woman from the congregation for an overnight fling, and then move on to the next church to begin again. Spurred by the assault of two sex workers that occurred while she was in Nashville, and the chauvinistic attitude of the pastor of a church there (he had invited her but became envious of the people's reaction to her), Myrtle decides to take up residence for awhile so that she could initiate a women's march against structural sexism and racism. Meanwhile, in a parallel plot, a famous R&B singer, Travis Lee, is in town at the same time and in need of spiritual healing after a violent breakup with her boyfriend. This leads her to Reverend Myrtle Black. After she seeks the minister's guidance, the two women develop a friendship, Travis lends her brand and energy to the cause, and the women struggle against mutual attraction as they labor together for social change. Eventually, they admit their feelings and begin a romantic affair that then creates the issue of disclosure in their otherwise very public lives and, for the first time in Myrtle's career, raises the specter of monogamy. The resolution unfolds through the ways in which the city, African American community, and the sex workers are affected by the march, as well as the choices Myrtle and Travis Lee make regarding the direction of their relationship and admission of their sexuality to their respective constituents.

The opening passages illustrate Myrtle's seduction ritual: from the pulpit she identifies an attractive woman who "exudes an aura of sex" in the congregation; she concentrates her energy on the woman for "signs" that the woman's interests are "aroused"; once sure the attraction is mutual, Reverend Black incorporates flirtation into the sermonic performances and lures the woman she has nicknamed "Magdalen" (for they have not actually met) to the front of the church for altar call (2).

> Magdalen was crying and trembling, wrapped inside the bat-like cape of Myrtle's robe. Myrtle felt the youthful body pressing against her and swallowed hard. Using the fullness of the robe to camouflage her movements, she tightened her arms around the tantalizing form and ground her hips into the girl, rotating them as she pretended to sway with her holy utterance to the worshipers: "Jesus-s-s is love!" [. . .] Was she imagining it, or were Magdalen's hips answering back . . . ? (6)

Indeed, Magdalen was responding to the altar call and her erotic attraction to the messenger. After a few seconds of this veiled foreplay, Reverend Black "expertly" presses an artery on Magdalen's jaw so that the girl fainted in her arms (6). Before the churchwomen can arrive to her aid, she revives Magdalen and invites her to a private meeting after services, to which the woman agrees. They later engage in a "long, stimulating night of lovemaking," after which the preacher muses that "the girl, obviously, was not a novice in the art of Sapphic loving" (9). She then moves on to the next revival service in another town to begin the ritual again. Critics have, justifiably, interpreted this scene as evidence that Reverend Black is disingenuous as a minister and that her behavior indicates religious authority can be as abusive and sexually exploitative in the hands of a woman as it has been with men.[3]

There is also a case to be made which takes into consideration that this is an illustration, however comical, of Reverend Black's negotiation of the homophobia in her religious environment. If we fail to recognize the secrecy necessitated by such an environment, we may too easily reduce Reverend Black's sexual encounters to mere sexual plunder. What some critics interpret as shallow, power-driven promiscuity could also be comprehended as the minoritized subject's subversive negotiation with oppressive forces. As we have seen in the previous discussion of gay Christians, queer spaces are not solely those zones estranged from heterosexual culture where queer people can experience full citizenship: queer people can transform a space or institution. When queer people participate in discourses and institutions that impugn non-normative identities, they can create spaces for queer citizenship there, too (Cobb, "Pulpitic Publicity" 285). So, in a rather comedic fashion, Shockley's closeted lesbian preacher exhibits queer citizenship in a heteronormative space by identifying and engaging the homoeroticism within the religious ceremony.

Reverend Myrtle Black *is*, technically, a power-driven dissembler, as critic Tomeiko Ashford characterizes her, because she is not "out" as a lesbian and so reaps the benefit of heterosexual privilege. Hers is a drive to maintain her sense of empowerment among male colleagues who presume her clerical inferiority and her sexual availability to them. She is driven by the need to preclude their efforts to disempower her through sexual dominance (through rape or conquest) and showmanship in the pulpit. This is not the same as an egomaniacal need to sexually dominate women; though that is a reasonable interpretation of the way the plot establishes monogamy/nonmonogamy as a binary of desirable/undesirable behaviors and which asserts in its resolution that a monogamous partnership in a publicly disclosed relationship is the most desirable. Meanwhile, I want us to consider the ways Reverend Black is in constant struggle against the forces of a heteropatriarchal tradition which advocates virginity and celibacy outside of marriage. Unlike her male counterparts, her participation in any sex act threatens to undermine her legitimacy in the eyes of parishioners.[4]

Reverend Black's behavior is informed by her awareness that the gay, lesbian, bisexual, and otherwise in-the-life populations are always already part of the church environment when she arrives. As Shockley explains in an interview, the black church "is filled to the pulpit with closet[ed] gays and lesbians" (qtd in Dandridge 161). So Shockley's point seems to be that the sermonic seduction is possible, not because Reverend Black's authority as a minister makes the spiritually weak women her easy prey, but because these women's sexual practices or orientations are such that they are already open to Reverend Black's magnetism. It is for and with this queer audience (or public) that Reverend Black engages in pulpitic publicity as she performs an innovative queer resistance to heteropatriarchy and heterosexism. What we witness in the pulpitic ritual of seduction is a closeted lesbian whose sex role is that of the aggressor. In other words, Reverend Black is a social extrovert who initiates contact with the women with whom she feels a mutual attraction. The church is but one forum in which she behaves this way. Over the course of the narrative, Reverend Black's growth as a character is measured by her willingness to step outside the comfort zone of apparent heteronormalcy and to put her body where her political and spiritual ideas are.

As the opening passage of the novel reveals, *Say Jesus* presents energetic, communal religious arousal as a spiritual expression that can dovetail into sexual desire. *Say Jesus* "institutes a goddess trope of feminine and matriarchal divinity" in its portrayal of the ministerial lesbian who provides healing to the masses (Ashford 297). Sermonic seduction is possible because sexual energy plays a large role in the passionate worship service. In *Race Rules*, Michael Eric Dyson eloquently illustrates this point in his discussion of sexual politics in the black church. Dyson traces the buildup and persistence of energy from the clapping, swaying and dancing induced by the choir that spreads through the building, to the pitch and fervor of the sermon, and including the parade of well-dressed bodies traipsing to the collection table and podium for announcements. The black worship service is, for Dyson, a ritual of religious arousal (88–89). *Say Jesus* captures and emphasizes, for affect, this electric, body-centric dimension of worship in several scenes.

Reverend Black caresses, fondles, and grinds her pelvis against responsive women, while her sexual acts are cloaked by the excitement and cacophonous sounds of the crowded church—and her flowing minister's robe. On one occasion, Reverend Black pulls up her robe to perform intricate footwork to the choir's "foot-stomping, earsplitting, body-shaking beat" (7). In the scene, soul talk manifests as blends of religious fantasy and erotic ecstasy:

> As the repenters filed up to her, she stopped to shake their hands, kiss and bless them. The music became more rocking, louder, and someone produced a tambourine which added to the beat. Myrtle's face was twisted in delirious holy flight as she began once more to wiggle her body and shuffle her feet in time with the music. She imagined herself an ancient Hausa queen performing religious rites around a fire in the African thicket. The movements and mind-image heated her spiritually and sexually, causing her thoughts to focus around the young thing and how it was going to be later. . . . [H]er rhythmic twisting movements happily carried her back to the girl whose eyes were riveted on her in fascination. (7)

Reverend Black's religious arousal bounces along a grid of sensuality and fantasy. She is affectionate with her fellow worshippers; but she soon loses sight of them as she is transported into an ancient rite of her African ancestors, which, historically, includes spirit possession, animism, and magic. As she meditates on the ancestors, Reverend Black embodies the syncretization of African cosmology—a paradigm in which human life is cyclical and the immortal soul exists in perpetuity, weaving through historical time and various life forms—with Christian beliefs.[5] As Reverend Black dances, she is propelled into visions of another life, a precolonial existence in the "African thicket," a vision that blends with sexual fantasy and "the release of tensions to God" (7). For Reverend Black and her potential lover, the holy dance doubles as a mating ritual.

A more subtle aspect of the soul talk, identified by Ashford, is that Reverend Black functions as a lesbian deity. Ashford recognizes a "reversal of Judeo-Christian theology" (297) by which Reverend Black rhetorically supplants Jesus as the savior. At the climactic moment of her sermon, she encourages those in need to submit to Jesus by calling his name and then joining her at the altar for prayer, blessing, or healing. By saying "Jesus" as they focus on Reverend Black, Ashford maintains, believers are actually naming Reverend Black as the savior. Ashford continues: "On the surface, the phrase acknowledges that there is a greater, more divine power than the preacher, while insisting on her earthly divinity. Reverend Black's imposition of her own spiritual dominion establishes her as the intercessor through whom believers access God" (298). Hence, she tells her follower to say "Jesus" as they feel her power. A nonreligious moment that Ashford does not mention but further solidifies her claim occurs when Reverend Black and her lover, Travis, engage in a sex act. Reverend Black mounts her and stares into her eyes; yet, as Reverend Black's fingers penetrate Travis's "moist crevice" it is God's name which she murmurs, effectively creating a reversal of the altar call (157).

Nonetheless, Reverend Black considers herself a holy vessel of God and is a genuine follower of the essence of Christian doctrine; in fact, it is the foundation of her feminist activism in the community. Throughout the novel, her negative critiques are reserved for sexist male preachers, pimps, white feminists, and homophobic black women. She uses the pulpit as a platform to broadcast a liberation theology through Christianity, to claim women's intellectual and spiritual equality in God's sight and, eventually, to equate coming out of the closet to being "baptized anew in the sight of our wonderful savior" (281). *Say Jesus* constructs a black lesbian spirituality that insists on human connectedness through sensuality and the pursuit of pleasure as much as it relies on Christian faith. It also constructs social responsibility as an expression of spirituality. Shockley's Reverend Myrtle Black uses her pulpit to influence her followers to join her in alliance with local feminist organizations in a demonstration sparked by the brutal assault of female sex workers. Through a coalition politics, she helped organized a women's march that publicized their demands from their state and local officials for more economic inclusion, stricter penalties for sexual assault and family violence, and access to abortion. Shockley uses the storyline to discuss some of the internal conflicts that have occurred in such intra-racial and multiclass coalitions and to point out the powerful influence a united front such as this can wield in the public sphere.

NONMONOGAMOUS BISEXUALITY AND BLUESWOMAN EVANGELISM: *THE COLOR PURPLE*

Probably the most famous of the women writers in this study, Alice Walker is a novelist, short story and children's book writer, poet, essayist, and an activist for protecting the environment, and human and animal rights. Her writing reflects that she was born and raised in Georgia, loves women sexually and romantically, and that she came of age during the Civil Rights Era. Central themes in her work include rural Southern culture and identity; the African American revolutionary spirit and struggle for justice and equality; multidimensional bonds of love between women; and the need for spiritual connection between people and across life forms. To date, she has published twelve (combined) novels and short story collections, four children's books, eight collections of poetry, and a dozen compilations of nonfiction writings. Recent works include: *Overcoming Speechlessness: A Poet Encounters the Horror in Rwanda, Eastern Congo and Palestine/Israel* (2010); and a memoir, *The Chicken Chronicles: Sitting with the Angels Who Have Returned with My Memories* (2011). Still very much engaged in global concerns, she posts dispatches from her travels regularly on her blog site.

The Color Purple (1984) is Alice Walker's third novel. It is in epistolary form, narrated by the protagonist, Celie, through her letters to God. In these letters, she documents the misery of incestuous rape, verbal and physical abuse, and loneliness. After being repeatedly raped by her stepfather, she is handed over, without her input or consent, to a widowed farmer, who turns out to also be an abusive person, with three children. Her development as a character occurs through the help of a loving community of women, including her husband's mistress, Shug Avery, and Celie's sister, Nettie. Through these experiences, she gradually learns to love herself, see herself as desirable, and understand her value and sacredness as part of a holy and wholly interconnected universe. The novel's endorsement by the National Book Award and Pulitzer Prize committees and development into a Hollywood feature film detonated a bomb of public and academic debates; boycotts of the film; the banning or removal of the book from libraries and school reading lists; and discussions about what kinds of black stories should be told in the mainstream.[6] In the main, adverse criticisms of the film (which also tie into reactions to the novel) have revolved around three issues: that the film does not examine class; that black men are portrayed unnecessarily as harsh and brutal; the consequences of this will be to further the sociopolitical rifts between the black men and women; and that black people as a whole are depicted as perverse, sexually wanton, and irresponsible (Bobo 43). What some readers deem as its depiction of "perverse" sexuality is my central concern with the novel, along with the postulations it puts forward regarding religion and spirituality.

Many critics analyze *The Color Purple* from the perspective of the narrator, Celie, as she journeys from "ostensible nothingness" (Haritaworn et al. 515) and "into a state of bliss and restoration" (Hankinson 320). Many writers have also identified how Walker posits a patchwork of black female strength and self-love in Celie's life from which she is able to stitch together her own identity and self-worth. It is also well established that Shug's role in Celie's life as mentor and "professor of desire and self-fulfillment" is particularly crucial to Celie's transformation (Berlant 838). My argument builds on those important observations as it adjusts our lens ever-so-slightly by zooming in on the particularities of Shug's transformative power and the implications of her belief system. I show that Shug's power lies in her blueswoman consciousness that informs and empowers her sexually and spiritually—an empowerment that allows her to claim an inextricable connectivity to the cosmos even as she is fully self-possessed.

"Celie, he say, you have my sympathy. Not many women let they husband's whore lay up in they house" (Walker, *Color Purple* 55). With these words, laced with indirection and scorn, Celie's father-in-law articulates the perception and judgment of the rural black community. His words are spoken to Celie but aimed at his son, Albert; for Celie has no authority in her marriage and, consequently, has no say in where her husband's other lover may lay. The focus of the father-in-law's critique is the *ménage à trois* in which Albert oversees Celie as she nurses Shug, Albert's beloved mistress and mother of his "outside" children, back to health. While it scandalizes the good Christian folk in the small Georgia town, the living arrangement is only the beginning of the queering, or destabilization of black sexual norms, that Shug's presence imbues: Shug and Albert are longtime off-and-on lovers who were "as hot for each other as two pistols" (270) and, on the occasion denounced by the father-in-law, had engaged in noisy sex in the bedroom and stealthy passion on the side of the porch within Celie's earshot.[7] Meanwhile, Shug also sparks a sensual flame with Celie, which culminates in a lesbian affair and facilitates Celie's spiritual empowerment. Eventually Shug abandons Albert, but returns to his house with her own husband, Grady—only to exit again with Grady, Celie, and another woman called "Squeak" in tow. Shug deposits and, for awhile, financially supports them all in her home in Memphis. Their new living arrangement illustrates Shug's emotional and sexual fluidity: Memphis is a "domestic, sensual, and spiritual space" (Russell 206) in which Grady and Celie share Shug as a romantic partner, while Grady is also enticed by Squeak. In most cases, these conflicts and overlaps would lead to disharmony in the domestic space, yet when Shug leaves for extended periods to work, "[Celie] and Grady and Squeak rattle around the house" (211) together. Later, Shug indulges in a whirlwind affair with the much younger Germaine, all the while maintaining an emotional connection to Celie through written communication. She and Germaine travel by car to visit Grady and Squeak, who, after leaving Shug's home, make a separate life for themselves in Central America. The kinship network in a group of ex and current lovers, and male and female partners—where there is much potential for jealousy and competition—is idyllic. Through these erotic openings, closings, intersections and diversions, Shug embodies the disruption of monosexual discourses and unidirectional models of sexuality represented by heterosexuality, homosexuality, and monogamy. The kinship network Shug constructs attests to her erotic power and, when contrasted with other characters, marks her as the most liberated and self-actualized character in the narrative. She is proposed to the reader as an idyllic figure of empowerment and self-definition, so Shug's sexual, emotional, and affective life is a complex configuration that requires some meditation. In what follows, I review some of the various models of sexuality that might articulate what Walker has so carefully drawn that it is neither easily managed nor easily named.[8]

Shug's queerness wreaks havoc on dyadic notions (good/bad or hetero/homo) of sexuality and could be described as polyamorous. Polyamory is "the assumption that it is possible, valid and worthwhile to maintain intimate, sexual, and/or loving relationships with more than one person [at once]" (Haritaworn et al. 518). Clearly, this is Shug's perspective: Once in Memphis, Shug lives with her lesbian lover and her husband, who falls in love with Squeak, an affair Shug acknowledges from its inception.[9] Therefore, Shug does exhibit a polyamorous disposition; however, it is important to me not to mute the bisexual nature of her affinities—same-sex attraction is not a presumed aspect of multipartner lifestyles. I could also use the term *bisexual polyamory*, but some prominent practitioners of polyamory insist that the designation implies something more than a nonmonogamous perspective on sexuality.[10] Elisabeth Sheff distinguishes it from other multiple-partner arrangements this way:

> It differs from swinging in its emphasis on long-term, emotionally intimate relationships and from adultery with its focus on honesty and (ideally) full disclosure of the network of sexual relationships to all who participate in or are affected by them. Both

> men and women have access to additional partners in polyamorous relationships, distinguishing them from polygamy. (253)

Polyamory as defined by these practitioners is not applicable because Shug's lovers do not necessarily enter into relationships with her fully aware of the sexual network in which she operates. Let us consider another set of relational possibilities.

Shug's interactions also reflect an African relational style called mati-ism, while her liminality invokes the Queen B(?) figure of African American folklore.[11] In the essay, "Mati-ism and Black Lesbianism," Gloria Wekker traces mati-ism from present day Afro-Surinamese culture to precolonial West African social traditions. It is a group dynamic in which one woman moves among several male and female partners that may not be aware of each other. Importantly, mati as a cultural phenomenon has no negative connotation. It simply is. Among mati women, a claim to a particular sexual orientation is irrelevant; the same is true of outness or disclosure of the relationship to others. Mati same-sex relationships are often characterized by their intergenerational nature and mentoring aspects, instead of differences in gender roles, such as butch-femme, though such gender expression differences are also visible in some cases.

Similarly, the African American Queen B(?) figure is a woman whose sexual politics indicate "the dismissal of false bilateral ordering of sexuality" (Stallings, *Mutha Is Half a Word* 170). She is a trickster figure who, like the Bad Man/Nigga of folklore and popular culture, is heroic because she operates outside of legal and/or moral boundaries. The variations of Queen B(?), which are the bitch, bulldagger, or bee, "[present] female omnipotence through sexual desire, sexual freedom and independence" (Stallings 172). Walker participates in the Queen B(?) tradition in the characterization of Shug as a woman who fulfills her immediate sexual and emotional needs with men but does not depend on or cling to them. Shug is, in her own words, "high natured" and prioritizes her erotic attractions where and whenever they occur (Walker 250). She bounces in and out of Albert's life as she pleases, and the marriage contract with Grady is not treated as an ironclad, monogamous "till death do us part" arrangement.

As the review reflects, a spectrum of terminologies and styles of nonnormative sexualities exists to help articulate Shug's emotional/erotic/romantic penchants. I use *nonmonogamous bisexuality* in hopes of capturing the specific design of her fluidity.

Shug's sexual disposition is articulated in *Color Purple* as part of her understanding of God, the universe, and humanity's relationship to both. Through her transmission of these notions to the people she loves, Shug functions as a type of blueswoman evangelist. The moniker *blueswoman evangelist* signifies the multilayered, intersectional relationship between the transformative powers Shug exerts in her private life and the public ministry of the blues music she performs.[12] Her blues consciousness is a secular religion, a liberation theology that informs her sexuality; indeed, they are branches of the same tree. In *Blues Legacies and Black Feminism*, Angela Y. Davis reminds us that there were three areas of African American life that were transformed dramatically in the post-Emancipation experience: the possibilities for travel, individual education, and the freedom to choose sexual partners. Because of these profound changes in the life of the black masses, travel and sexuality are ubiquitous themes in blues lyrics. So blues consciousness was shaped by and gave expression to this social transformation. Furthermore, because blues is an aesthetic of the psycho-emotional life—composed of moans, hollers, and an overall churchy aesthetic—it is considered the secular counterpoint to spirituals. According to this logic, if the spiritual is God's music, then Classic Blues, its sonic twin, belongs to the Devil.

However, African American expressive culture defies the simple sacred/profane binary. Jon Michael Spencer, author of *Protest & Praise*, argues that blues music's location outside of the church setting reflects its function as an expressive extension or variation of intense spiritual engagement. Spencer contends that "Christian religion was the sacred history . . . of blues people [while] blues and blues life subsisted within the larger sphere of Christianity" (109). That is, there are blues people who are church folk, and there are blues people among the jook-joint crowd; either way, the blues (as mood or philosophy) precedes utterance and is intrinsic to all spiritual striving. "God was the reference source in times of blueness, whether petitioned by the churched in black spirituals or by the unchurched in blue spiritual" (Spencer 112). Spencer explains the deeply religious experience of blues performance:

> It was the bluesman's religious demeanor that rebaptized profane space for the sake of the unchurched black blues community. Saturday night in the "juke houses" was their sacred time and place for the communion of blues confession, what Albert Murray

> designated "a ritual of human existence" and the "truth of black experience" as preached to them in the blues, was a way of rendering meaning to the cosmos by being brazenly truthful about it. (113)

But being brazen, especially in the realm of sexuality, was a male privilege in the 1920s. For women, it was stigmatizing. So, to those who subscribed to the sacred/profane dichotomy (which was most people), blueswomen were doubly debased by their participation in blues rhetoric. Blueswomen, particularly, represented love and sexuality in ways that often blatantly contradicted mainstream ideological assumptions regarding women and being in love. Davis catalogs the themes in blueswomen's lyrics as frustration with cheating men, the loneliness and jealousy of being the other woman, good and bad lovers, intimate partner violence, homosexuality, suicide, violent revenge, drunkenness, incarceration, and poverty. Although African American culture functions in a way that often blurs the line between sacred/profane spaces and performances, most church folk are invested in maintaining a clear rhetorical distinction between them. For those people, blueswomen represent an unchaste, unholy, "nasty" womanhood, as illustrated by the preacher's sermon in the novel.[13]

Walker situates Shug in the blues tradition by linking her to Bessie Smith, the first real superstar in African American popular culture. "First Shug sing a song by somebody name Bessie Smith," Celie writes, "She say Bessie somebody she know. Old friend" (72). The invocation of Smith's legacy is key to understanding Shug's position among the other women in the story. Bessie Smith is linked sexually to her professional mentor, Ma Rainey, whose lifestyle demonstrates elements of female masculinity, open marriage, polyamory and mati-ism (Phillips and Stewart 23). But she is not implicated by association alone. Smith was "known for traveling with a coterie of women-loving women, including a male impersonator, [and] she indulged her diverse sexual palate at buffet flats" (Phillips and Stewart 33).[14] Smith was the quintessential blueswoman who defied prescribed female roles and operated outside of moral boundaries. "In many regards," Jana Braziel observes, "Smith . . . embodied the very stereotypes continually (and negatively) associated with bisexuality—promiscuity, fickleness, lack of commitment, unpredictability, and illicit disregard for consistent or constant samesex and/or different-sex identifications" (6–7).

Through the Shug character, Walker combats the negative views of bisexuality by illustrating the ways fickleness and unpredictability are not inherently destructive traits. With Shug, the messiness and chaos of love and sex are nutrients in a garden of growth and healing. Her relationships exemplify the human complexity that June Jordan extols in her defense of bisexuality, a speech entitled "The New Politics of Sexuality." Jordan writes,

> Bisexuality invalidates either/or formulation, either/or analysis. Bisexuality means I am free and I am as likely to want and to love a woman as I am likely to want and to love a man, and what about that? Isn't that what freedom implies? If you are free, you are not predictable and you are not controllable. (14)

Shug is neither predictable nor controllable in her relationships with Albert, Celie, or Grady. She maintains her sexual autonomy and allows others theirs. After Grady and Squeak move away together, Shug becomes involved romantically with Germaine, a nineteen-year-old flutist in her band. She describes him as "a baby" that is "A third my age. A third my size. Even a third my color" (251). That would mean she is nearly sixty. Like the blueswomen she is patterned after, Shug simply ignores patriarchal ideology that privileges older men in intergenerational romantic pairings. Yet this freedom is not without its emotional consequences. Celie is devoted exclusively to Shug and feels betrayed by this romance. Nonetheless, Shug insists she has "got to have it" and so begs Celie for patience and understanding as the mating ritual runs its course (250). As I show later, Shug's nonmonogamous "high nature" is also part of her evangelism and serves to teach Celie how to love without possession.

But initially, the evangelism is articulated in soul talk. Soul talk manifests in the spiritual guidance Shug offers Celie, guidance that distances Celie from the constraints of sacred/secular divisions wrought by her Christian upbringing. In the oft-quoted "God love all them feelings" passage, Shug draws connections between sensual pleasure and cosmic connectivity (196). God is the creator of the senses, Shug explains, and therefore intended for humanity to experience the sensual aspects of life in pleasurable ways, such as admiring natural color patterns in a field of flowers, dancing to the music that moves you, and indulging in sexual orgasm. Further, by insisting that humans "come into the world with God," Shug reconfigures the creator/creation dynamic so that sacredness is not bestowed upon a chosen few (195). Such teachings release Celie from the religious obligations to attend church or perform certain rituals to attain

God's love, attention, or favor. The subtext of this conversation is the women's sexual relationship with each other. If mankind is a part of nature and nature is inherently sacred, Shug's perspective suggests, the naturally occurring erotic bond between the women is also sacred and blessed by the Creator. As was the case in Shockley's novel, these ideas regarding the life of the spirit are part of the author's feminist politics. "Men and their religions have tended to make love for anything and anybody other than themselves and their Gods an objectionable thing, a shame" Walker writes in *Same River Twice*, "But that is not the message of Nature, the Universe, the Earth or of the unindoctrinated Human Heart, where everything is profusion, chaos, multiplicity, but also creativity, containment and care" (171–172). Walker's Pagan interpretation of the "message of Nature [and] the Universe" is articulated by in a way that equates sexual ecstasy with spiritual ecstasy, a blueswoman's theology, which includes homoerotic and masturbatory experiences.

The link between the spiritual and sensual experiences is a large part of Shug's theological perspective. She encourages Celie to replace her image of a distant, solitary, anthropomorphic, masculine God with a permeating, genderless, divine energy that can be intuited. "[God] aint something you can look at apart from anything else, including yourself," Shug teaches (195). "[God is] Everything that is or ever was or will be. And when you can *feel* that, and be happy to feel that, you've found It" (195). She underlines the sensory aspects of her spirituality by folding the religious ecstatic moment into the erotic ecstasy of orgasm. Continuing, she testifies that when she found this understanding of the universe, it was on a day when she "was sitting quiet and feeling like a motherless child, which I was, [and] it come to me: that feeling of being part of everything . . . [and I] laughed, cried, and run all around the house," behavior that mirrors the passionate worship service (195). The spiritual breakthrough is linked to sexual release in her description: "I knew just what it was. In fact, when it happen, you can't miss it. It [feels] sort of like you know what, she say, [while she is] grinning and rubbing high up on [Celie's] thigh" (196). The blueswoman evangelist is a spiritual advisor and seductress: the erotic stimulation adds a sensual dimension to her testimony of love, God, and spirit. As they have been lovers for a while by the time they have this conversation, Shug understands exactly what "you know what" means to Celie—for it was she who introduced Celie to the prospect of clitoral orgasm. Celie recounts Shug's words in her diary (emphasis added):

> Listen, she say, right down there in your pussy is a little button that gits real hot when you do *you know what* with somebody. It git hotter and hotter and then it melt. That the good part. But other parts good too, she say. Lots of sucking go on, here and there, she say. Lot of finger and tongue work. (77)

The omission of gendered pronouns in this definition of orgasm creates imaginary space for Celie to insert Shug as the "somebody" to do the "finger and tongue work" in her pussy. Importantly, Celie will be the first to actually touch herself there. After this conversation concerning orgasm, Celie tearfully masturbates while listening to Shug and Albert make love (79). The first time the two women actually engage in sex acts, the details are left out. Celie simply says they kiss and touch each other. So, for Celie, the only logical reference to "you know what" when Shug rubs her thigh is the "little button" at the tip of Shug's fingers. By touching Celie's thigh during her testimony, Shug invokes the sexual pleasure Celie associates with those hands and claims that pleasure as an act of thanksgiving, praise, and connection to the Creator. In blueswoman theology, "God love all them feelings"; therefore, same-sex love and "you know what" are valid spiritual experiences, which can bring one closer to the Creator.

These are similar assertions to the ones I locate in Baldwin's works in a previous chapter. Indulging in those things that one finds delightful for spiritual reasons is a stark contradiction to the Christian dictum to "deny yourself" in exchange for sanctification and/or happiness in the afterlife.[15] The narrative shatters the ideological barriers between non-normative sexuality and spirituality and struggles to undo antagonisms between bodily pleasure and spiritual strivings. But this insistence on the sacredness of pleasure is a painful tenet for Celie to live by. For it means that she must accept Shug's pursuit of other lovers. When explaining to Celie why she must follow her desire for Germaine, she acknowledges Celie's lesbian orientation while asserting her own bisexual inclination: "He's a man. [Celie] write on the paper. Yeah, she say. He is. And I know how you feel about men. But I don't feel that way. I would never be fool enough to take any of them seriously, she say, but some mens [sic] can be a lots of fun" (250).

Though she knows Celie is hurt by it, Shug honestly and openly insists on her right to emotional and sexual freedom. According to Shug's gospel, derived partly from her blues consciousness, unidirectional sexuality is but one orientation, among others. Spiritual freedom is practiced as one's openness to the gifts of the universe or a conscious participation in Creation. The absence of Christianity's narratives of restraint and guilt creates space for the exploration, affirmation even, of Celie's lesbian identity *and* Shug's nonmonogamous bisexuality. Still, Shug seems more fulfilled overall than Celie. Shug praises God by "liking what she likes," while Celie learns to be contented as she waits for Shug's return (196).

Among the cast of characters in *Color Purple*, except Sophia perhaps, Shug has no lesson to learn about life, friendship, or God. She is the teacher in every scenario. So much so that even her absence is instructional. Shug is as capricious as she is powerful, and she often chastises her devotees. She brings love and then withdraws it, teaching the profound lessons of the blues (Marvin 422). While Shug travels with Germaine, for example, Albert and Celie bond through their mutual yearning for her. As Albert waxes philosophical about his lifelong devotion to Shug, he makes plain the differences between his discontentment and Shug's satisfaction:

> All I ever wanted in life was Shug Avery, he say. And one while, all she wanted in life was me. Well, us couldn't have each other . . . I got [the wife his father approved of]. Then [Celie]. [And] All them rotten children. She got Grady and who know who all. But still, look like she come out better than me. A lot of people love Shug, but nobody but Shug love me. (282)

Because he acquiesced to his father's demands for a respectable daughter-in-law, and even though he and Shug continued a clandestine affair for some years, Albert suffers spiritually and feels deprived of meaningful love. Shug, on the other hand, is not preoccupied with traditional romantic devotion. She indulges her desires with other men and "who know who all" in the name of self-love and because she rests assured that "God love all them feelings." In his expressed regret, "Albert represents those of us who listen to the regulatory voices around us, those produced by society, family, and/or religion, and internalized/perpetuated by loved ones, while we stifle, suppress, deny, or silence our own inner voice, that which speaks through desires" (Simcikova 51). Walker, in her role as priestess, sermonizes for a transformative paradigm, one in which we free ourselves from self-denial and the desire for mainstream acceptance. Shug personifies this message of emancipatory, revolutionary love.

In Walker's paradigm, "love is *the* revolutionary emotion, partly because it cannot be limited, cannot be compartmentalized, cannot be controlled" (qtd in Simcikova 126). This appears to be the message we find in Albert's transformation near the end of the novel. In Shug's absence, Albert's humanity expands. In his state of newfound spiritual clarity and intimate friendship with Celie, he falls in love with Celie and proposes they remarry, "this time in the spirit as well as in the flesh" (283). But Celie is a lesbian and, more importantly, does not entertain the possibility of another lover. So she, too, is frustrated, lonely, and jealous without Shug. Eventually, though, Celie's inner voice breaks through the solitude and imparts the wisdom of emotional commitment by which Shug already lives:

> Sometimes I feel mad at her. Feel like I could scratch her hair right off her head. But then I think, Shug got the right to live too. She got a right to look over the world in whatever company she choose. Just cause I love her don't take away none of her rights. [. . .] I miss her friendship so much that if she want to come back here dragging Germaine I'd make them both welcome, or die trying. (268)

The blueswoman evangelist is the center of the erotic vortex and benefits the most when her followers recognize her power, which is her deeply instilled sense of freedom. So through temporary moments of loss, they learn to love her without possession. Shug is the politicized ideal of the bisexual in that she is neither emotionally destructive nor spiritually restrictive. She models a life of love and spirit which reframes desire "in porous, nonexclusive ways" (Storr 146). When she returns to Celie and Albert, the *ménage à trois* that Albert's father so disdains is reconstituted. At the novel's close, their love flows in multiple directions and carries with it the promise of liberation and wholeness.

Soul talk and sermonic seduction occur very differently in the novels in this chapter. Shockley delivers a decidedly *lesbian* spirituality through a preacher who literally combines sexual pleasure with religious worship. She functions as an earthly deity, as she imposes her body between the believer and their sanctification. In Shockley's construction, the worship space motivates and underwrites romantic, political, and sexual relationships. Christian doctrine, as I have noted, is the foundation of the reverend's feminist activism in the community and her liberation theology is thoroughly Christian in its claim to women's intellectual and spiritual equality in God's sight. Meanwhile, for Walker's blueswoman evangelist, the act of worship is less relevant than recognizing one's sacredness in the context of an always-already hallowed universe. From that assumption, philosophies of social, sexual, and emotional justice are fashioned. The locus of spiritual energy and power is not assigned to any particular physical location. It is where you find it.

POSTSCRIPT

An important concern regarding the "praise god by liking what you like" spiritual principle is the notion that this kind of thinking leaves too much space for abusive relationships.[16] For some, it raises the following questions: What if "what you like" is hurtful to others, or creates an unhealthy or unethical sexual dynamic? Is God pleased by your pleasure no matter what the cost to others? That slippery slope perspective is only applicable when Walker's proposal is taken outside the context of the novel and her larger visionary landscape. *The Color Purple* contrasts Celie's relationship *with herself* before and after Shug's intervention. Celie's first sexual relationship was the years-long incest by Pa, who decided she needed to fill in for her mother's wifely duties. It was not consensual or pleasurable for her. Neither her body nor her children were her own. In addition, Celie's sex life with Albert is unremarkable except that she fantasizes about Shug occasionally. He "clam on top of me, do his business, in ten minutes us both sleep" (68), Celie complains, which means she did not imagine her pussy as hers; it was her husband's receptacle. Shug essentially gives Celie the keys to her own kingdom by introducing her to clitoral stimulation and orgasm.

In the conversation under question, Celie is especially troubled by the "dirtiness" of sex and God's response to human indulgence. This prompts Shug's response that God created sexual pleasure for us to know it—not to ignore it or condemn it. She ties this in with the pleasure that can be found in the beauty of all nature and that humanity's relationship to God is a reciprocal one: "People think pleasing God is all God care about. But any fool living in the world can see it always trying to please us back. . . . It always making little surprises and springing them on us when we least expect" (196). To please God is to acknowledge the gifts the universe provides. "I can lay back and just admire stuff. Be happy. Have a good time" (193). So praising god by "liking what you like" is a rejection of the religious orthodoxy Celie espoused, which aims to restrict the gratification of the female body, and to reduce a woman's sexual "place" to passive reproductive roles and on the receptive end of male desire. Shug asserts that God is pleased by our attainment of self-knowledge and self-love, some of which is derived through sensual pleasure. It is a gift to Celie's self-esteem and her sense of value to and within Creation.

A. Razak points out that Walker's broader artistic and activist vision, across the length of her writing, is one that insists on a sacred web of life that includes plants, animals, the Earth, the cosmos, the living and the dead. In a study of Walker's "visionary novels," Razak cites Walker's 1997 essay, "The Only Reason You Want to Go to Heaven is That You Have Been Driven Out of Your Mind," in which she expands on this notion:

> Everyone deserves a God who adores our freedom: Nature would never advise us to do anything but be ourselves. Mother Earth will do all that She can to support our choices, whatever they are. For they are of Her and inherent in our creation is Her trust. We are born knowing how to worship, just as we are born knowing how to laugh. (*Anything We Love* 25–26)

Laughter can be an expression of communal or individual joy, or it can be a weapon used to ridicule and punish. Following one's inner desires has similar parameters. However, if all life is equally sacred, there is no room for the toleration of unethical, unloving treatment of others.

CHAPTER FIVE

Neo-Spirit Narrative

"In the Life"

> There was no mortal that I could go to and gain instruction, so it pleased God in His love and mercy to teach me in dreams and visions and revelation and gifts.
>
> —Eldress Rebecca Cox Jackson, 1843

> Grace come to me in my sleep last night. . . . I catch the scent of Posner's Bergamot Pressing Oil, and that cocoa butter grease she use on her skin.
>
> —Jinx, circa 1980

Becky Birtha is the author of two volumes of short stories, *For Nights Like This One: Stories of Loving Women* (1983) and *Lover's Choice* (1987), and a poetry collection, *The Forbidden Poems* (1991), titled so, presumably, because the poems are told from the perspective of a black woman who has recently ended a long-term relationship with her white lover.[1] Penny Kaganoff notes in a review for *Publisher's Weekly* that *Forbidden Poems* "show[s] off Birtha's considerable ability to endow ordinary perceptions and occurrences with a profound significance" (77), but critical reception of her work remains sparse. Meanwhile, Birtha's work is widely anthologized, notably in *Home Girls: A Black Feminist Anthology* (1983); *Women on Women: An Anthology of Lesbian American Short Fiction* (1990); *Breaking Ice: An Anthology of Contemporary African-American Fiction* (1990); *Does Your Mama Know? An Anthology of Black Lesbian Coming Out Stories* (1997); and *Black Like Us: A Century of Lesbian, Gay, and Bisexual African American Fiction* (2002). Her most recent works are the children's books *Grandmama's Pride* (2005) and *Lucky Beans* (2010).

As part of the discussion of philosophies of the spirit, I analyze in this chapter "In the Life," which appears as the closing story in *Lover's Choice.* Within its few pages, the story presents a (literal) haunting lesbian desire and includes dreams and waking visions, which feature a lustful visitor from the afterlife; visits that spark blissful human-spirit and human-nature intimacies. But, before I do that, I spend some time reviewing the life and writing of a nineteenth-century preacher, Rebecca Cox Jackson, so that I may draw parallels between elements of Birtha's story and Jackson's autobiographical narrative, which was completed in 1864 and published in 1981 as *Gifts of Power.* My main assertion here is that in the narrative layers, the telling of a tale of transformational encounters with the supernatural, Birtha signifies on the structure and function of antebellum spirit writing genres, which were popular in the eighteenth and nineteenth centuries. These life writings include pamphlets, brief sketches, diaries/journals, and book-length memoirs that were intended to document the author's religious conversion and convictions, and to serve as a testament to the works of God. I begin with a brief discussion of the cultural function and literary structure of African American spiritual autobiography; then I shift to an argument that a form of black queer spirituality is visible in the fascinating journal of Shaker Eldress Rebecca Cox Jackson; and I continue into a comparative analysis of Birtha's short story to argue that the latter constructs a fictional adaptation (of Jackson's themes) that I call a neo-spirit narrative.

BLACK WOMEN AND THE SPIRITUAL AUTOBIOGRAPHY GENRE

Autobiography and memoir are literary forms that allow a writer to reflect on, defend, justify, and explain her life by way of a narrative map; it functions as a retrospective of the significant relationships and events that influence and connect the decisions and outcomes of that life. African American spiritual autobiographies and spirit narratives were written by freeborn and emancipated people in the eighteenth and nineteenth centuries and focus on spiritual awakenings and religious conversions. They tell a life story that documents the author's spiritual growth as well as the outward events of his or her life. These stories, like the ex-slave narratives, demonstrate that the literary space can be the place where one fashions one's own freedom. As William L. Andrews asserts in *To Tell a*

Free Story: The First Century of Afro-American Autobiography, the main difference between the ex-slave narrative and spiritual autobiography genres are their definitions of bondage and freedom. "In black spiritual autobiography the protagonist wishes to escape sinfulness and ignorance in order to achieve righteousness and a knowledge of the saving grace of God. In the slave narrative the quest is toward freedom from physical bondage and the enlightenment that literacy can offer" (Andrews 7). Commonly anthologized spirit narratives are the stories of Denmark Vesey and Nat Turner, enslaved preachers who rely on reading the extraliterary—"things unseen" or "signs in the heavens"—for direction in their violent rebellions against a brutal slave society. In both cases, their spiritual awakening is explained as the motivating factor or empowering force in the claim to a right to live as free people. Women preachers participated in this kind of testimony, too.

Black women authors used the spiritual autobiography to define and defend their call to preach—a defense necessitated by the derision they often garnered for having stepped out of their prescribed station in life. Katherine Clay Bassard explains in *Spiritual Interrogations* that for black women, bondage was an intersection of racial oppression in the larger society and gender inequality within black society. Their lives were circumscribed by a racist regime of laws and governmental policies and the limitations placed on women's roles in the public sphere. In the nineteenth-century context, it was considered undignified for women to speak to public, mixed-gender assemblies. Female leadership was acceptable in the blended public/private space of a "prayer band" or bible study meeting in a segregated, intimate, indoor setting. Likewise, the ministry was largely a male calling; women were itinerant evangelists, exhorters, and teachers who could deliver a sermon or a "word from the Lord" to other women, but leadership over an established church, and the pulpit space in the church building for that matter, were male preserves. So the empowering aspect of seizing on conversion discourse in a context of government-sanctioned slavery and church-sanctioned sexism, Bassard reasons, is the ability to challenge and change one's subjectivity within these institutions. She writes:

> For individuals socially "cursed" with a racialized and othered subjectivity, conversion represented one of the few discourses, and certainly the most prominent, holding the promise of a radical change in subjectivity. If one could move from "sinner to saint,"

> she/he could also move "from slave to free," [and] "from bondage to freedom." Thus conversion functions in early black women's literature both as an event and as a process for the revisioning of community. (Bassard 23)

Conversion functions as the "event and process" of reimagining the gender and racial order of things so there is cultural space for God to call on black women to act on their own and the community's behalf, just as He does male believers.

Furthermore, their harnessing of conversion discourse "challenges the performance of black womanhood prescribed as 'natural' by hegemonic discourses" (Douglass-Chin 11). For example, in the first woman-authored spirit narrative, *The Life and Religious Experience of Jarena Lee, a Coloured Lady, Giving an Account of Her Call to Preach the Gospel* (1836), Lee justifies abandoning her "natural" maternal duties by explaining that God "hid" the thoughts of her son from her so that she would not be distracted from the "holy energy," which propelled her away from him. Her impulse to preach, despite the disapproval and dissuasion of her pastor, was a divine calling, "like Saul of Tarsus was sent to Jerusalem," on a holy mission to spread the gospel (Lee qtd in Andrews 70–72). By analogizing her conversion experience and ministry with that of the biblical figure Saul, who becomes "Paul" after his conversion, one of the most influential voices in the New Testament, Lee transforms her example of womanhood from that of an uncontrollable, irresponsible mother to a preacher determined to do God's will (Andrews 70). Other autobiographies that deal with marital circumstances include *Memoirs of the Life, Religious Experience, Ministerial Travels and the Labours of Mrs. Zilpha Elaw* (1846); and *The Story of the Lord's Dealings with Mrs. Amanda Smith, the Colored Evangelist* (1893).

Spirit writing is a subgenre within spiritual autobiography, distinguished by the claim that literacy came about as part of the spiritual experience. People who had been denied access to formal education claimed to rely solely on divine intervention for their acquired literacy and composition skills; the act of writing was testimony to the power of God in their lives. Generally, the plot traced the author's journey from a state of ignorance to one of divinely inspired knowledge. This characteristic—that literacy as a type of liberty is gained through a spiritual experience—separates this life writing from that of Frederick Douglass, who marks his progress from slavery to freedom through access to books and instruction. An important figure among the spirit writing authors is Rebecca

Cox Jackson (1795–1871). She was a polarizing and controversial figure who was accused of "chopping up [black] churches" (Humez, "Introduction" 21) with her teachings regarding sexuality and her beliefs about the role of women in evangelical pursuits. Her journal documents a Christian woman's miraculous acquisition and practice of multidimensional literacy and demonstrates beliefs in the supernatural that displace much of what is considered traditional black church liturgy.

Jackson was Jarena Lee's contemporary and her ministry, too, was met with documented opposition from male clergy, but for considerably more reasons than just her desires for the same access (to audiences) and institutional respect that men preachers received. From 1830 to 1864, Jackson, a free black woman from Philadelphia, recorded accounts of her spiritual rebirth, out-of-body experiences, dreams, visions, prophecies, and supernatural abilities in a private journal. She did so because a spirit guide appeared before her and directed her to "write the things which I seen and heard, and write them as I seen and heard" (Jackson 170). Its rhetorical purpose appears to be to justify her conversion from the independent African Methodist Episcopal (AME) denomination to the Shaker sect of Christianity, and to defend against accusations of heresy and witchcraft. Some of the details of her conversion and the resulting struggle to fashion her own freedom enact a queering of religious discourse and spiritual practice. I apply a queer reading to the facts of her emotional life and the portal she enters through her "spirit eye," the implication of which is that Eldress Jackson may have authored the first black queer spirit narrative.

RELIGIOUS AND SEXUAL QUEERNESS: REBECCA COX JACKSON

Jean McMahon Humez is the editor of *Gifts of Power: The Writings of Rebecca Jackson, Black Visionary, Shaker Eldress*. Humez encountered the handwritten manuscript and Jackson's other dictated papers in the Shaker community archives in the Berkshire Athenaeum in Massachusetts and published them in 1981. In the introduction, Humez explains that during Jackson's sanctification experience, she was blessed with the gift of literacy and dispossessed, in its literal meaning, of sexual desire. Jackson had a revelation from God that "destroyed the lust of my flesh, and made me to hate it. . . . Of all things it seemed the most filthy in the sight of God, both in the married and unmarried, it all seemed alike" (17). In an entry titled "Release from Bondage," Jackson recounts for the reader how she broke the news to her husband: "I was commanded to tell Samuel I had served him many years, and had tried to please him, but I could not. And now from this day and forever, I shall never strive again. But I shall serve God with all my heart, soul, mind, and strength and devote my body to the Lord and Him only. And when I have done it, He will be pleased" (147). Humez interprets this entry as the moment in which Jackson, who is childless and therefore not bound by parental obligation, and for whom this is a second marriage, uses the religious experience "both to win independence from her husband and to justify her desire for independence" (Jackson 19). It is a logical supposition. The statement, that she "tried to please" her husband in the past and "could not," implies that sexual asymmetry was already a problem in their relationship. And with this revelation, God has given her permission to stop trying. Plus, she invokes biblical authority. In the subtext of her testimony lies Paul's obsessive biblical injunction against sex acts, which he calls "sins of the flesh," which recur throughout his letters to individual evangelists and members of various newly constructed Christian churches, as represented in the epistles to the Colossians, Romans, Thessalonians, and Ephesians. One verse in particular echoes in Jackson's entry: "So then with the mind I myself serve the law of God; but with the flesh the law of sin" (Romans 7:25). It is also no small point that Jackson's presence in the home and domestic labor were central to her family and, if it was her calling to travel and preach the word, this domestic arrangement was the first thing that needed to change.

Jackson's life revolved around two strong male personalities: her husband, Joseph, and brother and father figure, Samuel Cox, a prominent member of the Bethel AME church in Philadelphia. She was a seamstress who took in work from the community and was responsible not only for the upkeep of her husband's wardrobe, but also for her brother's household and children, because he was a widower (and she was living with him). Samuel resisted teaching her to read but agreed to read and write letters for her. A key moment in her text occurs when she recounts how deeply troubled she was when she realized he was not transcribing her letters in her exact words; he rebuked her harshly for challenging him about it. This moment is crucial because her conversion narrative is not a traditional journey from a sinful state of being to that of one who is saved. Rather, she shifts from a member of a religious family to spiritual agent and religious activist. Her *gift of power*, as she calls it, was just that: at around the age of thirty-five, her spirit eye was opened and enabled multiple literacies that would empower her to live independently of her biological (and legal) family. She found that she was able to "read" all kinds of texts, including the bible, future, weather, and minds. It seems almost a bonus "gift" that she was also freed of sexual desire for her husband. In one sanctified swoop, her dependence on and obligation to these men vanished. So empowered, she then took her message to the wider community and "testified against the churches" (137) for they were, in doctrine and custom, insisting on her submission to male leadership at home, inside the walls of their institutions, and in her religious conduct outside of formal church services—all of which she refused to do. From her perspective, the "persecution was raging" (158) from all directions.

First, Samuel and Joseph were displeased with this transformation; they, respectively, attempted to coerce her back into her "natural" place and punish her insubordination. Jackson records that her brother reproached her "as if he could tear me into pieces . . . like a lion" (151). Also, her husband became so incensed by her decision to end their sexual relationship that he "sought my life day and night" (145). (He would eventually accept her call to preach but was never able to regain her trust.) Soon, the local church leadership became alarmed because she began to draw large crowds as an itinerant preacher; and she refused to claim membership in any particular church, which, effectively, is a refusal to recognize institutional authority over her ministry. She held coed worship services in private homes, which usurped church attendance and defied the mandate that women evangelists could only preach to all-female audiences. This insubordination led to expulsion. Her defiance of Christian heteropatriarchy generated charges of "preach[ing] a false doctrine [and] part[ing] a great many men and their wives" (149). Male preachers wished death and destruction on her: "One said I ought to be stoned to death, one said tarred and feathered and burnt, one said I ought to be put in a hogshead, driven full of spikes, and rolled down a hill. These men called themselves preachers of the Gospel of our Lord and Savior, Jesus Christ" (149). According to her account, some ministers even threatened to expel church members who opened their homes to her during her travels.

Still, Humez surmises, "By far, the most threatening aspect of Rebecca Jackson's ministry in the 1830's, from the point of view of the established independent black churches, was her radical attack on the 'carnality' of the churches themselves" ("Introduction" 21). Not only does she reject her husband but, as the journal entry above states, she rejects all sex acts as sinful. In other words, celibacy is central to her message. This stance made her an outcast from the black Christian community because her message of celibacy was disruptive of the patriarchal construction of family *vis-à-vis* the woman's responsibility to regenerate the race and the assumption of natural male power over women. Humez continues: "In Jackson's eyes, they had failed to teach the demanding truth that holy living—which included celibacy—was the only way to follow Christ as was required. She developed her critique using Old and New Testament texts and her own experience as a basis, which caused intense controversy even within Holiness circles (21).[2]

An important aspect of her ministry is the displacement of tradition for direct communication with God, nature, and ethereal beings. In an endeavor to listen clearly to the voice of God, she learned to focus on her spirit eye, a prophetic clairvoyance that operated during waking and sleeping hours. She could read minds, hear conversations from across the city, and communicate telepathically. She became a medium and prayer healer who held séances and healing services. Wind, rain, and thunder spoke to her as the voices of God and spirit guides. Her visions and dreams were also prophetic; they would prepare her for upcoming negative encounters with hostile people or, in them, God would use symbols or divine beings to instruct, warn, quell concerns, or to make promises. In her dream life, she also was exceptionally mobile and otherworldly. Humez summarizes:

> Laws of nature are violated with ease, particularly in her accounts of visionary dreams. She soars, lifts, leaps easily into the sky, flies through the air, looks down from a great height, and can see things never visible from such a perspective before. She is given sudden, integrating flashes of understanding about the nature of the physical universe in visual form. She can leave the physical body behind, hold conversations with the angels, tour symbolic landscapes, and reenter the body again. (42)

At the height of accusations against her, Cox requested that ministers formally try her for heresy. When they refused, she cut off all ties to her biological family and the AME church. For the next ten years, she traveled and preached around Pennsylvania, northern Delaware, New Jersey, southern New England, and New York. During her travels, Jackson discovered the Shakers, whose religious views were similar to her own. Impressed by her spiritual gifts, they embraced her as a prophet, and she remained in the Watervliet, New York, community for seven years.

Jackson's narrative proceeds from her deeply held belief that her expulsion from the black church was God's holy plan in order that she be able to begin anew with other, more enlightened folk. So she foreshadows her immersion into the Shaker religion with the explanation that, in dreams, God promised her a new faith community:

> While I was under great sorrow and suffering about living a holy virgin life, everything seemed to stand in opposition to that life. Yet in me it was revealed, and all desire for carnal pleasure was slain. This made my life burdensome to me and to my husband, and to my friends . . . because I had to bear open testimony against all sin. . . .
>
> So I was buffeted, sometimes beyond description. The Christian Church would be set before me, with all their Bishops and Elders, all living in the works of the first Adam. I saw nobody lived the life I was called to live. I then entreated to the Lord to tell me why it was that I was called to live a life that nobody lived on the earth. Then in answer to my request, "I have a people on earth that live the life I have called you to live. . . . And if you are faithful, I will bring you to see them." (Jackson 136–137)

To live in the "works of the first Adam" is literal—in Genesis, the first, or original Adam was cast out of God's garden because of his sexual knowledge. Many Christian denominations call this the "fall from grace," and believe that it corrupted the entire natural world, causing people to be born into original sin, a state from which they cannot attain eternal life without the intervention of God. Jesus is sometimes called the "last" or "second Adam" and his model of ministry requires one to set aside the biological family.[3] Jackson attributes the sexist practices of the male leadership to their flawed biblical scholarship. Subsequently, the promise from God in the dream affirms her calling to ministry and justifies her commitment to lifelong celibacy by pointing out that the theological principles introduced to her by divine inspiration were not completely alien to others who were also drawing on Christian teachings. In fact, the Shaker belief system aligned nearly perfectly to hers: celibacy; the rejection of procreation for nonbiological kinship networks; female leadership in the church (and in the messianic narrative); and a belief that the individual believer is led directly by the voice of God are some of the pillars of the Shaker faith to which she belonged.[4]

From here, we can begin to see the emergence of a queer spirituality; that is, a nonheteronormative sexual practice that is directly tied to spiritual practice. On its face, her vow of divine celibacy, the ascetic desire to live "the holy virgin life" (137) even within marriage, in itself, lies outside the norms of heterosexuality.[5] Additionally, her spiritual abilities, as Bassard has demonstrated, rely on extraliterary (including numerology) and extrasensory engagements, which push the boundaries of modern Christian practices and evince traces of traditional African religions. The other integral aspect of her religious life documented in the journal are her years of companionship with another evangelist. This relationship moves the discussion beyond sanctified queerness into the realm of homoerotic spirituality.

After leaving the AME church, Jackson befriended Rebecca Perot, another free black woman, in 1836. From Philadelphia, the evangelists relocated to Watervliet, New York, in 1847, to join an established Shaker commune. Jackson was Perot's mentor and intimate friend. They were so connected to each other that the Shaker historical documents refer to them as one unit, "the colored Rebeccas" or "the two Rebeccas," and, in their isolated community, Perot was nicknamed "Rebecca Jackson, Junior." In 1851, after the federal Fugitive Slave Act became the law of the land, the Rebeccas broke away from the predominately white commune and co-founded a new one in Philadelphia for black women (believed to be a refuge for runaway slaves and, in the postbellum, newly freed people).[6] Together they revisioned the black church; one that structurally critiqued and competed with the male-centered and sexist hierarchy of the AME system (which also was a nucleus of abolitionist activism). Upon Jackson's death in 1871, Perot adopted her partner's name—they had been companions for more than thirty-five years. The new "Mother Rebecca Jackson" assumed leadership of the Philadelphia family, which survived another forty years.

Close readings of Jackson's dreams and visions that involve Perot reveal the ways in which erotic energies, so vociferously denied in her physical reality, are accounted for in the sensual and emotional imagery of her psychic landscape. In the first mention of the Perot in her journal, dated 1848, when Jackson was still living with her brother, she records a waking vision in which Perot was with her in bed and Jackson's husband appears as a threat to their solace:

> I thought I was in Philadelphia and Rebecca Perot was with me, in bed. I lay with my head to the west, and my face to the south, and Rebecca was behind me.
>
> As I was going to sleep I thought someone might come in while we slept. And I said, "Rebecca, go and get three forks, and fasten the doors." . . . Rebecca rose immediately, and as she put the fork over the latch, a man rushed against the door. I then arose and ran to the [other] door. And as I placed the fork over the latch, the man that used to be my husband rushed in, and I ran out. (210)

As the vision continues, Jackson flies above the scene and observes a different man, a Shaker "brethren," in the yard tossing watermelons into a deep well; they burst and splash on impact. When the well is full, an earthquake rumbles the ground and tosses both men onto rocks. The scene closes with a heroic Shaker deity approaching on horseback. Humez explains that many of Jackson's dreams reveal a fear of sudden violence because it was a common occurrence and threat of white violence was constant. I would add that her husband is a threatening presence in this particular dream because he had plotted against her life multiple times before she was able to finally free herself of him. "To mention all that I passed through *would fill this book,* but from that time [after the vow of celibacy], Samuel sought my life day and night. And if I had not had the gift of foresight given me at the beginning, I must have fell in death by his hands" (Jackson 145; my emphasis). Clearly, Samuel represents danger and violence.

Perot, on the other hand, is a figure of attachment, beauty, and deep affection. Jackson records two more visions of Perot, one that reveals an intense focus on Perot's hair and, in the other, Jackson visualizes herself "covered" in her bed by a "garden of excellent fruit" from which she feeds Perot (260–261). Fruit is a major motif, as the juicy round watermelons that are exploded by male violence and the sensual scene of being enveloped in a bed of fruit demonstrate. Dreams of fruit are commonly understood to symbolize erotic desire or emotional satisfaction. Watermelon particularly has connotations of lust and fiery passion. How the fruit appears or is handled in the dream determines whether it is a cautionary or festive symbol. The watermelon dream clearly reflects (the threat of) destruction and loss of an object of desire; while companionship on the bed of fruit suggests intimacy and abundance. Water is also an important theme; in dreams it generally represents the flow of emotional energy or life force and, similar to fruit imagery, its connotations are determined by the particularities of its appearance. The empty well that overflows with burst watermelons points to intense and overwhelming emotions—but about what or whom?

Sometimes water signals the rising doubts of the dreamer. Such as when Jackson dreams she and Perot "were in a house upon a rock together, and a storm arose, which made us feel that we were in great danger. . . . And I thought the storm . . . would carry us down to New York, and then our friends would see our good home, and our destruction also. . . . And the house stood firm because it was on a rock" (211). At other times, water signifies sanctification and the arrival of sought-after emotion:

> I dreamt that Rebecca and me lived together. The door opened west, and there was a river that came from the west and it ran eastward [. . .]—beautiful white water. I stood in the west door looking, westward on the beautiful river. I saw Rebecca Perot coming in the river, her face to the east, and she aplunging in the water every few steps, head foremost, abathing herself. She only had on her undergarment. She was pure and clean. . . . She looked like an angel, oh how bright! (225)

This dream predicts that they will live together, or is invoked by discussions they perhaps were already having about doing so at the time. Either way, it also conveys a connection in Jackson's imaginary among beauty, purity, and Perot's nearly naked body. Critics have debated whether, had they lived in a later period, Cox and Perot's relationship would have been interpreted as lesbian. I am not invested in that debate. My concern is not to argue for a lesbian identity or sex acts, per se, but rather to work from a critical perspective that provides a queer space of interpretive possibilities. Sexuality is not limited to genital contact and definitely does not begin with it. Sexuality involves attraction, fantasy, vibrational connection, and impulses that can occur before, during, after, or *instead of* physical contact. A reading of Jackson's journals as a ritual space that "calls for a redefinition of early African American women's spirituality and cultural performance" (Bassard 9) includes an acknowledgment that community, spirituality, and homoeroticism are fused in Jackson's transformative use of sacred literature.

Jackson's spirit narrative is the earliest example of black queer spirituality because it provides "a radical questioning of social and cultural norms, notions of gender, reproductive sexuality and the family" (Smyth 42). A queer analysis props open the window of possibility that Jackson's withdrawal from heterosexuality may have other, perhaps unnarratable, implications and outcomes than a life of celibacy—some of which are channeled into her psychic landscape. Did the Rebeccas share an erotic bond that was only viewed through a religious, and ultimately limiting, lens? Was there a sensual relationship that, because it lay outside of normative definitions of sex, maintained a theological space for a claim to celibacy? This cannot be known. What is clear is that through the gifts of the spirit, Jackson was able to claim a liberated identity and perform a type of freedom in religious rituals, which includes the occurrence of same-sex erotics through the lens of her spirit eye.

LESBIAN SPIRIT, CULTURE, AND SEXUALITY: "IN THE LIFE"

Bassard's chapter title for her discussion of Jackson's writing, "Rituals of Desire: Spirit, Culture, and Sexuality," echoes the holy trinity at the center of Becky Birtha's short story. "In the Life" reveals the struggle for black lesbian empowerment, agency, and subjectivity through the protagonist's negotiations with religious discourse. In a similar defense of so-called unnatural womanhood and the claim to spiritual virtue visible in the religious rhetoric of black women's spirit narratives, Becky Birtha's narrator describes her journey from loneliness and fear (of death) to a flourishing erotic connection with a beneficent, ghostly being, which facilitates her transformation from trepidation into eagerness. Birtha's text is a crafted work of fiction and cannot be defined as a spiritual autobiography or an act of spirit writing. I assert that the content, structure, and cultural politics extrapolate from the tradition outlined above, similarly to the ways in which *neo-slave narratives* are called such for their literary kinship to the ex-slave autobiography.[7]

"In the Life" echoes the concerns and justifications presented in *Gifts of Power* by detailing religious exclusion based on sexual practice and the displacement of the institutional church as the locus and authority of spiritual activity. It functions, rhetorically, to empower and affirm a black lesbian spiritual life that appears to be locked out of conventional religious paths. There are also parallels in the imagery. The first-person narrator is Jinx, a retired city bus driver in her seventies. Her account begins with a supernatural encounter with her dead lover's spirit:

> Grace come to me in my sleep last night. I feel somebody presence, in the room with me, then I catch the scent of Posner's Bergamot Pressing Oil, and that cocoa butter grease she use on her skin. I know she standing at the bedside, right over me, and then she call my name. . . . I'm so deep asleep I have to fight my way awake, and when I do be fully woke, Grace is gone. (289)[8]

As in *Gifts of Power*, the human-spirit interaction is vivid in its perception of scents and sounds. The construction of the phrase, stood "right over me," demonstrates Jinx's sense that Grace exists outside of the dream. When she does manage to wake up, Jinx makes her way down to the garden "half expecting Gracie to be there waiting for me, but there ain't another soul stirring tonight" (289). This suggests that she cannot access Grace in either a waking state or in deep sleep. The spiritual plane exists in the twilight between. We see that Gracie is a spirit-informant whose message, "I'm just gone down to the garden awhile. I be back" (289), has multiple meanings as this neo-spirit narrative situates the bedroom, garden, and dream life as spaces of secular mysticality from which Jinx gains direction.

Eldress Jackson had a similar relationship to her dream life and other states of consciousness. She would either go into a trance or have dreams in which her spirit eye revealed ancestral beings in her midst and allowed her to hear instructions that she would not benefit from or understand until much later: "In and with His wisdom, He saw fit to call and raise me up in this city as a living witness for Him and His work, the work of the latter day of glory. And although there was no mortal that I could go to and gain instruction from, so it pleased God in His love and mercy to teach me in dreams, and visions, and revelations, and gifts" (Jackson 96). An entry dated March 11, 1843, is especially analogous to Jinx's opening lines:

> In the morning I found myself under great power of God. An angel came in the room, and I found my body under strange

> feeling. I thought I was dying. I was seized with a trembling within and without my body, and I was then carried away. The earth trembled and a great storm came from the south. . . . And then I was all alone, and my vision ended, and I was very happy. (Jackson 178)

Although to different ends, both narrators illustrate a liminal space of consciousness in which spiritual visitation is possible, at times, and necessary.

Although visions of angels and spirits represent blurred states of in-betweeness, a clear binary exists between institutionalized religion and spiritual engagements. Specifically, a ceremony inside the material church structure is contrasted with the supernatural encounters in the domestic spaces of the bedroom and garden. Gladys, a neighbor, cautions Jinx, "You reaching that time of life when you might wanna be giving a little more attention to the spiritual side of things than you been doing" (293). The woman is a member of the local church and is suggesting that, at her age, Jinx may want to "get religion" or face eternal damnation. Jinx does not debate the neighbor's perspective but neither does the warning move her. "It ain't no use in arguing with her kind" Jinx tells the reader sarcastically, "[because they think] the Lord is on they side in every little disagreement" (293). When Gladys begins to quote bible verses, the narration cuts off the woman's proselytizing with ellipses and allows Jinx to take discursive control in an embedded narrative. Gladys wants Jinx to think about attending church soon. "Funny thing," Jinx tells us, "I been thinking about it all day. But not the kinda thoughts she want me to think, I'm sure" (293). To use Mae G. Henderson's words from another context, Jinx then steers the audience with counter discourse that "disrupts, rereads and overrides the conventional story" (358) of church as a welcoming space. She represents the heralded institution of the black church as more preoccupied with superficiality than in saving souls.

Thirty-five years earlier, Jinx and Grace attended an Easter service to appease Grace's cousin who accused the couple of being "unnatural and sinful and a disgrace to her family" (294). It was appeasement without surrender: "So Grace and me finally conspires that the way to get her off our backs is to give her what she think she want" (294). They conspire to display a cultivated butch/femme aesthetic to defy the regulation of gender roles imposed by the cousin's religion.[9] Jinx donned a man's suit "pressed fresh" and a "brand new narrow-brim dovegray Stetson hat" for the occasion (294). The cultural context of their "coming out" is a crucial element in understanding this as resistance and counter discourse. The Easter celebration observes the death, resurrection, and ascension of the Christian messiah; it is the doctrinal centerpiece of the religion. This holiday in the African American protestant tradition is second only to the Christmas celebration in terms of its heightened ceremony. Generally, new clothes, shoes, hats, and women's elaborate hairstyles are on parade. Family gatherings are common and the church building, as the site of communion, is usually overflowing with visiting/returning family and friends. It is likely that Grace and Jinx would have participated in Easter programs as children; yet, even if they had not, they would most likely be aware of its grandeur. So perhaps what Grace's cousin "think she want" is to overwhelm the lesbian sinners with the message of the holiday (the suffering of the Christ, his victory over physical death, and the promise of eternal life) and the scrutinizing gaze of the larger black heteronormative community who represent "proper" black families and "natural" gender alignment. Accordingly,

> [A]s soon as we get in the door, this kinda sedate commotion break out—all them good Christian folks whispering and nudging each other and trying to turn around and get a good look. Well, *Grace and me, we used to that.* We just finds us a nice seat in one of the empty pews near the back. But this busy buzzing keep up, even after we seated and more blended in with the crowd. And finally it come out that the point of contention ain't even the bottom half of my suit, but my new dove gray Stetson. (294; emphasis added)

The first component of Jinx's resistance is as the storyteller, for she assumes full interpretive control of the dynamics of this scene. Her version is that the commotion is "sedate" and that eventually they are "more blended in." Still something remains amiss. They learn precisely what when an elderly man in thick glasses "is turning around and leaning way over the back of the seat, whispering to Grace in a voice plenty loud enough for [Jinx] to hear, 'you better tell your beau to remove that hat, entering in Jesus' Holy Chapel.'" Jinx implies that his old age and sight impairment contribute to a misreading of her masculinity as maleness. Still, she complies with his indirect order. Immediately, from behind, a woman "grumbl[es]" that Jinx has "no respect at all. Oughta know you sposed to keep your head covered, setting in the house of the Lord" (294). This woman, on the other hand, recognizes the transgressive body before her. Both are spokespersons for the church and the broader black community's insistence on static, normative representations of men and women. The commotion then, according to Jinx, is that "the congregation can't make up its mind whether I'm supposed to wear my hat or I ain't." That is to say, they cannot easily categorize her gender performance and, therefore, cannot decide which gender norms to enforce. From then on, the entire church service is made to be a joke on the spectators. "I couldn't hardly keep a straight face all through the service," Jinx fondly reminisces, because "every time I catch Gracie eye, one or the other of us catch a sight of my hat, we off again. I couldn't wait to get outa that place. But it was worth it. Gracie and me was entertaining the gang with that story for weeks to come" (295). On the surface, this scenario is humorous, but when we consider the facts by themselves we can see that by controlling the narrative, Jinx has turned a situation fraught with anxiety, alienation, and vulnerability into a story about the folly of Christian folk.

To resist any complicity in the labeling of her gender expression and sexual orientation as sinful and shameful by Grace's cousin, Jinx refuses to tone down her butchness. This is an act of self-revelation in a literal procession of normative expressions of gender. Malinda Kanner's research into the "semiotics of butch" shows that the butch aesthetic is always interpreted as a distinctly sexual signifier. "Her sexuality is always salient," Kanner reports, "whether the context is sexual or not" (28). With Grace at her side as the site of her lesbian desire, Jinx's butch identity is further reinforced. Such reinforcement is not necessary though. "Irrespective of the imagination of the observer, the butch lesbian has stood out as the clear, visually declarative statement of attraction to other women," Kanner continues, "[because] the butch woman looks like who she is" (28). That is to say, by choosing to wear a man's suit and hat, Jinx intentionally looks like a woman who desires women. Thus, when they enter the church space together, they perform a refusal to disguise the nature of their relationship.

Another aspect of Jinx's resistance to shame is that she narrates the tale in a way that empowers her subject position and protects the audience from knowing the isolation she most likely experienced. Their entry was met with a bristling that rippled through the room—people were visibly nudging each other, whispering audibly, and turning in their seats. This is the epitome of alienation for the black queer subject: her blackness allows her full access into the cultural ceremony yet she is shunned from within the group. For, as Sally Munt reminds us, "the heterosexist gaze is intended to mark [the deviant]: the glance is a strike" (6). They are an unwelcome spectacle, even if, as Jinx retorts to soften the blow, that they are "used to that." Actually, the fact that they are accustomed to being stared at further underscores their general sense of self-conscious outsider status and does not necessarily diminish the weight of the church's gaze. It is an outsider status that simultaneously speaks sexuality and silences it, as the protagonist is defined, and then delegitimated (Munt 5). The empowering aspect of seizing narrative control in a context of church-sanctioned homophobia and gender policing is the ability to challenge and change one's subjectivity within these institutions.

To detract from the feelings of exposure they must have felt, no mention is made of the actual Easter program. The traditional church space is the ultimate site of validation for the homophobic, heteropatriarchal standpoint. Direct "quotes" of God's repudiation of same-sex sexuality usually abound in this space with critical impunity. What did the minister say? Did he take this opportunity of having visible lesbians in the audience to admonish their homosexuality? The "blind" old man and "grumbling" woman were attempting to chastise and shame Jinx by signifying on the placement of her hat. Were there any more direct or oblique remarks made about Jinx's deviant performance of femaleness? We cannot know because Jinx refuses to acknowledge the oppressive weight of the gaze by zooming in on the scopic exchanges between her and Grace. Hence, her power lies in *how* the story is told. The narrative view is pulled into a tight close-up of their loving, accepting, and protective gazes on each other, which effectively occludes and delegitimizes the master narrative of shaming and punishing gazes. This strategy denies the audience the opportunity to identify with the oppressor. It is alienation turned inside out.

In addition to the use of counter discourse, Jinx made retelling this story "to the gang" a means of empowerment for her lesbian community. The church public, with its reliance on bourgeois notions of propriety and ingrained reliance on normative gender expression, is cast as disorientated and unsophisticated when confronted with butch femaleness, and is situated in direct opposition to Jinx's counter public of lesbians who completely identify with the outsiders. Each act of retelling minimizes the penetrating gaze of the church until finally the judgmental crowd disappears altogether, eclipsed by Jinx and Grace's concentration on each other. This limits the audience's ability to comprehend how harsh the situation may have been for the couple. Although some anxiety is revealed in the statement, "I couldn't wait to get outa that place," their vulnerability is countered with the fact that they found a way to make the whole scenario "entertaining" for weeks afterward. This is a significant resistance to shame. By retelling this story this way, as (Jinx's) testimony and (Gracie's) witnessing, it becomes legend: the heroic butch/femme lesbians laugh in the face of the menacing church folk. Consequently, the church is rejected as a legitimate authority on proper gender performance and its religious message is completely obscured.

Hence, "In the Life" constructs the church space as an unusable and/or hostile environment to queer subjectivity, which amplifies the affirmative positioning of the home and garden as sites of secular spirituality. Melvin Rahming's study of diasporic African spirit-centered literature is supportive here. In a definition very similar to Hull's "soul talk" formulation, he outlines such literature as "concerned with spiritual cosmology and its organic relationship to individual and cultural circumstance" (2). Rahming aptly argues that the spirit-centered narrative is recognizable as such because it "holds up a mirror to human and cosmic spirit and to the spectrum of possibilities that emerges from human and cosmic interaction; [and it] testif[ies] to the authors' fecund awareness of cosmic interrelatedness, the unbounded locus of spiritual activity" (2). To the degree that it features soul talk and spirit-centeredness, Birtha's narrative joins Alice Walker's campaign in *The Color Purple* to upend the notion of the traditional black church as a transcendent space for all members of the black community.

Jinx's embedded narrative enables a dichotomous reading of the church/garden scenes as closed/open, inside/outside, and constricted/flourishing in terms of the queer subject's spiritual strivings. In the main frame of the story, Jinx documents her journey toward acceptance of death's inevitability and the spiritual growth that acceptance entails. When she begins her narrative, she speaks of her failing health and emotional status in analogous terms to the garden. "Gracie's poor bedraggled garden is just struggling along on its last legs—kinda like me. I ain't the kind to complain about my lot, but truth to tell, I can't be down crawling around on my hands and knees no more" (291). The garden was Grace's project and, in her thirteen-year absence, it has lost some of its liveliness. It parallels Jinx's weakening abilities to produce (energy, strength, desire, etc.) and the dwindling amount of light that falls on her backyard lot is a metaphor for her emotional demeanor. "Can't enjoy the garden at night proper nowadays, nohow," she laments. "Since Mister Thompson's land was took over by the city and they built them housing projects . . . you can't even see the moon from here. . . . Don't no moonlight come in my yard no more" (291). This mulling over of the state of her being through the yard/garden imagery is initiated by Grace's visitation discussed earlier; in fact, she followed Grace there.

Once near the garden, she is enveloped by nostalgic melancholia. This is the low point in the chronicle of her spiritual journey. We get a better sense of her foreboding when, immediately after closing the church tale, she begins to speak more candidly about her thoughts on dying. Indulging in a bit of signifying she assures us that,

> Far as life everlasting is concerned, I imagine I'll cross that bridge when I reach it. I don't see no reason to rush into things. I know Old Man Death is coming after me one of these days. . . . But I ain't about to start nothing that might make him feel welcome. . . . It might be different for Gladys Hawkins and the rest of them church sisters, but I got a whole lot left to live for. . . . When you in the life, one thing your days don't never be, and that's dull. . . . All these years I been in the life, I loved it. And you know Jinx ain't about to go off with no Old *Man* without no struggle, nohow." (295; original emphasis)

Jinx's discourse and spiritual philosophy are steeped in African American oral traditions. Semantically, she relies on proverbs and plays with shades of meaning; meanwhile, she reveals her belief, to return to Rahming's theory, in a spiritual cosmology and its organic relationship to individual and cultural circumstance. To the familiar listener, "I'll cross that bridge" is an unmistakable proverb. Yet there is another adage embedded in the line "I ain't about to start nothing." She cites a variation of the saying, "don't start no mess, won't be none," alluded to here to mean that prolonged contemplation of an idea/mood can manipulate the spirit world, so that the thought/act initiates (or starts) its physical manifestation (mess) in one's life. This is partly what Rahming means by "human and cosmic interaction." According to this worldview, focusing on death can tip the balance of the universe toward that outcome.

As is common in literature and folklore, death is personified as a suitor or leering man, awaiting his chance to pounce. This construction reflects her various states of being: emotional/spiritual unwillingness to succumb to death, her physical vulnerability as an aging woman against the strength of a man, and her steadfast pride in her lesbian identity.

Geneva Smitherman's thorough analysis of the stylistic patterns of black language further clarifies Jinx's articulation: "The speaker's imagery and ideas center around the empirical world, the world of reality, and the contemporary Here and Now. Rarely does [s]he drift off into esoteric abstractions; [her] metaphors and illustrations are commonplace and grounded in everyday experience" (65). Jinx contrasts her everyday experience of being happily "in the life" against the "church sisters" who are, presumably, more sexually repressed and considered more gender-appropriate than she. Time and again, Jinx is unapologetic for the kind of sexual being she has been/is, in resistance to the contrition expected by the church community, as represented by Gracie's cousin and Gladys. By loving "the life," Jinx simultaneously professes her desire to be alive and reiterates the joy and love she sustains as a member of her lesbian community.

This resistance notwithstanding, Jinx realizes that she is not immortal. "To tell the truth, though, sometime I do get a funny feeling bout Old Man Death," she confides. "Sometime I feel like he here already—been here. Waiting on me and watching me and biding his time. Paying attention when I have to stop on the landing of the stairs to catch my breath" (295). This "funny feeling" continues the spiritual narrative, the description of a deeper, soulful knowing, that is both physical and eerie. The phrase "been here" is what Smitherman designates a "grammatical intensifier" in Black English, as it modifies and emphasizes the preceding statement "here already." Not only does Jinx feel death approaching because of her age and ailments, but at times it is a lurking, familiar presence—in perpetual travel and having already arrived.

Eventually, Gracie displaces "Old Man Death" as a spirit-companion who leads Jinx toward a peaceful, gleeful anticipation of her metamorphosis, and the garden reflects as much. Grace appears twice more and, ominously, the garden/backyard space becomes a more prominent feature with each encounter. The first instance occurs on the evening of her talk with Gladys about church. Again, we find her in the liminal state of consciousness between sleep and wakefulness. Jinx is lying in bed when she hears sounds coming from the kitchen downstairs. She closes her eyes and,

> Just when I finally manage to doze off, I hear somebody footsteps right here in the bedroom with me. Somebody tippy-toeing real quiet, creaking the floor boards between the bed and the dresser. I'm almost scared to open my eyes. But it's only Gracie—in her

> old raggedy bathrobe and a silk handkerchief wrapped up around all them little braids in her head—putting her finger to her lips to try and shush me so *I won't wake up*. (Birtha 295; my emphasis)

Perhaps Jinx does not wake up, but she does speak to Grace, coaxing her to join her in bed. Grace replies that she needs to attend to the insects in the garden since its nearly daybreak. "I be back before you even know I'm gone," Grace assures her. Eventually Jinx tires of waiting and leans out of the window into a startling reality: Gracie is not there, and neither are her clothes in the closet. These realizations and the dreary sight of gathering storm clouds trigger an "awful funny feeling" and the need to "see what's what" (296). Again Jinx is led down into the garden to convene with nature. She spends time in the garden picking peaches and tomatoes until it begins to rain.

Rain, thunderstorms, and floods are prominent water symbols in Eldress Jackson's spirit narrative also. Her conversion scene is particularly similar in its transition from feeling as if her "soul had come into the chamber of death" (Jackson 72) to a triumphant spiritual connection to the environmental elements. Apparently, Jackson had an intense aversion to thunder and lightning. In 1831, during an alarmingly noisy storm, she believed God was angry with her, potentially seeking to kill her with lightning, and that she was not yet prepared to die. After much hand-wringing and praying, her fears subsided and her perspective on the meaning of lightning changed:

> [T]he cloud bursted and heavens [sic] was clear. And the mountain was gone. My spirit was light, my heart was filled with love for God and all mankind. And the lightning, which was a moment ago a messenger of death, was now the messenger of peace, joy and consolation. And I rose from my knees, ran downstairs, opened the door to let the lightning in the house for it was like sheets of glory to my soul. (Jackson 72)

Jackson makes it, literally, through the storm, to find her way back to God. Afterward, she is able to fellowship with nature and hears the voice of God in the wind. While Jinx does not gain such gifts of power, the weather and garden are metaphors for her changing attitude.

The final visitation occurs the very next night and, therein, all the elements of the story meld together. Jinx returns home to find the front door unlocked. Believing the intruder is still there, she searches every room but finds no one. She lies in bed, uneasy for awhile and eventually drifts off to sleep. Then, unsurprisingly, "The next thing I know, Gracie waking me up" (299) with kisses. Descriptions of this visitation are rich with a sensuality that is absent from earlier scenes. "I can feel the laughing running all through her body and mine," Jinx gushes, "[. . . and] my whole body is all a shimmer with this sweet, sweet craving" (299). Jinx's sexual arousal is punctuated by the weather. While her "blood is racing [and] singing," the sky is "wide open—the storm is throbbing and beating down on the roof . . . pressing its wet self up against the window. . . . And I run my fingers down along her breast, underneath her own nightgown." The emotional range of the church scene is mirrored here as Jinx's night began with her in an anxious, fearful state and leads to her vulnerability being buttressed by a scopic exchange. Grace lies beneath her, "smiling up at [her] through the dark, and her eyes is wide and shiny" (299–300).

The paragraph ends with ellipses, an indication of the unnarrated but continued lovemaking. The story picks up again in the postcoital moment. Jinx wakes up alone and it is dark and rainy outside. The downpour of rain is also a metaphor for transformation, for her emotional status and attitude about death have reversed since its passing. She interprets the experience as a glimpse into the afterlife, one that she wishes to join sooner than later. Death is no longer an old man coming to steal her soul, but an erotic intermingling of the elements, the universe enwrapping her and Grace in its embrace, and baptizing them in its wetness as they share in each other. "Like a flash I'm across the room," Jinx says, "*knowing I'm going after her*, this time" (300; italics added). The "knowing" in this scene is her reception, without reluctance, to literally following Grace into the earth, the spirit world, or the world of the dead.

The sensuality remains as heightened as the urgency to find Grace in the garden: "The carpet threads is nubby and rough, flying past underneath my bare feet, and the kitchen linoleum cold and smooth. . . . I push through the screen" (300). The garden is now a luxuriant environment, no longer the bedraggled, suffocated lot readers encounter in the story's beginning:

> The storm is moved on. That fresh air *feel good* on my skin through the cotton nightshirt. *Smell good*, too, rising up outa the wet earth, and *I can see* the water sparkling on the leaves of the collards and kale, twinkling in the vines on the bean poles. The moon is riding

> high up over Thompson's field, spilling moonlight all over the yard and setting all them blossoms on the fence, to shining pure white. (300; my italics)

Jinx undergoes an epiphany induced by the Lordean concept of erotic knowledge. Jinx's sensual contact with Gracie caused a surge of spiritual clarity that is inextricable from her wide-eyed appreciation for the beauty of the landscape. The erotic is not a question only of what we do, Audre Lorde theorizes, "it is a question of how acutely and fully we can feel in the doing" (54). The sky's orgasmic fervor has settled into a gentle caressing of the earth. The air, water, and light fondle the foliage to illustrate the various stages of life, the ways that separate entities work in concert to form wholeness through a cyclical, symbiotic, nurturing relationship.

Again, we find parallels to Eldress Jackson's journal. In a dream dated March 12, 1843 (a day after the angel dream quoted above), flowers rain down from heaven:

> All the house, trees, and everything else disappeared. And then the rain changed from cotton to sweet-smelling flowers. There was one clap of thunder and a great noise in the heavens. . . . This was a little white flower. They fell in bunches, the flower in between two beautiful green leaves. I stepped to the door, picked some up, tasted them. Their taste was sweet, just like the smell. I then put some in my bosom, but I am not able to tell what they smelt like. The whole air was perfumed with their odor, yea, with their heavenly smell. . . . Then there came a sound from heaven which had never been heard before and in that storm came streams of light. And they came in the form of hoops, bright as silver, passing through the shower of flowers. They went like the lightning. They were moved by female angels and they were beyond the tongue of mortals to describe their heavenly appearance.

At the end of this aromatic and graphic dream of whiteness shot through with silver streaks of lightning, are crowds of "colored people" who represent the shifting desires of the Eldress. She relays later in the entry that realizes that she wants to devote time to being "useful to my people" in the surrounding black communities. Her decision to pursue this mission begins a new chapter in her ministry. It is a decision delivered to her in a medley of sights and sounds in a dream recorded with deep feelings of wonder and pleasure.

Similarly, Jinx's connection to the Earth calms her. As the earth sparkles, twinkles, and spills about her, Jinx becomes serene and contemplative. "I'm just gonna stay right here on this back porch," she decides. "And hold still. And listen close. Cause I know Gracie in this garden somewhere. And she waiting for me" (300). The finality of this last "knowing" suggests that Jinx may already be dead when the story closes. Perhaps, as Gracie's touch moved past the layers of Jinx's clothing, she was removing emotional and intellectual barriers between the living flesh and the disembodied spirit, which would allow Jinx to fully open herself to the experience of dying. When considered from that angle, the lovemaking is the act of crossing over into the afterlife. In this way, the story illustrates Lorde's erotic knowledge pushed to its furthest extent. Jinx's death then is a return to life, a reconnection to being in the life with Gracie, as opposed to letting go of it in exchange for a Christian heaven.

Finally, Birtha's tale also revises the teachings of the "first Adam" and the "fall from grace" that Eldress Jackson so willingly discarded in her conversion experience. This is a turn *to* Grace, a lesbian spirit guide who epitomizes erotic spirituality in an act of sacred union. Sexuality is the bridge to the garden and to grace/Grace. Sexual knowledge does not send one away from blissful cosmic interaction; it pulls one in deeper.

Following Joycelyn Moody's claim in *Sentimental Confessions* that the spiritual autobiographies in her study produce a theology because each text, in its own way, interrogates divinity; theorizes the nature and function of the divine; and engages, interrogates, resists, and endorses the texts of other theologians (18), it is my hope that this chapter lays the groundwork for more discussion of how and where the production of theology in LGBTQ fiction, unwittingly perhaps, revisits the spirit narrative tradition. I propose that the neo-spirit narrative in this book produces a theology that interrogates what it means to be spiritual and theorizes that the divine supernatural operates in the lives of the unreligious. Becky Birtha renders various supernatural encounters in the bedroom, the dream life, and the garden to theorize "the unbounded locus of spiritual activity" (Rahming 2). The spiritual encounters and ecstatic experiences are used to critique homophobic religious exclusion and to redefine the role of sexuality within the spiritual experience. It leaves the reader with the notion that sacredness, if not God, is in the details of everyday life.

PART III

Nontheist Cosmologies

CHAPTER SIX

Humanist Zealotry

Parable of the Sower and *Parable of the Talents*

> The dichotomy between reason and faith is often given emphasis in humanism, with humanists taking their stand on the side of reason. Because of this, Religious Humanism should not be seen as an alternative faith, but rather as an alternative way of being religious.
>
> —Fred Edwords, "What is Humanism?"

> All successful life is
> Adaptable,
> Opportunistic,
> Tenacious,
> Interconnected, and
> Fecund.
> Understand this.
> Use it.
> Shape God.
>
> —Lauren Olamina in *Parable of the Sower*

According to Samuel Delany, science fiction's most famous and prolific African American author, science fiction's marginality in literature is its most forceful and distinguishing aspect. From the far corners of the literary stage, sci-fi writers can be the most honest and most effective (qtd in Dery 189). Octavia Butler's ideas flourish there. She uses sci-fi and fantasy genres to interrogate the human impulse to oppress others, and to highlight the erotic possibilities that exist in the relationship between the victimizer and victimized. It is a major feature of her imaginative project to disrupt, interrogate, and restructure how the "sexual" is posited in the African American literary imagination (Hampton 89). Butler (1947–2006) is often referred to as the grand dame of science fiction because she was the first woman writer to break through to popular readership in the white male-dominated field. Her first story, "Crossover," was published in the 1971 *Anthology of Speculative Fiction and Criticism from the Clarion Writers' Workshop.* She would return to the highly competitive and prestigious workshop numerous times as a teacher. *Patternmaster*, her first novel and the first title of her five-volume *Patternist* series, was published in 1976, followed by *Mind of My Mind* in 1977. Others in the series include *Survivor* (1978), *Wild Seed* (1980), and *Clay's Ark* (1984). With the publication and popularity of the neo-slave narrative *Kindred* in 1979, Butler was able to devote herself full time to her writing career. She won the Hugo Award in 1984 for her short story "Speech Sounds," and in 1985, "Bloodchild" won the esteemed Hugo and Nebula Awards for science fiction literature. Her other books include the *Xenogenesis* trilogy (now called *Lilith's Brood*), and a short story collection, *Bloodchild and Other Stories* (1995). *Parable of the Sower* (1993), the first of her *Earthseed* series, was a *New York Times* Notable Book of the Year. The book's sequel, *Parable of the Talents* (1998), won a Nebula Award. In 1995, Butler was awarded a prestigious MacArthur Foundation "genius" grant. Her final novel is a vampire tale, titled *Fledgling* (2005).

Sexuality, justice, and the ethics of domination are central themes in her oeuvre. Perhaps this is why, as Lewis Call argues, what Butler has to say can *only* be said from the margins (279). In his analysis, Call characterizes the cosmic "dance" between the immortals, Doro and Anwanyu, in *Wild Seed* as one in which they alternate "mastering and enslaving one another in a permanent spiral of mutual desire" (284). One is also reminded of a subplot in *Kindred*, in which a nineteenth-century female slave is twisted with guilt after submitting to a sexual relationship with her master for survival purposes. She is attracted to him in spite of the brutality he regularly inflicts on her on an interpersonal level and, on a structural level, in his maintenance of the slaveocracy. Also, *Fledgling* features a hybrid human-vampire being who embodies a discourse of ethical domination and consensual symbiosis by occasionally asking her human food source for permission to feed/and or "turn" them. Many humans willingly relinquish their sense of autonomy and individual freedom for an entwined physical, emotional, and erotic dependency with a being that can protect or end human life in a given situation. We could also point to the disorienting premise of *Lilith's Brood* that introduces readers to three biological sexes: male, female, and the "ooloi." Ooloi bodies are able to manipulate genetic material and, in the reproductive act, unify human genes with other species. In each new generation, the offspring differ greatly from their parents. *Fledgling* and *Lilith's Brood* blur the line between pleasure and danger in their narratives of pansexual (interspecies, interracial, and homosexual) border crossings, which underlie explorations of other, equally complex, ideas. Remaining true to form in the *Earthseed* series, *Parable of the Sower* and its sequel *Parable of the Talents*, Butler weaves a tale that continues this leitmotif as the characters resist the forces of spiritual and environmental slavery. This chapter argues that Octavia Butler contributes to the epistemology of black queer spirituality through the specific humanist leanings of her minister character in the serial.

In the *Earthseed* series, Butler weaves a tale that maintains the pleasure, danger, and domination leitmotif of her oeuvre as her characters resist the forces of oppressive religious, political, and commercial regimes. Particularly significant to a discussion about the diversity of African American worldviews and spiritual perspective is the way the *Earthseed* serial provides a curriculum of human survival with humanist principles. Beginning with a focus on the serials' (ir)religious ideology, this examination of the erotic experiences and worldview of Lauren Olamina, the cross-dressing, gun-toting minister reveals a narrative propelled by religious humanist rhetoric combined with elements of voyeurism and masochism; the outcome of which, to repeat Gregory Hampton, further disrupts and interrogates how the sexual is posited in the African American literary imagination. After the analysis, I propose that the ways the black female protagonist survives dangerous situations adds fresh perspective to the political uses of depicting the black body in pain in literature.

RELIGIOUS HUMANISM: "AN ALTERNATIVE WAY OF BEING RELIGIOUS"

According to the *Humanist Manifesto III*, published in 2003 by the American Humanist Association, humanists generally seek a purposeful, ethical life without religious prescription; they embrace modern science, democratic principles, human rights, and free inquiry. Yet, some humanists behave as other established faith-based groups and structure their lives within a system that provides fellowship, instruction, and community. This behavior is characterized as "religious." So there is no major distinction between humanist belief systems, only the degree to which they express their humanist principles as a way of life. Fred Edwords is the former executive director of the American Humanist Association and past editor of the *Humanist.* To date, he serves on the faculty of the Humanist Institute. In an online essay, "What is Humanism?," Edwords expounds on the definition of religious humanism. As he explains it, humanist thought becomes a religious force when its principles underpin the social life of its believers:[1]

> Religion is that which serves the personal and social needs of a group of people sharing the same philosophical worldview. To serve personal needs, Religious Humanism offers a basis for moral values, an inspiring set of ideals, methods for dealing with life's harsher realities, a rationale for living life joyously, and an overall sense of purpose. To serve social needs humanist religious communities (such as Ethical Culture societies and many Unitarian Universalist churches) offer a sense of belonging, an institutional setting for the moral education of children, special holidays shared with like-minded people, a unique ceremonial life, the performance of ideologically consistent rites of passage (weddings, child welcomings, coming-of-age celebrations, memorials, and so forth), an opportunity for affirmation of one's philosophy of life, and a historical context for one's ideas. (n. p.)

In other words, religious humanists are considered "religious" because they have institutionalized their beliefs through ceremonies, community life and work, interpersonal relationships, and the critical engagement of ideas in published writing and group study. The signal difference, then, between theologically based religiosity and reason-based religiosity is the organizing principle of the belief system. Hence, Edwords asserts, "Religious Humanism should not be seen as an alternative faith, but rather as an alternative way of being religious" (n. p.). From this perspective, humanism is religiously anti-theology.

In fact, a central tenet of humanism is the rejection of divine beings and supernaturalism. It emphasizes human ethical and moral responsibilities in relationship to all living beings and the planet. One's inner voice or conscience, lived experience, logic, emotion, and scientific reasoning are considered the most reliable sources of guidance and explanation. As an "alternative way of being religious," it is the endeavor for purposeful living in the absence of theism. From this perspective, God-talk perpetuates ancient myths, superstition, and dogmas; meanwhile, humanism offers an alternative to human powerlessness through its emphases on activism, cooperation, and peaceful conflict resolution. "Humanism teaches us it is immoral to wait for God to act for us," declares Unitarian Universalist minister Kenneth Phifer in "The Faith of a Humanist." Phifer continues: "We must act to stop the wars and the crimes and the brutality of this and future ages. . . . Humanism tells us that whatever our philosophy of the universe may be, ultimately the responsibility for the kind of world in which we live rests with us" (qtd in Edwords). Phifer's discussion proceeds from an assertion in the *Humanist Manifesto III*: "We accept our lives as all and enough, distinguishing things as they are from things we wish or imagine to be" ("The Unfolding" 4). So religious humanism, at bottom, eschews any directive to please a deity or seek reward in an afterlife; a stance that is neither nihilistic nor fatalist but, rather, a vision of the future as within the grasp of human power through collective consciousness and action. Although it is beyond the scope of this chapter to enumerate the history and perspectives of the various factions, many practitioners within organized sects of humanism contest the notion that their beliefs and moral directives constitute a religion in the way Edwords describes it. Nonetheless, some of the established tenets of religious humanism clearly inform the ideas, which are expressed in the *Parables.*

Many of these principles emerge in Butler's *Earthseed* series through the exploration of human-cosmic interaction from the perspective of people whose faith in Christianity fails to improve their outlook, daily living, or hope for life on the planet. The average, poor, or working class citizen has no real sanctuary because natural resources are scarce and most human interaction has devolved into defending against or avoiding roaming bands of animalistic, predatory folk. It is a society in which the desperate violently prey on even the most fleeting moment of vulnerability in others. From within this growing chaos, Butler's high priestess of the Earthseed ministry emerges; hers is a voice of humanist reasoning and activism that can best be described as a zealous advocacy of human self-rescue cloaked in theist terminology.

EARTHSEED: THE DISBELIEVER'S BELIEF SYSTEM

At the center of the *Earthseed* series is the voice of Lauren Olamina, a black girl who receives a vision at the tender age of twelve that vastly contrasts with her Baptist upbringing. For three years she quietly cultivates her new worldview through journal writing. The structure of *Sower*, the first novel in the series, extrapolates from the spiritual autobiography genre where the reader is exposed to all of the author's fears, motivations, dreams, and observations in chronological fashion. Interposed are her humanist-inflected revelations, which eventually are published separately under the title, "Earthseed: The Book of the Living," and, consequently, are transformed into a sacred, preacherly text. The verses, her "collection of truths" (*Talents* 180), create a cultural movement in which Olamina becomes its revered (and equally despised) prophet. Earthseed first and foremost asserts a belief in human agency and responsibility.

The Earthseed doctrine asserts two main principles: (1) the true nature of God is the ever-changing universe, and (2) the destiny of Earthseed (the believers who accept the first principle) is to save humanity by colonizing other inhabitable planets. Although there is abstract god-talk in *Earthseed*, such as, "the Universe is God's self-portrait" (*Sower* 315), no part of the theology renders God an interactive, anthropomorphic being that must be worshipped, or answers prayers, or bestows faithful followers with a peaceful afterlife. The Holy Trinity, Ten Commandments, Mosaic Law, and gospels according to Jesus' disciples are all erased. In fact, Olamina cunningly subverts the very theological terminology she utilizes: "God" is defined alternately as chaos, change, and humanity's impact on humanity and the environment. Along with theist language, prayer is retained as a meditative activity that centers the self and focuses one's resolve "to accept and work with the shapes that God imposes on us" (*Sower* 25). In other words, one should not pray for external intervention but to become attuned to the environment in which you live and take on situations with problem-solving skills and/or a proactive approach. It is a religious practice of humanism because it involves creating communities around these principles, and is intended to change the direction of the future for the human species.

Also from Olamina's Baptist tradition remain the concepts of free will and humanitarian service. She proposes that spiritual investment in an external supernatural power source renders people too passive and less responsible to each other. God is Life, according to one *Earthseed* entry, and your response to Life defines your relationship to God:

> A victim of God may through learning adaption / Become a partner of God / A victim of God may / Through forethought and planning/ Become a shaper of God. / Or a victim of God may / Through shortsightedness and fear / Remain God's victim / God's plaything / God's prey. (*Sower* 31)

So self-reliance and active shaping of one's reality is central. One should do so religiously. At times, *Earthseed* echoes the Humanist Manifesto outright as it "deals with ongoing reality, not with supernatural authority figures" (*Sower* 219) and suggests to the reader that "to shape God, [one must] shape Self" (*Talents* 235). Though it may contain some traditional religion-inflected terminology, Earthseed is religious humanism, a disbeliever's faith system.

Some literary critics construe Earthseed as progressive Christianity; a denomination emptied of traditional intolerance and misogyny. Other readers have interpreted Olamina's character as a Christ figure.[2] Butler's repudiation of this interpretation notwithstanding,[3] it is an easy leap of logic to make as a reader: the novels' titles invoke Matthew 13 and Matthew 25, respectively, wherein Jesus uses allegory to instill the importance of ministry and faithful service. And like Jesus of the Christian bible, Olamina is a storyteller, teacher, and philosopher whose radical break from the family's faith tradition elevates her to a deity in the minds of future generations.[4] Furthermore, Butler closes each novel with the recitation of its biblical namesake; so, the last words readers encounter in each *Parable* novel is the direct quote of its corresponding Christian parable.

Even so, Earthseed diverges from a Christian theology and worldview in multiple ways. To begin, as one critic put it, Earthseed is a doctrine of radical reciprocity, which should not be confused with the Golden Rule (Miller 356); for there is something more complex about it than equality and empathy among humans. Earthseed believers worship at the altar of one's sense of purpose, one's place in the community and larger cosmos, and the preservation of humanity through shared resources. Another important difference lies in the fact that, unlike Jesus, Olamina does not insist on being the single conduit to the sacred. She emphasizes the multiplicity of truths that exist in the world. Whereas Jesus is quoted as saying, "In my Father's house, there are many mansions" to which he promised to go and prepare a place in Heaven for his followers (John 14:2), Earthseed provides a unifying, purposeful life here on Earth, and the hope of "A *real* heaven, [peaceful, secure life on other inhabitable planets near Earth] not mythology or philosophy" (*Sower* 261; original emphasis). That is, Olamina asks her converts to release their imaginations from the Heavenly Father and host of angels to define God as the universe in all its processes, as well as a source of "infinite potential" (*Sower* 270). Humans are neither saints nor sinners but, rather, "flesh that is self aware, questing, problem-solving" (*Sower* 151). These ideas echo Phifer's insistence, noted earlier, that "it is immoral to wait for God to act for us." It is the humanists' responsibility to rise to the challenge and be their own deliverers.

Earthseed also reflects humanism in its lack of speculation on a spiritual afterlife. The mystery of death remains an unknown or is, simply, the unknowable and, therefore, is unaddressed in Earthseed worldview. Perhaps a focus on such matters would distract people from working toward the destiny of interplanetary travel and species revitalization. Whatever the reason for it, this glaring absence and the human-centric essence of the doctrine, as Hampton notes, are what make the Earthseed theology flawed and dangerous from the Christian characters' perspective. In *Sower*, militant fundamentalist Christians perceive Earthseed as the teachings of an antichrist, which, technically, it is, and they seek to destroy every root and branch of it.[5] "The absence of absolute laws or universal truths," Hampton explains, "suggests the presence of ambiguous space, unanswered questions, and chaos, the very things that Christianity often associates with sin and tends to combat" (86). Olamina suffers dearly for her beliefs at the hands of fundamentalist crusaders. After being identified as a heretic, she is held in the Camp Christian Reeducation Facility, "an amalgam of concentration camp, religious training and slavery" (Stillman 21). As she evolves in her role as itinerant preacher, Olamina's suffering becomes an exercise in spiritual self-defense and self-preservation, a nexus of gender and sexual queerness, philosophical zealotry, and adaption as survival strategy.

REALNESS AND GENDER PASSING AS STRATEGIES OF SURVIVAL AND RELIGIOUS SEDUCTION

Gender passing is part of Olamina's survival strategy. The *Earthseed* serial begins in a postapocalyptic United States in the 2030s, where no public space is safe from the threat of violence: sexualized aggression, physical assault, enslavement, torture, and dispossession are constant threats to the migrant as well as the insulated home dweller. The richest few Americans have moved off-world (the neo-suburb is outer space) and those left on Earth are falling deeper into a life of perpetual terror and despair. Early in the chronicle, Olamina begins a migration north to escape the lawlessness of her California hometown. Roving gangs and lack of police protection necessitate survival strategies for anyone traveling by foot and living on the road. As a child, Olamina was been trained in weaponry by her father (it is a rite of passage in the postapocalyptic environment) and so is very comfortable handling guns and shooting to kill. Still, the predators in her midst, mainly dogs and men, must also be defended against through a presentation of indomitability. "Every direction was dangerous," Olamina narrates, "but there was more danger where there were more people. In the night, a woman and three kids might look like a gift basket of food, money, and sex" (*Sower* 154). To decrease the chances of attack, she diminishes the evidence of her femaleness by shaving her hair close, donning baggy menswear and renaming herself "Cory."[6] "I'm big enough and androgynous-looking enough to get away with it," she brags to a friend (*Talents* 337). But it is not enough to simply wear men's clothes and a short haircut to successfully impersonate a man. Gender passing requires the ability to appear "seamlessly similar to a male, publicly and privately" (Maltz 277). As R&B singer Cheryl Lynn famously intoned, it's got to be real. So, for safety and survival reasons, Olamina seeks to achieve an embodiment of masculinity which reveals no clues of her femaleness to the naked eye—a type of butch realness. Subsequently, her experiences as a male impersonator launch her humanist ministry into the realm of gender and sexual queerness and forge a convincingly seductive masculinity.

In lesbian subcultures, and broader drag culture in particular, butch realness describes a biological female who is convincing in her presentation of masculinity (Halberstam 246).[7] It is defined as a presentation of female masculinity that cannot be distinguished from male masculinity, whether it functions as a costume for a show or the daily routine expression of butch identity.[8] In either case, gender passing is not legitimated without an audience. In an excellent study of the performance/performativity of female masculinity, aptly titled "Real Butch," Robyn Maltz delineates the triangulated relationship between gender passing, stone butch realness, and audience:

> Passing, as used in the context of both race and gender, describes a situation of intelligibility in which the perception of the race or gender of the passing subject is actually a misreading. To pass effectively, a subject is (mis)read as "real." In the case of a passing female, to be read as genuinely male. Race and gender passing require stable, legible markers so that the passing subject can acquire, master, and perform the appearance and nuances of the appropriated race or gender. Passing is a public (and sometimes private) legibility and requires a spectator in order to legitimate the pass. (277–278)

The legible markers of black masculinity that Olamina would have to acquire, master, and perform in order to achieve butch realness as "Cory" include a passable voice quality, a recognizably male gait, and context-appropriate responses to women and other men.

Readers are assured of Olamina's graceful transition to a male presentation through several references to her size, strength, and hardness. She brags of her bone-breaking ability in fistfights (*Sower* 11–12). As a teenager, she "towers" over her stepmother (*Sower* 104); in a crowd of women, her height distinguishes her (*Talents* 317); and, even at age fifty-eight, after her gender-passing years are over, she still appears "big and strong [and as though she could] be hard with just the smallest change of expression" (*Talents* 398), according to her daughter. Hardness, as Olamina's daughter uses it, conveys an array of "unfeminine" traits, including stoicism and emotional toughness. Each of these traits is part of Olamina's survival toolkit. In her own words, she "[tries] not to let my face show anything. . . . Sometimes people say I look grim or angry. Better to have them think that than know the truth. Better to have them think anything than let them know just how easy it is to hurt me" (*Sower* 13). Olamina's realness and hardness shield the true vulnerability that exists, as we see later, just beneath her skin.

Her passing is legitimated because she is able to move freely, in close contact and often in conversation among men and women as "Cory." Olamina performs her male persona for months and, during this time, makes her way from California to Washington living a "laborer's life" (*Talents* 298), in which she is hired on a daily basis for painting, gardening, and carpentry work in exchange for food and boarding. Men who perceive her as a young black male seek ways to establish their sexual dominance, even though the position as potential employer is already one of power. One man propositions Cory for oral sex in exchange for a night's rest on the man's property. Another elderly male employer reminisces about his days of sexual conquest as a young musician while he monitors Cory's work on his farm. Women either suspect Cory is a potential predator or are drawn in by his "arresting eyes" and seductive appeal (*Talents* 380). So gender passing is a successful survival mechanism for a black woman traveling by foot on the dangerous open road. But this is no ordinary woman: Olamina/Cory is a preacher in perpetual search for followers and power. In her quest for both, butch realness and zealotry form a powerful instrument of religious humanist seduction.

An example of how realness and zealotry intersect occurs when Olamina exploits a woman's loneliness and obvious sexual attraction to Cory in the name of advancing the goals of Earthseed. To tell this part of the story, Butler's use of multiple narrators in the second novel, *Talents*, allows the reader to see Olamina from contrasting and, often, competing perspectives. The adult voice of her daughter, Larkin, is retrospective, written after Olamina's death, and interprets her mother as a dangerous religious fanatic who was rightfully feared for her relentless pursuit to abandon planet Earth. "The more I read about Earthseed," Larkin laments, "the more I despised it" (*Talents* 380). Larkin's skeptical tone frames the chapter in which Olamina exploits an erotic bond, which was facilitated by her butch realness. (Henceforth, I will use male pronouns to refer to Olamina's transmale identity.) In a conversation with Len, a female traveling companion, Cory realizes that the time spent working for people should also be utilized for recruiting more disciples. It would be a rebirth of the flock after the escape (from slavery) and dispersal of the original group. Nia Cortez, a forty-ish, single woman is selected for the first attempt at recruitment. Cory and Len spend the day weeding Nia's enormous vegetable garden and, after a meal, the three converse as Cory draws a sketch of Nia's face. As they sit on the porch together after dinner, Cory focuses intently on Nia's features and glances back and forth to the sketch pad, while poetic Earthseed verses fall gently from his lips. The verses intrigue Nia and she begins to ask questions. Cory's oratory performance and flattering artistic drawing coax Nia into allowing the traveling couple to stay on for the night. The opportunity for more intimacy is important: the minister has decided that Nia's background as a teacher would be useful in the training of future Earthseed children. So he continues to subtly inflame Nia's sexual attraction.

After establishing Nia's trustworthiness, Cory reveals himself as a biological female. Nia stares intently at Olamina's face but, alas, the familiar cues and traits of femininity have vanished beneath the masculine expression of the Cory persona. In an attempt to thwart the tension, Cory/Olamina redirects the conversation. But Nia is preoccupied with the struggle to discard her rising desire:

> "But you . . . ," she said. "I can't get over it. I still feel . . . I still feel as though you were a man. I mean . . ."
>
> [Cory:] "It's all right."
>
> [Nia] sighed, put her head back and looked at me with a sad smile. "No, it isn't."
>
> [Cory:] No, it wasn't. But I went to her and hugged her and held her. Like Len, she needed to be hugged and held, needed to cry in someone's arms. She'd been alone far too long. (*Talents* 371)

Throughout the scene, Cory/Olamina stimulates and channels the erotic energy into a commitment to Earthseed. Even so, the physical contact raises the possibility of a sexual encounter:

> To my own surprise, I realized that under other circumstances, I might have taken her to bed. I had gone through 17 months [imprisoned] at Camp Christian without wanting to be with anyone. I missed [my husband]—missed him so much sometimes that it was an almost physical pain. And I had never been tempted to want to make love with a woman. Now, I found myself almost wanting to. And she almost wanted me to. But that wasn't the relationship that I needed between us. (*Talents* 371)

This passage reveals that Olamina exploits the erotic as a binding and mobilizing impulse between humans (spiritual connection), but ultimately determines sex acts (physical connection) as superfluous in a humanitarian crisis. Second only to daily survival, expanding the Earthseed following is her purpose. For it, too, she believes, will lead to a greater human survival. In Olamina's view, the erotic is only useful as an instrument of religious seduction. Standing on the precipice of lesbian desire, she turns away, insisting that it will only create a conflict with the religious work to which she is most committed.

For the Earthseed cause, Olamina spends the following two days stirring Nia to the point of tears by sharing the painful and violent history of the Earthseed community children who were stolen/lost to the Christian outlaws. The goal is to secure Nia's property as a sanctuary for future generations. "I never suggested it," Olamina confesses shrewdly, "but I did all I could to open ways for her to suggest it" (*Talents* 372). Nia eventually volunteers her house to the future vision of the Earthseed community. Larkin reports, in a resentful and disapproving tone, that her mother was highly successful in getting these kinds of donations to the Earthseed ministry:

> I found that Earthseed was a wealthy sect that welcomed everyone and was willing to make use of everyone. It owned land, schools, farms, factories, stores, banks, several whole towns. And it seemed to own a lot of well-known people—lawyers, physicians, journalists, scientists, politicians, even members of Congress. (*Talents* 380)

Meanwhile, inside the narrative frame of Olamina's journal, Olamina/Cory maintains the role as Nia's comforter while seeming to struggle with the boundaries they've agreed on: "I held her once more when she cried. I kissed her lonely mouth, then put her away from me. [. . .] That was very compelling, somehow, that complete acceptance and trust. It was hard for me to leave her" (*Talents* 372). Yet, clearly, the larger humanitarian mission takes precedence over any insular relationship she could cultivate with Nia.

Although the urgency of Olamina's religious mission hinders her from exploring these same-sex desires further, it is important that her reaction to discovering them is not about gender taboos, shame, self-loathing, or denial. As a heretofore-heterosexual woman who values the lessons gained from lived experience, she simply marvels at her newfound capacity for sexual fluidity and then diligently returns to the business of affecting change in the world.

HYPEREMPATHY AS SPIRITUAL SELF-DEFENSE

Olamina's queerness is more complex than a transgender trek up the west coast. To further complicate matters, Butler deploys aspects of bondage/discipline/sado-masochism (BDSM) to produce a paradigm in which Olamina cultivates a way of seeing and being seen that is an offense and defense mechanism, a sexual agency, and spiritual self-defense that blends voyeurism and masochism.

Olamina's voyeurism and masochism manifest through "delusional hyperempathy," a genetic condition. It is the vulnerability to which she refers in the quotation above regarding her need to convey hardness. With this disease, Butler revises a common sci-fi trope and transforms it into a weakness or disability: The traditional empath can connect psychically with a person and thereby experience the other's thoughts and feelings as his own; that is, the empath can truly empathize. However, Olamina's condition is a "neurochemically-induced delusion" (*Talents* 12), in which she feels the pain and pleasure that she is able to observe in others. She calls it, simply, "sharing." She can observe an injury or interpret the body language of a person and share in the perceived emotions or sensations. In other words, watching people triggers her imagination and, in a millisecond, perception becomes a visceral reaction. For Olamina, to gaze on an emotional scene is to submit to its power, to be overcome by it. It is considered a disability because it is a congenital brain disorder, which occurred *in utero* due to her mother's drug abuse. It is also a disability because it easily undermines her ability to protect herself in combat, for example. As she causes her opponent to lose consciousness, so, too, will Olamina begin to black out—a vulnerability that could easily become her undoing in a society of normalized public violence. She also experiences a sensory transference of other people's sexual and erotic dispositions. So in the realm of sexuality, hyperempathy equates to voyeurism. Let me explain.

I suggest voyeurism as a way to interpret hyperempathy precisely because it connotes an erotic component and a sexual agency, both of which are visible in the narrative. My focus here is on the implications of hyperempathic abilities for Olamina's sexuality and, later, how that ties into her spirituality. In psychoanalysis, a voyeur is defined as someone whose *primary* means of sexual or erotic gratification consists of looking at the sexual organs/activities of others without their knowledge or a passive observer of sexual acts.[9] In the case of the secret observer, an erotic charge is derived from the sense of power and control gained from the anonymous intrusion. Olamina's voyeurism manifests in three ways: in the ability to share in others' erotic experiences by merely viewing them; the secrecy surrounding her disease, to the extent that it operates as a closeted, non-normative sexuality; and the agency she ultimately displays in regard to her ability that, arguably, is its own form of power and control in an otherwise unpredictable and violent environment.

Masochism, the tendency to find pleasure in one's own suffering, is subtly entwined with Olamina's voyeuristic behavior. The evidence lies most saliently in her descriptions of her imprisonment by a radical Christian militia. It was their mission to capture and "reeducate" religious dissidents; for them, a black woman preaching about shaping one's own reality was a dangerous threat. To the soldiers for/of Christianity, she represents a desire for religious autonomy that must be disciplined and controlled. To that end, Olamina and her followers are placed in pens and affixed with leather collars programmed with an electric charge. Prison guards (called teachers) use the electric shock to punish and discipline insubordinate or insufficiently servile prisoners. When this happens, Olamina shares in the pain of her fellow prisoners as well as the erotic charge of the teacher with his finger on the button. In her recounting of this experience in her journal, Olamina reveals that there are guards, all male, who indulge in the sadistic pleasure of punishing the Earthseed followers. She is aware of their erotic responses to applying electric shock (called *lashes*) because she is sucked into their pleasure:

> There are a few men here, though . . . who lash us until they have orgasms. Our screams and convulsions and pleas and sobs are what these men need to feel sexually satisfied. I know of three who seem to need to lash someone to get sexual pleasure. Most often, they lash a woman, then rape her. Sometimes the lashing is enough for them. *I don't want to know this as clearly as I do know it, but I can't help myself.* These men feast on our pain. (*Talents* 233; my italics)

In addition to sharing the visual pain of her fellow prisoners and the vicarious pleasure of their torturers, Olamina was also raped. When she discusses her sexual assault in the Christian camp, she decries her inner "twisted, schizoid ugliness," which is the ability to identify equally with her rapist's "wild intense pleasure" and her own sense of violation (*Talents* 234). By this time, she has learned to control her sharing (by averting her eyes quickly enough to prevent the onset of hyperempathy) and thereby exercise some agency under duress. This agency is visible in other moments, sexual and nonsexual, where she averts her gaze, such as when female prisoners perform sexual acts on each other on a pallet next to her in the prison; and during a fistfight in which she pummels a thief into unconsciousness. Ultimately, sharing is as much a type of power to be wielded in times of struggle (or extreme vulnerability) as it is a weakness to be exploited by enemies.

The implications of Butler's portrayal of erotic exchange in the midst of violation, anguish, and disempowering situations in the *Parables* are complex. In the next section, I discuss the "shaping and sharing" humanist paradigm as a radical reimagining of black survival and resilience, which conflates humanist philosophy with ontological concerns. Olamina's response to her environment blends humanist self-sufficiency with a complex spiritual agency that places black female subjectivity in conversation with previous explorations of the relationship between erotics and violence in African American literary studies.

IMPLICATIONS OF EROTICIZED SUFFERING, OR THE BLACK BODY IN PLEASURABLE PAIN

Butler's illustration of eroticized suffering is the Earthseed doctrine functioning as spiritual practice. Put another way: In her daily attempt "to accept and work with the shapes that God imposes on us" (*Sower* 25), perhaps Olamina's hyperempathic gaze is best understood as a spiritual defense mechanism in the face of multiple forces of violence that are intent on destroying her. In the context of African American literary studies, Butler engages the tradition and ongoing discourse about uses of the black body in pain or as a victim of violence in literature.

On one hand, the *Earthseed* series continues the tradition of eighteenth- and nineteenth-century slave narratives that cataloged the instruments of violence in the slave system and depicted the black body as victimized by racial hatred and demoralized by an un-Christian system. Tales of estate sales, whips, chains, hot irons for branding, and elaborate muzzles and yokes litter their pages to reveal the lie of the so-called benevolent institution. Embedded within a few of these narratives is the suggestion that sexual or erotic desire played a role in acts of physical violence that were perpetrated against enslaved people. For example, Harriet Jacobs' *Incidents in the Life of a Slave Girl* (1861) is generally celebrated for its illustration of the enslaved woman's ability "to exercise a measure of freedom within the restrictions of [her] oppression" (Gates and McKay 279) by using her sexuality "with deliberate calculation" (Jacobs 83) to manipulate two white men and avoid being raped. This rhetorical project required that she depict herself as a debased woman in order to explain to white middle-class Christian readers that slavery was inherently a system of recurring moral debasement. It is a counterargument to the widely held belief that black women were naturally and intentionally lascivious—and therefore different from the inherently virtuous white woman.

In a chapter titled, "The Trials of Girlhood," Jacobs writes that her owner attempted to coerce her into sexual submission when she was twelve years old: "He told me I was his property; that I must be subject to his will in all things" (Jacobs 45). In making this claim to her body in addition to her labor, Dr. Flint, Jacobs' master, was speaking a social and legal truth. In literal pursuit of this claim, he stalked and harassed her as she moved about the house and plantation, all the while divulging the details of his sexual imagination. "He peopled my young mind with unclean images, such as only a vile monster could think of," Jacobs laments (44). Meanwhile, her owner's wife doles out her own jealousy-inspired brutality against the young Harriet. In a desperate act of reclamation, Jacobs takes on a secret white male lover in the hope that, by denying her owner's claim to her virginity, her sexual desecration will, subsequently, douse his fiery desire for her. *Incidents* is a case in which the black body under duress and mental anguish is utilized in literature to demonstrate how the slave system precludes black women's entry into a state of pious chastity, which is so highly regarded in middle-class white culture. It also identifies white male desire for black women (as opposed to the black woman as temptress) as the root of the so-called miscegenation that created tension between white and black women in domestic interactions.

Also, as Saidiya Hartman points out, Jacobs highlights the mundane (as opposed to the spectacular) uses of force and violence in slave culture, the "scenes in which terror can hardly be discerned" (4) because they are part of the everyday routine. As part of the larger abolitionist discourse, Jacobs' representation of sexual violence demonstrates, according to Hartman, the white man's full enjoyment of the slave as thing" (86). So, as part of (and arguably, as the initiators of) this discourse in African American literature, slave narratives depict the black body in pain or as victims of violence to condemn the perpetrators and demonstrate black resistance to this paradigm (or resistance to "thingification," as Aime Cesaire theorizes in *Discourse on Colonialism*, the theory to which Hartman alludes).[10] Butler uses the attacks against her protagonist's personhood to make similar arguments.

Butler's novels also engage the discourse in literature by black men that acknowledges sadism and voyeurism as inherent to the experience of the perpetrators of racial violence. For example, in James Baldwin's "Going to Meet the Man," a sexually impotent white sheriff becomes successfully aroused only after reminiscing about the castration and lynching of a black civil rights activist. Baldwin thereby employs the connection between erotics and human suffering to indict and shame perpetrators of racially motivated violence as sexual sadists who enact their fear, envy, and desire for black bodies in these events and, by extension, in their sex acts with white women. Baldwin's perspective is an extension of Frederick Douglass' insinuation in *My Bondage and My Freedom* (1855) in the description of the overseer who "was cruelly deliberate, and protracted the torture, as one who was delighted with the scene" (22) as he whipped Douglass's topless, screaming Aunt Hester while her hands were tied.

Butler's work also intersects with Debra Walker King's critical study of African American literature that deals specifically with depictions of racial hurt and pain. In *African Americans and the Culture of Pain* (2008), King defines pain as "a boundless perception woven intricately from experiences of physical, mental, and emotional wounding and trauma that threaten one's ability to move safely into survival and wholeness. It is any experience that threatens the soul" (16). Pain, then, is the result of trauma, whether physical, emotional, or spiritual. Relevant to this discussion are King's findings as they relate to the characters' (in her study) responses to pain, for they resonate with Butler's portrayal of Olamina. King analyzes narratives by black male writers that engage pain and racial hurt through portrayals of male characters who maintain their dignity through silence as a technique of self-restraint. She explains that male characters often allow the flow of tears but refuse to cry out when whipped or beaten. King asserts that, for the silent sufferer, a tear represents weakness leaving the body. In such scenarios, the perpetrator may read the victim's silence as complicity but black onlookers (in the text and reading audience) will recognize this as part of a long-standing survival strategy (self-containment), which means more than simply living through the experience. "Suffering in silence binds individuals to their communities through an agreed-on mandate for uniform behavior, a bodily hexis that raises the sufferer to the level of hero or martyr" (King 93). It is the embodiment of Paul Lawrence Dunbar's poetic injunction to "wear the mask" in spite of our collective and individual "tortured souls."

Self-containment as a strategy "offers black people a claim to moral superiority over those who inflict pain," King explains (94). In the study, King identifies a distinction between "inert silence," which she believes can be another type of wounding, and that of "silent mobility, which can be conceived as action" (19). Silent mobility is defined as:

> [A] movement beyond suffering that acknowledges racial hurt without public expressions or personal submission to the limitations pain imposes[, and so] *silence emerges as a defensive strategy,* a mobility that allows torture victims some control over the way they experience and navigate moments of pain and racial hurt. It is a way of rising above victimization, if only symbolically. (King 91, 93; my italics)

These ideas align Butler's masculine female character with black male characters' responses to torture and racial hurt in literature. For Olamina, too, practices a self-defensive silence to survive imprisonment, electrocution, and rape; and, thereby, denies her captors the satisfaction of gauging the extent of her pain.

Ultimately, Olamina's tactics for self-preservation and containment go beyond silent mobility and the discourse of condemnation for the perpetrators of violence. She has the ability to split herself into dual consciousnesses: that of the victim and the victimizer simultaneously. The ability to identify with the perpetrator, to stand in his place as he positions himself in complete control over her life, mitigates the trauma and its subsequent pain, and creates a sense of control. This defense mechanism, in its apparent passivity, can be mistaken for defeat but serves as a deceptive barrier against the oppressor. It is Ralph Ellison's "agree[ing] em to death" (*Invisible Man* 16) inscribed on the body; a kind of going-along that facilitates survival. Even if her sense of control is a delusion, Olamina's power to keep the self intact in the face of danger and wounding is completely real.

When Olamina enacts the submissive gaze, she diminishes and expels pain. This brings us to the other theoretical perspective on pain that dovetails with King's work. In *A Defense of Masochism*, Anita Phillips maintains that the sexual masochist does not collect pain into the body, but instead serves as a conduit for pain. Pain moves through the body and spills out through orgasmic release. The masochist survives intact and renewed precisely because she is willing to suffer.[11] This is more than a sexual disposition; it is a worldview:

> If one believes . . . that violence is an ever-present force, surging around and through everyone, masochism could be seen as a

> contrary way of confronting it. By making oneself the focus for a controlled version of that violence, one for a moment grasps it physically, lives through it, acts as an escape route for it. The masochist plugs into the electric current of social rage to combine its crackling spark with his or her own eroticism. . . . If the world is a violent, mean and sordid place, the masochist rejects transcendence as a way of handling it. The only way out is through. (Phillips 148–149)

In relating this insight, Phillips provides another dimension to Olamina's erotic experiences during torture and rape. The submissive gaze is a kind of suffering that absorbs and expends pain as a way of controlling it before it can dominate, if not obliterate, the queer subject's self-control.

In the *Earthseed* series, then, Butler theorizes that victims of trauma need to rely on internal resources that can keep them in a state of perpetual spiritual remission. It is the shape of God in the self.

CONCLUSION

> and in the brief moment that is today
> wild hope this dreamer jars
> for i have heard in whispers
> talk of life on other stars
>
> —Audre Lorde[12]

Butler credits two cultural catalysts for this narrative: the "fundamentalist religion-driven national politics" (qtd in Francis 121) exemplified by the evangelical preacher Pat Robertson's presidential campaign, and the rolling back of environmental protections that began during President Ronald Reagan's administration.[13] The tone and outlook of the *Earthseed* series are pessimistic, but beneath the cautionary tone of Butler's crash-and-burn forecast of American culture lies the "wild hope" expressed by the speaker in an Audre Lorde poem above. *Parable of the Sower* and *Talents* plea for the transformation of the collective consciousness, and for a life on other stars of cultural, political, and spiritual destinies. "And I think the best way to do something else is to go someplace where the demands on us will be different," Butler explains in an interview. "Not because we are going to go someplace and change ourselves, but because we will go someplace else and be forced to change" (qtd in Francis 71). Through the lens of spirituality, the "someplace where the demands on us [are] different" is inside our own pain as it connects, empathetically, to the pain, suffering and well-being of others. This is the paradigm shift from individual to community member.

Yet on the individual level, the *Earthseed* series is a curriculum of survival through absorption and catharsis, renewal and self-empowerment on multiple levels. I reiterate that this is a type of spiritual practice. Though Olamina appears to be completely disempowered, emotions, sensations, and people move through her body and are utilized in the pursuit of transformation, and suffering becomes a tool of power and sustenance for the inner self. Through this humanist paradigm of the renewed and renewable self, Butler's gun-toting, gender-passing, revolutionary evangelist aims to liberate humanity from its passive religions, and acceptance of war, corporate greed, and irretrievable damage to the ecosystem. It is imperative to the Earth's inhabitants that capitalistic individualism be replaced by a zealous love for mutual cooperation and survival. When social forces push back and attempt to silence and punish us, Butler's minister commands that the only way out of pain and the threat of destruction is to go through it.

CHAPTER SEVEN

Reciprocity as Spiritual Ethos

The Gilda Stories

Jewelle Gomez is an acclaimed novelist, essayist, playwright, and poet whose work reflects her racial and feminist consciousness, as well as her lesbian identity. Her entry into the literary world began with self-published poetry collections, *The Lipstick Papers* (1980) and *Flamingoes and Bears* (1996), both of which are lesbian-themed and woman-centered. The title of her third collection, *Oral Tradition* (1995), is a double entendre that further reflects these politics. Gomez is best known, however, for her 1991 vampire novel *The Gilda Stories*. It broke ground with the first black lesbian vampire heroine in American literature. Like Butler, Gomez participates in a white male-dominated field of fiction in order to invent a black heroine who transcends popular ideologies. In a 1993 essay, "Black Lesbians and Speculative Fiction," Gomez reflects upon the fact that, although the women's liberation movement of the 1970s and 1980s produced women writers interested in creating feminist and lesbian (and lesbian feminist) utopias and surrealist fiction, "few Black lesbians . . . have made the leap into the unknown" (949). In a genre that is considered "the product of dreams of what life might be," black lesbian representation is necessary, Gomez insists, because "[our] wishes are larger and richer than most people have been able to imagine. In our speculation about the future[,] the vision of the struggle is often quite brutal, but the vision of the triumph is equally fantastic" ("Speculative Fiction" 954, 955). Indeed, the struggle is brutal in *Gilda Stories*, but its impact is balanced by a vision of hope, emotional triumph, requited desire, spiritual uplift and sanctuary in a life-threatening ecological and social environment.

Inspired by the intense mourning she experienced after the death of her great-grandmother, she based *Gilda Stories* on her family's ethnic makeup and history. For this work Gomez was awarded two Lambda Literary Awards (in fiction and science fiction categories).

Since then, she has published *Forty-Three Septembers*, a collection of nonfiction essays, in 1993. Although it mostly contains autobiographical accounts of her family life and coming of age, it also displays her skills as a pop culture and literary critic. She recounts her relationship with her father; explores the variations of influential womanhood and beauty in her family; recalls the firsthand experiences of protest marches and other momentous realizations that forged her feminist identity; connects her Catholicism to her attraction to vampire mythology; asserts the importance of black lesbian and gay visibility in popular culture, history, and literature; and includes an exposition of the life and work of Lorraine Hansberry. In 1996 she adapted *Gilda* into a stage play entitled *Bones & Ash*; it was performed by the Urban Bush Women in thirteen cities across the United States at such theaters as San Francisco's Yerba Buena Center for the Arts, the Walker Arts Center in Minneapolis, and the Joyce Theater in New York. Although Gomez continues to publish short stories and plays, *The Gilda Stories* (hereafter *TGS*) continues to be her most influential and famous work.[1]

The protagonist of *TGS* is able to lead multiple lives over a two-hundred-year span. The story begins in the antebellum South, 1850 Louisiana, in the protagonist's human life. She is a runaway slave, not yet a vampire, called only "Girl" by the narrator. She stabs her would-be rapist in self-defense and runs away from the plantation and, consequently, leaves her biological family behind forever. Alone and covered in blood, the girl is rescued and finds sanctuary in a brothel run by Gilda, a three-hundred-year-old white woman vampire, and her Lakota Sioux female companion, Bird. In a sensual scene of *ménage à trois*, the pair "turn" Girl, and she takes her benefactor's name. The rest of Gilda's lives are spent searching for a place to call home and for greater meaning in the world. The 1890s find herself in San Francisco, where she meets others like her and learns the subtleties of what it is to be a vampire. She lives on a farm in Missouri in the 1920s. In Boston in the 1950s, she owns a hair salon. She is a New

York jazz singer in the 1980s. The final chapters take place in the future, in a polluted and decaying America. Vampires are hunted for their blood by the rich and who have learned of its ability to extend their own lives.

As it was for Butler's protagonist in the *Parable of the Talents*, the harrowing threat of extinction and the perpetual search for sanctuary are also major themes in Gilda's life journey. Gilda negotiates an environment in which she is feared and despised, and the plot is driven by her search for cultural, material, and psychic survival in response to "state and global power apparatuses that employ systems of racial, sexual, and national subjugation {which are} . . . brutal and painful" (Munoz 161).[2] Over the course of the novel, Gilda learns a survival code that advocates co-existence; embraces sustainability; and emphasizes the value and sacredness of all life forms. In addition, Gomez inserts African American history and culture, and lesbian sexuality into the center of a white and mostly male landscape of conquest fantasies and xenophobic anxiety.[3]

In "Transubstantiation: This Is My Body, This Is My Blood," Gomez explains that she has shed her belief in the Catholic doctrine of her upbringing, but that it instilled in her a passionate commitment to a higher power that directly relates to the moral code upheld by the vampire community in her novel. "That passion was transformed into a belief in human rights and the interconnection of all living things" (*Forty-Three* 72). These passions are conveyed through Gilda's trials and life lessons. She is in search of love, community, and reciprocity, and, in her world, sustainability is sacred and morality is measured by how one values the life of others. These are the virtues by which the spiritual ethos of the text is constructed. The ideas conveyed about community and mutual responsibility in this novel are slightly different from the humanist principles in Butler's *Parables*. Gomez's text highlights ethical relationships between dominant and subordinate groups in society and involves spirituality without god-talk. It also produces a paradigm of the margin.

In "Choosing the Margin as a Space of Radical Openness," bell hooks argues that marginality necessitates and informs a critical oppositional perspective to the ideological, cultural, and political views that are formed in the center or dominant culture. The perspective from the margins, hooks maintains, can be a valuable space in which to cultivate and maintain one's resistance to domination. I will show how TGS operates in a paradigm of the margin through an emphasis on social, emotional, and cosmic justice. Of particular importance to this paradigm are depictions of the erotic bond between the black woman vampire and other people/vampires of color. While the vampire species as an archetype is soul-less (and thereby perceived as a terrifying purgatory existence for the human consciousness), Gomez infuses her undead characters with a spiritual foundation. So the narrative is propelled by the entwined themes of moral consciousness, family, community, the individual's responsibility to the self, and the struggle for survival by a minority population in an increasingly antagonistic and violent world. It is my overall view that Gomez puts forth a definition of spirituality in which reciprocity, fairness, and self-love are central. First I discuss the role of reciprocity in spirituality and, following that, propose a theory I call *homoerotics of talk* as a way to interpret the main character's spiritual journey.

RECIPROCITY AS SPIRITUAL ETHOS

Gilda, the protagonist, belongs to a community of vampires that insists that the taking of blood from a human need not be a murderous or purely selfish act. Gilda is instructed by her mentor, Bird, to recognize the weaker species of humans, on which the vampires rely, literally, for life support, as beings whose existences matter beyond the capacity they serve for the vampires. Therefore, the act of feeding is seen as an exchange of psychological/emotional needs rather than a unidirectional self-serving encounter. In a conversation with Bird, Gilda is taught to create a psychic and emotional connection with the spiritual inhabitant of the host body:

> And as you take [blood] from them you must reach inside. Feel what they are needing, not what you are hungering for. [In exchange,] You leave them with something new and fresh, something wanted. Let their joy fill you. This is the only way to share and not rob. It will also keep you on your guard so you don't drain life away. (50)

It is imperative that she perceive her feeding through an ethical lens; that she be morally unable to take her fill of blood and discard of the human body or rob it of its humanity by "turning" it into a vampire, as is the traditional narrative. Gilda must infiltrate the consciousness of the human and locate "something wanted" on the emotional shelf, and replace that sense of lack with a sense of fulfillment. Simultaneously, the feeding vampire allows the human's "joy to fill [her]" so that the encounter is uplifting for both parties. This politics of exchange signifies a "consciousness, ethos, lifestyle, and discourse which privileges the [human] spirit" (Ryan 23). The "share and not rob" ethos is, for the naturally rapacious vampire, a lesson in self-discipline and reciprocity that also insists on respect for the vulnerable human community.

"Share and not rob" is the core thread and major spiritual philosophy at work in the text. Because they are endowed with hypersensitivity, psychic and hypnotic powers, and unstoppable strength, vampires are the dominant species. Yet the group Gilda is part of chooses not to dominate. Instead they practice an ethics of reciprocation: this vision of ethical power relations sets them apart from other vampires in the novel and in the tradition of vampire fiction. Traditionally, the vampire character is representative of middle- to upper-class status—a corrupt but admired position in the capitalist system. And, generally, physical prowess is a metaphor for the social and economic power wielded by such groups. The powerful social position of the seductive, contaminated vampire in the mythology is no accident. "[The archetype] tells us that part of the inherent metaphorical material in society's dreams of vampire narratives is social, and involves questions of social justice, power, exploitation, race and class, as well as the more obvious gender conflict" (J. Johnson 75). Gomez asserts reciprocity as the radical revision of the vampire/human relationship and, symbolically, wealthy/poor, majority/minority, privileged/underprivileged relations. When the feeding vampire infiltrates the human consciousness, she literally sees into the life perspective of the oppressed so that she (as a former human) cannot ever lose sight of what it means to live that life. The ethos of reciprocity insists that the vampire resist the "colonizing mentality" in their power relations with humans (hooks, *Yearning* 145).[4]

Time and again, the humans on whom Gilda feeds need hope, faith, inspiration, or some other type of happiness to fill their emotional void. So as Gilda feeds on her victims, she un-victimizes them by reorganizing their thoughts so that their happiest memories or deepest loving desires are foremost in their minds when they recover. A suicidal person can recover from the feeding with a renewed sense of purpose and a positive outlook on life. In one such scene, as Gilda trolls the streets hungry for blood and lonely for companionship, she is drawn by the muffled sobs of a depressed and isolated human woman. As Gilda "rummaged" through the girls thoughts, she was most saddened by the fact that "the woman was devoid of dreams. She had no fantasy or embellished aspirations on which to affix her daily life" (122). As Gilda feeds on the sleeping woman's body,

> In return she offered [the young woman some] dreams. She held the girl's body and mind tightly, letting the desire for future life flow through them both, a promising reverie of freedom and challenge. The woman absorbed Gilda's desire for family, for union with others like herself, for new experience. Through these she perceived a capacity for life and an open door of possibility. [. . .] The young woman began to cling to life and experience the urge to project into a future. (123)

This is nothing less than a spiritual healing in which both beings are renewed and rejuvenated in the process. For the woman's "resurgent dreams cast a new glow on Gilda's life: in giving dreams she had recaptured her own" (124). So then the soul-less, parasitic, murderous vampire is recast as the principled heroine and mystic, as the gifted spirit worker who invades one's dream life to bless it; as the one who drags you to the brink of death only to intensify your life force. In *TGS*, the human encounter with certain enlightened vampires is a resurrection, a transformative experience, which occurs at the intersecting planes of life and death, where natural and supernatural forces connect in the sacred act of giving—exchanging—life force.

QUEER KINSHIP, HOMOEROTICS OF TALK AND SELF-LOVE

Gomez's lesbian spirit-worker vampire is also a dark-skinned black woman who travels and lives among predominately white (human and vampire) populations. This state of racial otherness, which tends to bring much attention to her in the antebellum period, produces a paradigm of the margin even before Gilda is indoctrinated into the vampire spiritual ethos. In Gilda's childhood, her mother had spoken often of their Fulani ancestry and culture that had existed in a "natural rhythm of life without bondage" (10). Memories of an African homeland and culture passed down in the oral history distinguished the enslaved people from the white enslavers who, according to her mother, "were not fully human" (12). White men were "beasts" and white women could be as dangerous as their men (12). So while the cultural politics of the novel support multicultural alliances, the narrative also asserts the salience of race in the lived experiences of black people.

Kinship networks are formed or, rather, transformed in *TGS*, as Shannon Winnibst successfully argues in "Vampires, Anxieties, and Dreams: Race and Gender in Contemporary US Culture." Winnibst maintains that the bloodletting and bloodmixing in the novel occur across gender, racial, sexual, and species boundaries for reasons that recast the tropes of miscegenation and contamination into a symbol of eternal love. I quote:

> No longer a matter of nature or biology, kinship becomes a particular mode of reading the many flowing affections, affinities, connections, and intensities that circulate amidst bodies in the world. Often in interracial exchanges, Gilda and her family carefully mix their blood with those whom they love and with whom they wish to live eternally. [. . .]By the end of the story, tellingly 2050, this realm of the eternally undead, filled with mixed-race queers, has become the singular savior for a technologically induced apocalypse. (Winnibst 12, 13)

"Mixed-race queers" is an appropriate characterization of Gilda's chosen family, and the erasure of sociocultural barriers. Winnibst's words signify a crucial aspect of the intervention Gomez enacts. Yet, it is more significant in the context of my argument that even though an erotic current connects each of the family members, Gilda's choice for an eternal romantic partner is another phenotypically black woman. My examination of the major relationships within the kinship network reveals that *TGS* constructs a narrative of racial solidarity that emerges within the resemanticized "blended family" narrative. I call this same-sex intra-racial dynamic a black female homoerotics.

The concept of a black female homoerotics is guided by two theoretical principles. The first is Audre Lorde's theory of the erotic as an inherently political force that is the combination of emotional, intuitive, experiential, and intellectual knowledges, which is where I begin.

Though I mention aspects of it (erotic knowledge) in previous chapters, it is necessary to be more expansive of her argument here. Lorde's views in "Uses of the Erotic" advance the theory that erotic knowledge is a transformative power in the lives of women, "an assertion of the lifeforce of women . . . [and] creative energy empowered" (*Sister Outsider* 55). This definition identifies a specifically female power to love herself to the point of acting with passionate agency on her own behalf. Importantly, Lorde urges readers to consider how the homoerotic bond is inherently spiritual and is the convergence of physical, emotional, and psychic expressions. She advocates for an understanding of same-sex desire as foundational in feminist community building and in the formation of political alliances against oppression. Her articulation of erotic bonding challenges the dominant heteropatriarchal narrative, which deems female sexual energy benign when shared solely with other women; considers such energy a source of shame when wielded too confidently; or, if acknowledged as power, restricts sexual energy to sexual situations; and attempts to police it through compulsive heterosexuality. This formulation is reclamation of women's creative life force as a sacred power that is activated by, for, and with other women. The erotic is a unifying force, "a form of love that unites life with life" (Baker-Fletcher 204).

Further, it bears repeating that Lorde argues that when a woman recognizes the erotic in her life as a spiritual inclination, it can function on multiple levels of her existence: as a bridge to sharing deeply any pursuit with another person; energy that intensifies an experience; a deep and irreplaceable knowledge of her capacity for joy; and a reason to stop being satisfied with suffering and self-negation (*Sister* 56–58). These ideas are expressed in the context of feminist activism so that she, in effect, extends the feminist premise that "the personal is political" to say that the political can also be spiritual. Lorde hereby theorizes a politicized spirituality, a "woman's creative energy empowered" that is connected to, driven, and enhanced by her knowledge of what brings her pleasure. In one fell swoop, she proposes a significant integration of female political, spiritual, and sexual selfhood that recognizes the possibilities wrought by pleasure, desire, and creativity in liberational work.

Karla Kaplan builds on Lorde's theoretical foundation in *The Erotics of Talk: Women's Writing and Feminist Paradigms* as she identifies "erotics of talk" as a feminist narrative technique that ties pleasure, desire, and liberational work together in fiction writing. According to Kaplan, a protagonist's imagining of and/or search for the ideal lover is symbolic of "finding, imagining, or projecting ideal listeners" (18). The ideal listener is the "sine qua non of [the protagonist's] sexual and individual desire" because it is one who will assume the speaker is an equal, will be a fully engaged hearer and, therefore, appropriately responsive (18). Through the protagonist's search, the narrative constructs an ideal that reflects the reciprocity, fairness, and justice that is lacking in the character's life, and it directs the reader's attention, Kaplan argues, to the author's politics. So the protagonist's talk with individuals in the narrative represent an eroticized and politicized "talking back" to power structures, social movements, and other texts.

Kaplan demonstrates how Zora Neale Hurston highlights black female marginality and a desire for social equity through Janie in *Their Eyes Were Watching God*. Janie's ideal listener is Phoeby, her "kissin' friend" who, when Janie is "longing" for self-revelation, is "eager to *feel and do through* Janie" (Hurston 6–7; emphasis added). Within the dynamic of their conversation, Janie's longing to represent her reality is met with her listener's equally intense eagerness to know the sights and sounds of the journey, to feel and do it in her own imagination. Thus, the kissing metaphor is not only a description of a deeply intimate relationship, but it also signifies their mutual cultural, gender, and emotional literacy. With Phoeby, Janie can feel the full capacity of conversational joy because there is no cultural or intellectual gap to overcome: they live in the same symbolic universe. The main narrative framing of the novel is situated in this linguistic universe as Janie shares with Phoeby the story of her journey where she struggles for self-determination and self-expression. Theirs is a conversation about failed conversations. According to Kaplan, it is a key political strategy that Phoeby is the single listener with whom Janie is satisfied. She asserts, "Insofar as that imagined ideal listener is both gendered and limited (either to one person or one instance of fulfilling exchange), finding one's ideal listener/lover works to criticize the cultural conversation these texts both emulate and disrupt" (Kaplan 18). In other words, Hurston's character speaks her racial, gender, or sexual desires into cultural fissures so as to demonstrate that the fissures exist and, perhaps, to affect change. Hurston writes to participate in liberation struggle.

Erotics of Talk provides a vital assessment of the "discursive reciprocity" in *Their Eyes Were Watching God* and is central to my argument here. However, I want to mention a revelatory statement that (although minute in Kaplan's overall argument) highlights the very tensions regarding imagined audience, and the reader's identification/positioning with/

against the text that she takes up in her analysis of women's literature. Kaplan is "discomfort[ed]" by the implication in Hurston's novel that Janie's ideal listener "is not someone who masters discursive fairness or learns the skills necessary to recognize the concrete particularity of someone who is different" but rather is someone "practically interchangeable" with herself (119). Ultimately, (and unfortunately for white people and urban blacks, it seems) Hurston's ideal listener/lover/reader is southern, rural, black, and female. Kaplan complains at length:

> But remembering that Hurston allegorizes such a reader as not only black, female, from the same background as Janie and with similar experiences, but also as operating from a position of sympathy[,] . . . sensuality and erotic openness to Janie[,] . . . generosity and nurturance[,] . . . protectiveness[,] . . . and finally discursive passivity (the willingness to remain a listener, not to demand an exchange of places, not to insist on telling her own story as well), *we must conclude that her depiction is an exaggerated idealization*, just as all objects of romantic desire and fantasy are exaggerated and idealized. (118; my emphasis)

Kaplan attempts to mitigate her rejection of Hurston's mirror-gazing desire by rendering it as equally "exaggerated" as any other romantic fantasy, but the repetition of the phrase only makes her rejection all the more obvious. Idealization is inherently exaggerated, so to deem this particular figuration as redundantly so, suggests that although Kaplan may be able to "recognize the concrete particularity" of black women, she cannot fathom the possibility that two black women who share the same socioeconomic, geographic and linguistic background may find in each other a mother-lover bond, in which they also may also alternate between dominant/subordinate erotic roles.

It is not an uncommon other-as-self trope in African American women's literature. Kevin Quashie has called this identification a kind of "girlfriend selfhood" where the girlfriend is the "other someone who makes it possible for a black female subject to bring more of herself into consideration" to the extent that "the boundaries between the two become fluid and sometimes collapse" (18, 19). Phoeby's interchangeability with Janie is the reflection of self that validates Janie's formulations about southern, rural, erotic womanhood. From a queer standpoint, girlfriend politics constructs a liberated homoerotic space. Overall, I agree with Kaplan's assessment that while the traditional husband/wife dynamic *within* Janie's metanarrative leaves much to be desired for Janie, the pleasure of the oral/aural consummation of the main narrative frame with Phoeby leaves both women gratified; evidenced by the following exchange: "So Ah'm back home agin and Ah'm satisfied tuh be heah," Janie says in closing, and Phoeby "breathed out heavily, 'Ah done growed ten feet higher from jus' listenin' tuh you, Janie'" (Hurston 182). Their relationship is the home space, a paradigm of the margins in which they both experience spiritual intensity and freedom, and are both lover and the beloved.

Erotics of Talk affirms "Uses of the Erotic" in that it reveals how Hurston's highly sensual language pinpoints her own desire for black female readership/companionship and identifies the same-sex bond as a space of egalitarianism and multilayered gratification. For it is the profound familiarity between the women, their interchangeability, which forges the erotic bond. Hence, all of the other conversations in the novel are inferior when held to the standard of this one. As I demonstrated in previous chapters, it is, as Lorde surmises, the acquisition of erotic knowledge that creates such a standard because it changes one's expectations of the height and depth of all "feeling and doing." Lorde's philosophy intersects with Kaplan's feminist narrative theory in women's novels that illustrate the desire for female listener/lovers. This intersection of the political erotic and discursive erotic encoding forms a black female homoerotics of talk.[5]

Kaplan provides a model for understanding the kind of conversation Gomez imagines she is having with her readers. What does it mean for a woman's creative work to foreground her *desire to be desired* by a black female reader? What cultural conversation(s) does Gomez reconstruct and critique in a novel that spans two hundred years in the life of an African American vampire? What are the terms by which she formulates the ideal listener/lover? What images does her desire conjure? If desire is shaped differently according to gender and sexual orientation, as Judith Roof asserts in *A Lure of Knowledge: Lesbian Sexuality and Theory*, then it may differ in respect to other criteria as well (qtd in Kaplan 17). The narrative arc in *TGS* presents a homoerotics of talk, as the first few relationships in the kinship network effectively teach Gilda, through lack, the qualities she seeks in an ideal listener/lover. Gomez/Gilda's desire differs from that of Hurston/Janie because it as much a yearning for sexual contact and romantic love as it is a longing for gender and cultural identification.

The most prominent and enduring relationship Gilda has is with Bird, her "maker" or parent vampire. Yet their metaphysical and psychic bond is not enough to sustain her. With Bird, she learns to feel close to her lover in spirit—by remaining in sync psychically and emotionally.[6] It marks the beginning of her developing erotic knowledge. Gilda was a runaway slave at age fourteen and found refuge in the brothel owned and operated by Bird and her white female (vampire) lover. Bird befriended and mentored Gilda, taught her to read and write in English and French, and to speak the Lakota language fluently. Theirs is a very intimate bond in which "Bird had opened herself to [Gilda] as she had with no one else" (28). It was Bird and her lover, the first Gilda, who brought the protagonist Gilda into their vampire network in the 1850s and from whom Gilda acquires an altogether new meaning of family. The narrator emphasizes the moment of transformation, and all blood exchanges, as sensual, erotic, and emotional. As Gilda is being prepared for the crossing over into a state of the undead, she "feel[s] herself opening to ideas and sensations she had never fully admitted before" (43). She is told to think of people she loves in order that she become hopeful about the inconceivable lifetime that was being offered to her. As she recalls memories of her biological mother, the thoughts mingle with her budding feelings for Bird:

> Her mother's hands reaching down to pull the cloth up to her chin as she lay on the mattress filled her vision. Her mother's darkened knuckles had loomed large and solid. Something she had not articulated her love for. She remembered hearing Bird's voice for the first time in the house announcing the entertainment. The deep resonance sent a thrill through her body. (44)

The "deep resonance" of her desire for Bird is a vibration that Gilda will entertain again and again on her life's journey. Bird is the vampire to whom she is first bonded in blood and they openly commit to remain together; however, Gilda's first lesson in the life is that being "together" has many meanings.

Bird dedicates her life to the repatriation of land to her human relatives, the dispossessed Lakota tribe. This political work requires her to travel for years at a time. Bird's extended absences create a dynamic in which physical contact becomes an elusive desire or short-lived encounter. After Gilda's initial feeding/exchange, which is her birth as a vampire, they live together for forty years but then are separated for more than sixty because of Bird's life of activism. It is the beginning of Gilda's separate journey into self and, as it was for Hurston's Janie, it is a journey that shapes and helps articulate her deepest desires. She realizes that "Without Bird she was floating out of control on a dangerous sea. Once again she needed to give shape to a world that was beyond her comprehension, much as she had been forced to do when her mother died" (111). When they reunite after the lonesome decades, the reader learns that the women have not "taken each other in as fully as they could" (139). They desire to "cement their family bond" through a blood exchange that constructs a share-and-not-rob recital and restructures the traditional vampire feeding scene altogether.

The bloodletting occurs after they have recently fed on humans and is carried out to quench a deeper thirst. The narration illuminates the erotics of the girlfriend/mother/lover bond in that, "This was a desire not unlike their need for blood, but she had already had her share. It was not unlike lust but less single-minded. She felt the love almost as motherly affection, yet there was more. As the blood flowed from Gilda's body into Bird's they both understood the need—it was for completion" (139). This scene captures their ascent into profound and ambiguous ways of knowing and seeing. They spent decades building a friendship, sharing family history, taking long walks, embracing each other, but only pondering the sexual energy that flares between them. Their union creates energetic ripples as "[t]he ancient rhythms of the Lakota and Fulani peoples vibrated the air around them as they rocked together in each other's arms" (137). Bird strokes Gilda's face and neck, "sparking a tingle inside her thighs" (139). She whispers in a "mesmerizing" tone as she "spoke of her life and aloneness, her fear of being without anyone, always pushing away those she loved" (139). Bird admits to the loneliness of the migrant activist's life and the dread/desire of needing another person. As is the convention in vampire mythology, the dynamics involved with feeding on another's body is an erotic and precarious interaction for the bitten: the sharp teeth sinking into the wrist, armpit, thigh or neck is a metaphor for sexual penetration, which can connote either consent and trust among partners, or rape—the unsympathetic domination by another. The bitten party is at the mercy (or unmerciful whim) of the biter. But Bird and Gilda exchange blood in a way that mimics traditional narratives of motherhood instead of phallic penetration. The vampires take turns sucking "at a delicate slash just below the breast of the beloved, giving birth to immortality through a deliberate mixing of blood and blurring of race" (Winnibst 13).

As each digests the life force of the other, they create a home space in which they can nurture their bodies and further cultivate their desires.

The narrator maintains a paradigm of the margin wherein cultural codes and expressions that are demonized by mainstream (in this case, human) discourses are interpreted from the vampire's perspective: "To an outsider, the sight may have been one of horror: their faces red and shining, their eyes unfocused and black, the sound of their bodies slick with wetness, tight with life. Yet it was a birth. The mother finally able to bring her child into the world, to look at her. It was not death that claimed Gilda. It was Bird" (140). The alien other, the parasitic creature considered a threat and source of contamination from the "normal" perspective, is recast as a life-giver, a mother lovingly delivering a newborn. Blended with the maternal aesthetic is the erotic, spiritual nature of their exchange. The slickness of their bodies creates a sound, a sly suggestion of sexual friction and the slippery bloodiness of afterbirth. This is spiritual rapture vampire style: their "tight" bodies are satiated with life force as emotion, imagination, and muscles contract and release in mutual embrace. In the home space of marginality, they can see each other from the inside out, through openings of all sorts.

Even so, as the vampires search for completion in each other's bodies, their dialogue reveals the shortcomings of the present-absence Bird represents.

> Where have you been? [Gilda asked.]
>
> I've always been behind you. I returned to those of my people who survived the terrible years. Offering my knowledge and strength where it might help, relearning how to be with my own people. How to be alone. Even there on the plains I listened for you. (141)

Bird's ability to listen and intuit Gilda's needs is a key aspect of her loyalty. In times of trouble or doubt, Gilda hears Bird's voice or feels her presence near her. Gilda constantly yearns for her but, sadly, is almost always physically without her. Bird's absences are so sharply painful for Gilda that theirs is a cultural conversation that falls short of the ideal.

Gilda, like Hurston's Janie, has a mirror-gazing desire for same-sex partnership. She and Bird have geographical, racial, and economic interests that serve to bridge their lives, but also represent the dissimilarities that become keen points of departure in their lifestyles. Gilda, a Fulani descendant, was an illiterate, fugitive slave when she met Bird, who was financially independent when they met. Plus, Bird is an activist for repatriation of Lakota people to their ancestral tribal lands. The guiding principle, to "share and not rob," applies to them in the sense that love, time, blood, and even rescue is given and taken sparingly. As a guide-of-spirit (as opposed to spirit-guide, because she remains in a body) Bird "lingered over [Gilda] as she would a child. She whispered sweet words to her as she might a lover" (140). Yet she also balances her time for grassroots work and self-reflection. She shares of herself without robbing any of her life's priorities of their deserved attention. As one friend tells Gilda, "You think of it as running away from you. For [Bird] it may simply have been running to other things that are most important" (77).

The narrator further describes the bloodletting and exchange as a dance of ancient rhythms. I propose that their entire relationship is one such dance. Bird's activism and Gilda's dreams and memories of her slave past represent what bell hooks calls the "politicization of memory," which is part of the paradigm of marginality. The novel "is expressive of the need to create spaces where one is able to redeem and reclaim the past, legacies of pain, suffering, and triumph in ways that transform the present" (*Yearning* 147). *TGS* is the author's critique of the changing same, to borrow Deborah McDowell's borrowed phrase, of the nonwhite, nonhetero female subject's struggle against oppression, as well as her desire for love, acceptance, and a place to call home. Gilda's two-hundred-year passage through time is reflected by her multiple subject positions: from enslaved and illiterate, to fugitive, and then to student; and after the transition to vampire: activist, salon owner, vocalist, and novelist. These roles and time periods reflect the limitations set by hierarchical oppressions within the American society, as well as a progression of collective black women from dependent object into independent, self-fashion-ed/-ing subjectivity.

Gomez inserts this narrative of progress within a dystopic landscape in which the United States grows gradually uninhabitable for poor people. By the last chapter, in the year 2050, humans have abused the Earth's resources to the extent that it is considered "wasteland country" (234) and the wealthiest classes live in space stations that hover above the planet. Those left behind must suffer through injurious ecological systems that have decreased the life expectancy of all life forms in major industrial cities and their immediate surroundings in the United States. To make matters worse, the humans have discovered the regenerative powers of vampires and, those who can, pay hunters to capture them. And so Gilda's life comes full circle: "There were many rumors: the life being offered was service, not servitude or destruction. It was said that only those who resisted sharing their blood were dealt with harshly" (234). But Gilda, having been the game of bounty hunters before, recognized that "This horror was slavery come again" (235). The vampire populations are in constant migration for fear of being captured for profit and forced to reproduce for/with the owner class. So Gilda is again in hiding from the constant threat of patrollers "using telepathy, sonar body tracers, and decoy tricks" (238) to enslave her. Gomez's narrator articulates the perceptions of African Americans who retain cultural memories of slavery, "pattyrollers," sharecropping, and lynchings. The narrative voice iterates a strong distrust of the parasitic relationship between institutions, such as the military, sports, and science (i.e., the Tuskegee experiment, forced sterilization) and black populations. Gilda's situation reminds us, in Stuart Hall's words, "The past continues to speak to us. [. . .] It is always constructed through memory, fantasy, narrative and myth" (395).

The novel constructs a remarkable erotics of talk between Gilda and a politically conscious heterosexual man that serves to reflect true revolutionary potential. Gilda meets Julius in 1971 and they bond over memories of sit-ins and the recent death of activist George Jackson in prison. Jackson's death is a deliberate context for their meeting, for it marks the downswing of the Black Nationalism's sway in black popular culture. As a preface to the friendship being forged in these scenes, this reference also serves to remind us that, for many, the decade of the sixties was, in regard to rhetoric and visible leadership, the moment of the Black Man. "Now that freedom, equality rights, wealth, [and] power were assumed to be on their way," Michele Wallace remembers in *Black Macho and the Myth of the Superwoman*, "[the black woman] had to understand that manhood was essential to revolution—unquestioned, unchallenged, unfettered manhood" (13). Up to that point, the most publicized agendas and strategic goals to end racial oppression placed male-defined priorities in the forefront and, although women were organizing and incrementally transforming American culture, heteropatriarchal voices were often given a more visible social platform. So their perspectives often obscured any gender-specific issues that women had been articulating since slavery. Wallace continues: "When she stood by silently as he became a 'man,' she assumed that he would grant her long overdue 'womanhood' [. . .]. But he did not. He refused her" (14). What resulted was a political betrayal that fueled bitterness along gender lines in coalitions and organizations. "The result has been calamitous. The black woman has become a social and intellectual suicide; the black man, unintrospective and oppressive" (Wallace 13).

While Wallace overstates the case a bit (and has been diligently taken to task for it), even the biographies of activists such as Septima Clarke and Ella Baker affirm that the enforcement of heteropatriarchy in civil rights organizations necessitated the creation of gender-segregated sociopolitical spaces as a strategy for women in the later generations to create platforms in which to define and implement liberation strategies for themselves.[7]

Also, the Combahee River Collective Statement, originally published in 1978, explains what necessitated the outgrowth of a black feminist movement from other social justice movements:

> Black feminist politics also have an obvious connection to movements for Black liberation, particularly those of the 1960s and 1970s. Many of us were active in those movements (Civil Rights, Black Nationalism, the Black Panthers), and all of our lives were greatly affected and changed by their ideologies, their goals, and the tactics used to achieve their goals. It was our experience and disillusionment within these liberation movements, as well as experience on the periphery of the white male left, that led to the need to develop a politics that was anti-racist, unlike those of white women, and anti-sexist, unlike those of Black and white men. (Reprinted in Smith, *Home Girls* 265)

For further insight into the ideological tensions between popular black liberation philosophies of the 1960s and feminism, we need only to turn to one of the most prominent voices from one of the most influential activist groups in the United States at that time. In a dispatch dated August 15, 1970, originally published in *Panther*, the official weekly publication of the Black Panther Party, one of the organization's founders, Huey P. Newton, encourages members to reconsider their homophobic and sexist attitudes. Even though black women can be as homophobic and loyal to patriarchy as any other group, Newton's mode of address makes it clear that he is speaking to the male readership:

> During the past few years strong movements have developed among women and among homosexuals seeking their liberation. There has been some uncertainty about how to relate to these movements. Whatever your personal opinions and your insecurities about homosexuality and the various liberation movements among homosexuals and women (and I speak of the homosexuals

> and women as oppressed groups), we should try to unite with them in a revolutionary fashion. I say "whatever your insecurities are" because as we very well know, sometimes our first instinct is to want to hit a homosexual in the mouth, and want a woman to be quiet. We want to hit a homosexual in the mouth because we are afraid we might be homosexual; and we want to hit the woman or shut her up because we are afraid that she might castrate us, or take the nuts that we might not have to start with. (*Huey P. Newton Reader* 157)

His essay was part of a recent shift (end of the 1960s) in the framing of the Party's gender politics and, I would argue, was made necessary by overwhelming resistance to the notion of gender equality that was being propagated in its recent articles and reflected in the visibility of the group's female leadership.[8] In it, Newton implores the men to recognize a woman's right to be free and the homosexual's right to use her or his body in any way they want (158). Yet, as the ordered beating of a female member by Newton revealed, the rhetoric and lived politics did not always line up. Elaine Brown spells out, in her memoir *A Taste of Power*, that the beating of the woman, Regina Davis, was a "clear signal that the words 'Panther' and 'comrade' had taken on gender connotations, denoting an inferiority in the female half of [the Panthers]" (445). So for many factions of the women's movement, the 1970s ushered in a new paradigm in which men were considered "the enemy" of women's liberation. This is the sociopolitical context, as the references in *TGS* to "nation building" and "dashikis folded at the bottom of a trunk" (169) allude to, in which Julius and Gilda met across lines of shared struggle and mutual distrust. Through the evolution of their friendship, the narrative constructs Julius and Gilda's conversation as one in which two people with different revolutionary aims are able to aspire to the unifying ideals forged in organized resistance.

Their story begins when Gilda rebuffs Julius' sexual advances. "Gilda found her comfort with women. That's just the way it was" (174). In spite of herself, she is lured by the gravitational pull between them and is confused by it. "It was certainly not the first time a man had prepositioned her," the narrator explains. "She had passed off their suggestions so easily, though, that they usually never remembered they had made them. What was upsetting her then?" (174). She realizes that even though she has constructed her private life in a way that generally excludes men of any species, she is still, at bottom, joined to them. As thoughts of Julius "reached out to her through the night air" (174) she opens herself to the idea of bringing him into the life. But first some ground rules have to be set. Gilda makes it clear that she wants nothing more than friendship. Julius quickly releases his initial ambition and admits that their attachment is much more valuable to him than sexual conquest. "I can't imagine life without you somewhere near me," Julius pleads. "If it's as a friend and not a lover, then let it be that" (184). As she succumbs to her own feelings of attachment to him, Gilda articulates clearly the type of companionship she is offering. "It is commitment as you've always fantasized it—in college dormitories when you talked of revolution, in the theater when they speak of changing the world," Gilda promises. "The reality of it can never be as one imagines" (191). The key terms in this pledge are commitment and revolution. As a vampire, she has lived many lives and, by 1971, has acquired wisdom beyond her apparent years. Becoming intimate with Julius brings back painful memories of betrayal and failure. Gilda recalls that,

> Most of the men we marched with ran out of liberation ideas. They had a big dream about black men being free, but that's as far as it went. They really didn't have a full vision—you know, women being free, Puerto Ricans being free, homosexuals being free. So things kind of folded in on top of themselves. (170)

Gomez constructs in this conversation a critique of the movement and, as part of her wish fulfillment, a moment between men and women that bell hooks suggests never occurred on a large cultural scale. What if, this scene asks, after things "folded in" men began to appreciate the frustrated voices of the women who had marched with/for them? What if women, when given the opportunity to speak to a man about male domination, choose not to recede into silence or to rely on separatism? bell hooks concedes that this kind of "talking back" was never collectively undertaken by feminists. "The next stage would have been the confrontation between women and men," hooks asserts in *Talking Back: Thinking Feminist, Thinking Black*, "the sharing of this new and radical speech: women speaking to men in a liberated voice. It [is] this confrontation that has been to a grave extent avoided" (129). Gomez's characters do not avoid the opportunity for confrontation and complicates perceptions of the black lesbian feminist stance. It exemplifies what bell hooks articulates is a varied and multidimensional context of "longing to love" between men and women:

"Whenever this longing to love exists there is present the possibility that the forms of discourse within patriarchy that estrange and alienate women and men from one another can be resisted, that a context for dialogue can be created, that a liberatory exchange can take place" (*Talking Back* 131). When Julius accepts Gilda's proposal (for friendship and the vampire life) they become a model of liberatory exchange in that the "share and not rob" principle negotiates nondomination and reciprocity. They produce a counter-hegemonic discourse between black feminism and black male liberation, which offers readers an alternative perspective, a paradigm of the margin in which such alliances are produced as acts of kinship building and love building, which do not require separatism or heterosexual identification. The scene between Julius and Gilda reiterates Lorde's assertion that such cultural work is nonetheless erotic. Also, in the act of feeding/exchange, they revise Hurston's "kissin' friend" metaphor:

> She opened her eyes and her arms; Julius lay in them like a child. She ran her finger gently over his face and neck, enjoying the softness of his skin. . . . She encircled him with her arms, kissing his eyes and nose. She felt his pulse begin to race as she passed her hand over his chest. She pressed her lips to his in a gesture that was full of the excitement she'd held inside herself for so long. It was a kiss both passionate and chaste, leaving Julius feeling like a child in her arms, yet still a man. When she sliced the flesh on his neck, he opened his eyes in shock but did not try to pull away. His body trembled, then lay still, as the life drained from him into her. Gilda stopped, bit her own tongue, and kissed him hard, breaking the skin inside his lip. She thrust her tongue into his mouth. [. . .] He began to suck at [her] blood insistently, finally understanding the power that moved between them. Electricity surged through him. (191–192)

This is a portrait of how a lesbian can embrace a heterosexual man in a passionate, liberated exchange of power, respect, and uninhibited affection. The kiss is a bond of coalition building. The power that moves between them is an unlimited (and potentially infinite) space of liberated consciousness. This passage also reinforces Gilda's desire for a female lover. Her insistence that theirs be strictly a platonic, although affectionate and erotic bond is an expression of her lesbian sexuality that leaves the female reader at the center of desire. As Kaplan's research proved, the quest for an ideal lover requires the failure of those that precede that lover's appearance. The reader is rewarded with Gilda's ideal listener/lover in the last few pages of the novel.

In the year 2050, the United States is a degenerating, decaying environment. The wealthy "off-worlders" occasionally ship charitable donations of food down to the planet while the remaining poor on Earth "work themselves ill to accumulate enough money to bribe their way to life" (241). A sustainability agenda eludes the government, and grassroots activists working for a livable planet are scoffed at in the streets. Disease and death are widespread because human immune systems cannot adapt quickly enough to the ever-increasingly toxic environment. In the meantime, vampires remain immune and their regenerative powers have been discovered by the humans who had believed their existence a myth for multiple millennia. The hunters have become the hunted, as the saying goes, and Gilda is a fugitive from desperate humans. It is in this context that Gilda finds her ideal listener/lover, Ermis. As she takes cover in what she believes is an abandoned condominium, she senses Ermis is in the room with her, dying from an intentional drug overdose. Ermis is a black woman whose complexion is "as dark as Gilda's" with hair "cut in a loose, curly old-fashioned Afro. It was deep brown [. . .] soft, nappy hair" (244). Ermis is attempting suicide because she has succumbed to "the fever of desperation" (234); as such, she symbolizes misery and helplessness. She also represents the dying potential for black female companionship.

Gilda resuscitates her, mainly to satisfy her own hunger for blood but, as she does so, another desire is kindled. "She was appalled by the thrill of pleasure that shot through her at the warmth of the woman's mouth, and a small cry of sadness escaped her. Gilda waited no longer. She pulled back the light quilt tucked around the woman's chest, and her own breasts pulsed with excitement, desire, and shame" (244). The shame seems prompted by the guilt of reviving the woman "who had chosen death rather than wait for death to choose her" (244). Vampires also respect one's right to die. So in deciding to not simply feed on the body of a dying woman, she exchanges blood with her and so "turns" Ermis without her consent. Even without the phallic symbolism it is a nonconsensual and violent act. Contemplating the meaning of her actions, Gilda "looked inside [herself] to reassure herself that she had not done an evil thing" (246). To mitigate her shame and guilt, Gilda offers the recovering

Ermis a chance to complete her suicide. Ermis chooses to live. Once Ermis is fully revived and thirsty for blood, she "did not wait but pulled Gilda to her on the wide living room floor beneath the starless sky" and their exchange is not only an erotic one, it involves oral sex: "This time Gilda's lips explored the whole of Ermis' body shamelessly before sharing the blood that gave them both life" (246). The sexual, erotic, and blood unions complete, the emotional bond is solidified when Gilda reveals that the miniscule amount of hope that she found in Ermis' consciousness during the initial feeding was something she was beginning to run low on in her own life. "I needed that in you," Gilda confesses. "I wanted the chance to be with you" (247). So they become lovers and partners on the run for freedom. Their relationship is a testimony to the multiple dimensions of the erotic: political, spiritual, physical, and the powerful aesthetic of embodied, sensual, intimate desire (Kirk-Duggan 222).

In the struggle for liberation, to paraphrase Kevin Quashie, black women loving black women is serious, dangerous, necessary, and revolutionary business (28). As they travel thousands of miles southward "by hovercraft, then by foot, packhorse, and then on foot again" their conversation and experiences reflect the alternating roles and complementary aspects of strength and weakness in their relationship" (247). During a resting period, for example, they are ambushed by vampire hunters and Ermis carries a sedated Gilda strapped to her back for several days. "Your courage is great," Gilda compliments her. Ermis replies: "I couldn't leave you any more than you could leave me" (251). With that, the mutual desire for survival, protection, sanctuary, and home space is confirmed.

The final assertion of the cultural specificity of their erotic synergy is in the reference to the African American music tradition and the ways it is an intrinsic part of each of their beings. Upon a visit to the opera, Gilda's mind drifted from the highbrow European aesthetics to the "monumental rhythms and the urgency" of the plantation music she left in her past (93). Also, one of Gilda's personas was a jazz singer/songwriter. A few pages of the novel are dedicated to a moment in which the "piercing notes" from a cornet player "wrapped themselves around her body" and induced a feeling of "oneness" with the black humans in the room. As she listened "The web of music bound them through the ages, through the dark, until there was but a single future for them" (122). And so we have come full circle regarding the role of the sacred songs in constructing queer spirituality.

For Ermis, the twenty-first-century African American, the sacred music tradition is the most readily available. In one of the first conversations they have, Gilda reminds Ermis that she is not obligated to remain physically close to her or to remain alive. "I believe I'll run on," is Ermis' reply, a reference to the gospel song made popular by the group the Mighty Clouds of Joy. More of the lyrics include:

> I believe I'll run on / See what the end will be / I believe I'll work on / Find out what's waiting for me. / I see ten thousand stories / And glories and dreams / I see angels right here on Earth / I see laughing and growing and loving / And knowing what life is worth

As I stated in the first chapter, gospel music involves a theology of the black experience in the United States. Cheryl Kirk-Duggan further explains, "Gospel songs include a theology of grace where one can be intimate with God and know liberation, and a theology of survival where God assists one daily, despite monumental oppression" (228). In a single lyric, Ermis evokes a theology of hope, survival, and grace and, simultaneously, queers the lyrical text by expressing it as a confirmation of her willingness to seek happiness in a future as a vampire. She expounds on how much a part of her immediate heritage this use of *double entendre* is when she reminisces about her parents. They had not been religious folks but were often sighted "crooning 'Steal Away to Jesus,' snuggled together on the front porch swing as if it was a romantic ballad" (252). Just as her parents had, and the innumerable struggling black people before them, the vampire couple makes a slight interpretive adjustment to fit their context. They are the hunted species, forced to steal away in the cover of night, pushed further underground, further into the margins of society, in order to keep the threat of (in)humanity at bay.

Ermis is the ideal listener: a fully engaged hearer and appropriately responsive. Her presence provides Gilda with renewed connectedness to the Universe, as is indicated in a scene reminiscent of Jinx's postcoital transformation in the garden in Becky Birtha's short story in Chapter Five. Still on the run,

> They crossed the mountains side by side. A few more stars showed themselves, giving them assurance Gilda stopped short and looked up at them with admiration, as if they could look down and see her. She felt her lungs expand with the air scented by the thick foliage. The nights itself seemed green as the rustle

> of leaves grew louder. [. . .] She looked more closely at an enormous leaf, reaching forward from the darkness. The light veins and soft curves of its outline offered a universe unto itself, a wonder as yet unexplored. (251)

As a metaphor for the ideal black lesbian existence, the vampire couple lives a life founded on ethical, reciprocal nurturing of all life force. In addition to their love of black life that is reflected through their desire for each other and their valuing of African American cultural traditions, they also see the environment as sacred, even as it decays before their eyes. The path to safety is more than a route by foot; it is a path guided by the natural elements that protectively shroud the women at night, and the rocks, caves, and thick forests that conceal them during the day. To reciprocate, Gilda admires the starry sky and leaf the same way Shug Avery admires the swaying purple flowers in a field (Chapter Four); the way Jinx admires the glistening dew on the tomato vine (Chapter Five); and the way Arthur admires the intoxicating sweet funk emitted by Crunch's aroused body (Chapter Three). Their lives are enriched by a spirituality that is sensual and inherently erotic.

The dialogue, plot, and narration construct a spiritual ethos, which is also a love ethic. *TGS* envisions the erotic life of the black lesbian as ultimately engaged with a love of self and as that which reiterates girlfriend selfhood. This is an ethical principle, a black female homoerotics, which articulates sociopolitical and erotic solidarity with black women and black culture, and coalition with other minority cultural movements. The narrative involves a vision of hope, emotional triumph, requited desire, spiritual uplift, and sanctuary. Eventually they reach the horizon of (presumed) safety at the Peruvian border and are greeted by the silhouettes of Gilda's racially diverse and multicultural circle of vampire friends, including the black male, Julius. Although it is not clear how long they will be safe from the hunters, the closing passage is hopeful in its decree that "Gilda was no longer fleeing for her life" even as it indicates that she must continue to reside in the margins (252).

In closing, I revise Hortense Spillers' description of the science fiction/fantasy genres: *The Gilda Stories* is a black lesbian narrative that returns us to what we know in a way that we had not known and experienced before. We know that spirituality is a politics, lens, and ideology in African American literature and that black male vampires have existed as protagonists in African American creative works (mainly film) before this novel. *TGS* participates, or repeats the themes, in the tradition with a signal difference: the vampire character, previously characterized as evil, even if sympathetic, regardless of skin tone, has been appropriated for black queer spirituality and resistance. Gomez fuses an archetypal immortality to black lesbian identity in a way that expands the landscape of black queer possibility into infinity.

Closing Thoughts and Suggestions for Further Reading

> Jesus might love you, this you might know, but being made love to by a woman like Pauline puts the love you fantasized about then in new perspective. Obviously Pauline is doing loving like Jesus couldn't and wouldn't. At least not in the version handed down to the adoring and gullible.
>
> —Susannah in *By the Light of My Father's Smile* by Alice Walker, 110

Writing has always been an integral aspect of the African American liberation struggle. The literature presented in this book attests to this, as these writers intervene into discourses that rely on the specious black/gay or people-of-faith/people in-the-life binarisms. I have highlighted how various formations of homoerotic spirituality makes such binarisms irrelevant because they construct a "radical creative space which affirms and sustains our subjectivity" (hooks, *Yearning* 153) as racialized beings, spiritual beings, sexual beings, citizens of the world, and children of the Cosmos—simultaneously. What these writers present to us, ultimately, is the pervasive presence of an LGBTQ-affirming stance, which further diversifies African American expressions of spirituality.

In conversation with the broader culture, Gay Christian Narratives propose, for example, that believers do not have to choose between creating a false (repressed) self and being cut off from among their people. These stories relate that believers who experience same-sex desire, or whose gender expression is nonconforming, can maintain an active membership in the Christian community by employing the revisionist tradition of the black church, a tradition that is their rightful heritage. Popular novels that take up this theme include Laurinda D. Brown's series of "lesbians in the church" books. In her debut novel, *Fire and Brimstone*, Brown integrates lesbian motherhood, cycles of silence surrounding intra-family rape, bisexuality, and same-sex domestic violence to portray fuller lesbian lives and to engage complex networks of black female oppression. Also, E. Lynn Harris emerged in the 1990s with his novel, *Invisible Life*, about wealthy black men who secretly engage in homosexual and bisexual behaviors. It foregrounds religious homophobia and the impact of AIDS on black men, and initiated a string of bestselling novels from the author until his death in 2009. Poets Essex Hemphill and Lenelle Moise, and musicians Prince and Michelle Ndegeocello also commonly explore (and queer the conventional) biblical and Christian perspectives in their artistic expressions. In fact, poetry as a genre awaits our discovery of its contributions to queer spirituality, as I have chosen to focus solely on fiction. Depictions of Christian-identified queer characters are probably the most abundant narratives.

Nonetheless, many writers dramatize folk theologies, blues-inflected cosmologies, and Pantheist perspectives. For, as James W. Coleman demonstrates in *Faithful Vision*, literature is a reflection of how these beliefs vary but are always carried alongside Christianity in the words and doings of black people (if they do not displace it altogether). Such depictions, referred to here collectively as *philosophies of the spirit*, propose that sacredness is where you find it and with whom you make it. But perhaps that is an oversimplification. Maybe it is better to say that sacred spaces for blues people (à la Amiri Baraka) are constructed through everyday rituals of faith and spiritual expression. For further reading, an important and impressive range of syncretized theologies appears in the work of playwright and poet Sharon Bridgforth. She integrates images of ancestral presence, homoeroticism, and black southern rurality in a work she describes as a performance novel, titled *love/conjure blues*. The novel is a "reflection of the ways that Black people have used artistic expression to transmit stories of survival. [It] re-imagines the traditional role of the Griot. Asserts queer as sacred. Claims the blues as ritual-in concert with Ancient practices and new creations" ("love/conjure blues" n. p.). Bridgforth continues to indulge the queer southern black and spiritual in *Blood Pudding*, a drama set in New Orleans. Ntozake Shange also imagines that the South is a supernatural space in *Sassafrass, Cypress, and Indigo*, a novel about a family of sisters steeped in South Carolina Geechee culture and which features a spectrum of female sexuality. Plus, it almost goes without saying that any novel by Alice Walker published after 1989 imagines female sexuality through a lens of spiritual engagement. The passage quoted above is taken from her novel, *By the Light of My Father's Smile*, which is narrated in part by a spirit who observes and sometimes guides his two daughters, one of whom is bisexual, as they live out the end of their lives. True to all of her cultural and political affinities, Walker's tale in *By the Light* is interwoven with testimony, refutations, (re)visions, and the assertion of paganism as the natural, most self-loving way of life.

I have also shown how some writers trouble the waters by aiming to "get rid of God" in order to place nontheist discourses, egalitarian paradigms of cooperation, or a love ethic at the center of black queer liberation politics. These ideas have circulated among a nearly invisible (as such) minority of nontheists within the African American community, going back to the era of slavery, for whom the concept of God does not resonate with their reality. In the quest for justice and freedom, this outlook demands that we search within ourselves for goodness, morality, and love, and that we empower ourselves to address the problems that plague our society. The manifestation of these ideas was first examined in the 1983 publication *Black Literature and Humanism*, a critical essay collection edited by R. Baxter Miller. And, more recently, theologian Anthony Pinn published *The End of God-Talk: An African American Humanist Theology* (2012). Some of the most famous literary figures mentioned in either book include Frederick Douglass, Langston Hughes, Toni Morrison, and Gwendolyn Brooks. Though, in this book, I focus on a single work of science fiction by Octavia Butler, the reader seeking more formulations of queerness and secular ethics or nontheist expressions of spirituality in that genre will find that Butler and fellow speculative fiction author, Samuel Delany, construct Earthly societies and intergalactic communities across the breadth of their respective oeuvres in which black bodies, black consciousness, black spirit, and spectrums of sexuality are fused in challenging and ingenious ways. A place to begin is Butler's *Patternist* series or Delany's *Tales of Neveryon* collection.

In the Life and in the Spirit offers up this archive of artists, theorists, and characters as the presence of knowledge, visions, and schematics that further expand our understanding of black strivings against emotional and sexual bondage. Across African American expressive culture, we have always imagined ourselves free, and I bring you these irreverent, "indecent," heretical freedom dreams that minister to black queerness and worship the rising spirit of desire. For they convey a sense of community and wholeness derived from the love of sensuality and self that extends outward into the environment and other living beings.

Notes

PREFACE

1. The website no longer displays the message I quote in this passage (I began this research in 2006). As of June 2013, the mission, and possibly the name, of the Exodus International ministry has changed. After thirty-seven years, the founder, president, and self-proclaimed "ex-gay," Alan Chambers, has had a change of heart regarding the official policy on the treatment of people who experience same-sex desire. He issued a formal apology to all gays and lesbians expressing that "Exodus is an institution in the conservative Christian world, but we've ceased to be a living, breathing organism. For quite some time, we've been imprisoned in a worldview that's neither honoring toward our fellow human beings, nor biblical." See Ed Payne, "Group Apologizes to Gay Community, Then Shuts Down 'Cure' Ministry" (*CNN*, July 8, 2013). For reactions from the evangelical Christian community, see Melissa Steffan, "Alan Chambers Apologizes to Gay Community, Exodus International to Shut Down" (*Christianity Today*, June 21, 2013).
2. Examples of state and national organizations that defend monogamous heterosexual marriage as the only morally legitimate model include Alliance for Marriage, American Family Association, Concerned Women for America, Family Research Council, Focus on the Family, Liberty Counsel, National Organization for Marriage, and Renew America.

3. In 1996, President William Clinton signed the Defense of Marriage Act (DOMA), which provides that no State shall be required to give effect to a law of any other State with respect to a same-sex marriage. It also defines the words *marriage* and *spouse* in monogamous heterosexual terms for purposes of Federal law. To date, there are twenty jurisdictions (nineteen states and the District of Columbia) that recognize same-sex marriages, and four states that allow some form of same-sex union recognition (civil unions or domestic partnerships). Meanwhile, in 2013, the U.S. Supreme Court ruled DOMA unconstitutional under the Fourteenth Amendment, which has opened the door for lawsuits against those states that do not treat all legal marriages equally under the law.
4. President Obama signed the repeal of this legislation on December 22, 2010.
5. In addition to "Theorizing Spirit: The Critical Challenges of Elizabeth Nunez' *When Rocks Dance* and *Beyond the Limbo Silence*," Melvin Rahming published a series of essays in which he models his spirit-centered methodology. See "Towards a Critical Theory of Spirit: The Insistent Demands of Erna Brobder's *Myal*"; "Phenomenology, Ontology, Epistemology and Spirit: Caribbean Perspective in Ann Petry's *Tituba of Salem Village*"; and "Reading Spirit: Cosmological Considerations in Garfield's Linton's *Voodoomation: A Book of Foretelling*."
6. This is not to say that the role of spirituality in the lives of black LGBT people has not ever been documented. Ethnographic and historical studies exist that provide centuries of evidence of openly same-sex-loving and gender nonconforming people who have served in leadership roles or held important positions in their spiritual communities. A good starting place would be Will Roscoe and Stephen Murray, *Boy-Wives and Female Husbands: Studies of African Homosexualities* (Palgrave 1998); Randy Connor, *Queering Creole Spiritual Traditions: Lesbian, Gay, Bisexual, and Transgender Participation in African-Inspired Traditions in the Americas* (Hayworth Press 2004); or Yvette Flunder, *Where the Edge Gathers: Building a Community of Radical Inclusion* (Pilgrim Press 2005).
7. My work does not introduce the notion that African American LGBTQ literature participates in the signifying tradition by queering the "black experience" or black church. Charles Nero laid the foundation for my work when he made those claims in the classic 1991 essay, "Towards a Black Gay Aesthetic: Signifying in Contemporary Black

Gay Literature." *In the Life and in the Spirit* is the first book-length study of the phenomena and expands the discussion into women's writing and recent narratives.

8. James Baldwin's novel, *Just Above My Head* (and arguably his other tragicomic works examined in Chapter Three), is the exception to my "no crisis narratives" approach. The central queer character in the novel is killed in a bathroom.

CHAPTER ONE

1. Hurston, Douglas, Thurman, Nugent, Hughes, Gwendolyn Bennett, and John P. Davis, collectively known as the *Niggerati*, expressed their resistance to the censorship (defined as the limitation of topics/themes accepted) they experienced when their work was showcased in *Crisis* (magazine of the NAACP; edited by W.E.B. Du Bois) and *Opportunity* (of the National Urban League) magazines; both held contests that led to wide promotion and sponsorship from white patrons for its winners. The Niggerati also resented the respectability politics of racial uplift ideology in general, and made all of this clear in their collaborative production of the short-lived literary journal *Fire!!* in 1926. In addition to Nugent's homosexual-themed story, the issue included illustrations of working class blacks, sex work, gambling, nudity, and nonjudgmental use of black vernacular.
2. Tim Wirth, Nugent's literary executor, published Nugent's collected works in *Gay Rebel of the Harlem Renaissance.* In the introduction, Wirth points out that Nugent was highly influenced by the Greek pedaristic tradition in philosophy and visual arts, and authors in the nineteenth-century Aesthetic Movement. This list includes Oscar Wilde, Aubrey Beardsley, and Ronald Firbank, whose guiding artistic principles were the primacy of sensuous beauty and emotion over moral or political sentiments, and over linearity and perspective. Nugent's short story, "Smoke, Lillies, and Jade," shows clear evidence of these principles.
3. In the introduction to *Gay Rebel of the Harlem Renaissance*, Wirth quotes Nugent as saying that "Harlem was very much like the [Greenwich] Village. People did what they wanted to do with whom they wanted to do it." Wirth explains that in the social matrix in which Nugent moved, extramarital dalliances and same-sex affairs were an open secret but that Nugent was less secretive about his interest in men

(21). For more information regarding Nugent's negative treatment by publishers, see Alice Randall's commentary in her review of Nugent's novel, *Jigger Man* in "Tales of the Jazz Age," *Los Angeles Times*, April 24, 2008. Also see Ellen McBreen's article, "Biblical Gender Bending in Harlem," *Art Journal* (Fall 1998): 22–28. Christopher Vitale discusses the reasons Nugent was a problematic and therefore overlooked figure for the Black Arts Movement generation of the 1970s, which had successfully revitalized public and academic interest in Langston Hughes, Zora Neale Hurston, and Countee Cullen in "The Untimely Richard Bruce Nugent" (NYU 2007), an unpublished dissertation.

4. A more thorough (or differently focused) analysis would also consider the context of Roman culture at the time, which Nugent had studied. The culture of pederasty, sexual relationships between adult men and adolescent boys, was commonplace among men of high social and military stature.
5. For a thoroughly contextualized analysis of Nugent's drawings and paintings, see the unpublished dissertation, "The Untimely Richard Bruce Nugent" (NYU 2007), by Christopher Vitale.
6. We still live in an era in which HIV and AIDS present major challenges to medical research and treatment communities and in which infection rates continue to rise at alarming rates. By "AIDS Era," I mean the panic-stricken "pandemic" decade of the 1980s and early 1990s where an HIV-positive status was a literal death sentence.
7. Initially, Acquired Immune Deficiency Syndrome (AIDS) was called GRID, an acronym for Gay-Related Immune Deficiency Syndrome by the mainstream news media because of medical reports that tied it to homosexual men. Unmesh Kher of *Time* (March 21, 2003) reports in a series titled, "80 Days that Changed the World" that on July 27, 1982, at a meeting between activists, federal bureaucrats, and the investigative team from the Centers for Disease Control, GRID became AIDS. Other sources: "A Cluster of Kaposi's Sarcoma and Pneumocystis Carinii Pneumonia among Homosexual Male Residents of Los Angeles and Orange Counties, California" in *Morbidity and Mortality Weekly Report,* 31.23 (June 18, 1982): 305–307; Randy Shilts, *And the Band Played On,* p. 121; and Carl Bean, *I Was Born This Way*, p. 228.
8. In her definition of womanism, Alice Walker asserts that feminist work need not be separatist "except, periodically, for health." This is a tacit acknowledgment of the challenges and risks to one's spiritual

and physical health that are inherent in liberation work. Occasionally, black women will have to separate from black men and/or white people to heal themselves. Likewise, Tinney insists upon a homocentric church into which gays can retreat from heterosupremacist environments to rebuild their spiritual fortitude. One of his goals was to eventually gain "mutuality, equality, and reciprocal relationships" (74) with their heterosexual and nonblack institutional counterparts. But first he had to serve his congregants' needs and to ensure they remained "truly and unquestionably Christian" by "doing and redoing theology" in a separatist fashion (76–77).

9. A recent development in the inclusive church movement is the founding of the Unity Fellowship Church (UFC) denomination, which maintains African American worship styles. Bishop Tonyia Rawls of UFC Charlotte, North Carolina, relates in a published study that the UFC movement is a direct response to the alienation of LGBT Christians from traditional black church communities, an alienation that she believes results in "physical, spiritual, and moral damage that robs believers of their community and faith, and robs the community of potentially strong contributors and members" (327). In every Sunday service, congregants say aloud to themselves and each other, "You are a Beautiful Creation of God" (Rawls 329). This affirmation, in addition to an inclusive theology, constitutes a counter narrative to the oft-cited Leviticus abomination text and the general onslaught of judgmental rhetoric that exists in conservative churches. Relatedly, Bishop Carlton Pearson, a heterosexual ally and former Pentecostal minister, published *The Gospel of Inclusion* (2009) and *God Is Not a Christian Nor a Jew, Muslim, Hindu* (2010) after he was shunned by his peers within his denomination. His current ministry is based on his spiritual revelation, which dissuades a belief in Hell or an exclusionary, punitive God. His followers include LGBT people of diverse faiths.

10. Although I spend a bit of time detailing the influence of Black Theology in the sections that follow, my research also benefits from a body of scholarship on African American literature and religion that is not situated in that field. Most of these publications focus on nonfiction genres from the eighteenth and nineteenth centuries, such as Joycelyn Moody, *Sentimental Confessions: Spiritual Narratives of the Nineteenth-Century African American Women*; Katherine Clay Bassard, *Spiritual Interrogations: Culture, Gender, and Community in Early African American*

Women's Writing; Kimberly Rae Connor, *Imagining Grace: Liberating Theologies in the Slave Narrative Tradition*; and Cedric May, *Evangelism and Resistance in the Black Atlantic, 1760–1835.* This area of literary study provides nuanced explorations of the sociopolitical ambitions, which emerge at the intersections of race, gender, sexuality, and religious expression in African American literature to which I am greatly obliged.

11. According to religious studies scholar Dwight Hopkins, black male theologians were responding, in part, to their white counterparts who were debating in religious journals and at academic conferences the role of religion in the Civil Rights Movement (7–9, 54–55). For a fuller historical contextualization, see Hopkins' textbook, *Introducing Black Theology of Liberation* (1999). Much of this section on Black Theology is informed by his extensive and well-researched work on the subject.
12. For example, Elias Farajaje-Jones (now Ibrahim Farajaje) outlines an "in the life theology," which "grows out of the experiences, lives, and struggles against oppression and dehumanization" of nonheterosexual religious folk (*Black Theology* 140).
13. See Traci C. West, "A Space for Faith, Sexual Desire, and Ethical Ministerial Practices" in Pinn and Hopkins, 31–52.
14. ACT UP is an acronym for Aids Coalition to Unleash Power; federally funded AIDS research, increased access to life-extending medication, and protective federal legislation were its central focuses. Fed Up Queers was New York–based and –focused, meaning they targeted local, state, and public violence against sex workers, trans and gay people, and NYPD brutality and corruption generally. Queer Nation mobilized around ending homophobia by increasing lesbian, gay, and bisexual visibility. These groups represent a collective ethos that reclaimed *queer* as a term of empowerment and collective identity for nonhetero-sexual identities, as well as gender nonconformists.
15. For concerns regarding the de-specification of sexual identities see the work of Gloria Anzaldua, Elizabeth Groscz, Sherrie Inness, Leo Bersani, Cathy Cohen, Clare Hemmings, and Stacy Young. For discussions of its fragility as a politics, see Biddy Martin, David Phillips, Jeffrey Escoffier, and Julia Parnaby.
16. In 1995, Lauren Berlant and Michael Warner co-authored a notoriously equivocal address to the Modern Language Association, which aimed to dispel the belief that queer theory is really a theory, meaning

it could not ever truly be housed in academia and separated from its political roots. They suggested it would be better thought of as "commentary," which seeks to bring into being a population "that can afford sex and intimacy in sustained, unchastening ways" and that can "comprehend their own differences of privilege and struggles." "What Does Queer Theory Teach Us About X?" *PMLA* 110 (1995). For examples of how queer theory is perceived as having lost its activist way, peruse the reviews of Lee Edelman's *No Future* and Judith Halberstam's *In a Queer Time & Place.* Also, Linda Garber bemoans this state of affairs and so retraces and reclaims the lesbian feminist political roots of queer in *Identity Poetics.*

17. Queer theory has two competing histories. One narrative is that the phrase was uttered at a conference by Teresa de Laurentis as part of a critical rumination regarding the need to animate and unsettle some of the guiding assumptions in lesbian/gay studies. From there, the story goes, it became a theory in search of a school of thought, which led to differing definitions and formulations. Others insist that a retroactive claim to the school of thought was possible because a queering of sexuality studies was already underway, operating in the feminist work of Judith Butler and Eve Sedgewick. For a more precise genealogy of queer theory and queer politics, see Annamarie Jagose, *Queer Theory: An Introduction*; Steven Epstein, "A Queer Encounter: Sociology and the study of Sexuality," *Sociology Theory* 12.2 (1994): 188–202; and William Turner, *A Genealogy of Queer Theory.*

18. Black studies has been critiqued by feminist thinkers for its masculinist, heterosexist, and misogynist paradigm. For examples in literary studies, see Barbara Smith, Deborah McDowell, and Joyce A. Joyce. Meanwhile, foundational queer theory texts rely heavily on Michel Foucault. Critics, such as Robert J.C. Young in the essay, "Focault on Race and Colonialsm"; and Ann Laura Stoler, *Race and the Education of Desire* take Foucault to task because his Eurocentric articulations of nineteenth-century institutional discourses ignore racial dynamics. Discussions of the white bias in queer theory have led to critical correctives, such as Ian Bernard, *Queer Race*; Ruth Goldman, "Who is that Queer Queer?"; and Urvashi Vaid, "Inclusion, Exclusion and Occlusion." Regarding black queer studies, Nicholas Boggs compiled a bibliography in *Callaloo* 23.1 (2000): 479–494. More recent titles include: Sioban Somerville, *Queering the Color Line*; Johnson and Henderson, *Black Queer Studies*; Stefanie Dunning, *Queer in Black and*

White; David Gerstner, *Queer Pollen*; L. H. Stallings, *Mutha' Is Half a Word*; and Roderick Ferguson, *Aberrations in Black.*

19. Joseph Beam was the first to use "in the life" as a book title. He was not able to trace the history of the term but justifies his usage thusly in the preface of the anthology: "The word-of-mouth, oral tradition of the African-American community often makes it difficult to locate the etymology of a word or phrase. *In the Life*, a phrase used to describe 'the street life' (the lifestyle of pimps, prostitutes, hustlers, and drug dealers) is also the phrase used to describe the 'gay life' (the lives of black homosexual men and women)" (12). The phrase is also used throughout the documentary film by Albert and Allen Hughes, *American Pimp* (1999), a text that includes an historical tracing of the sex trade in African American urban centers from the 1920s to the 1990s. The term was appropriated in 1992 by a white-owned television production company, In the Life Media, which was founded "on the premise that visibility in media is vital to achieving equality and social justice for LGBT people" (*In the Life Media* n. p.). The show was featured on public television for twenty years.
20. Many people participate in same-sex sexual activities and maintain a heterosexual identity. *In the life* is not an identity, it is a descriptive umbrella term whose meaning is determined by the speakers and context.
21. Beam and several of his contributors cite the writing of Audre Lorde, Barbara Smith, and "black feminism" as sites of empowerment. They were among several lesbian feminists who participated in writer-activism by editing anthologies, publishing poetry, polemical essays, and novels, and founding specialized journals and presses.

CHAPTER TWO

1. There is always, necessarily, a bit of resistance to free-wielding references to the "black church" because the historical, institutional, and cultural terrain the phrase attempts to cover is expansive and patchy in the United States. Nonetheless, these histories, physical structures, and religious cultures have commonalities that do allow for a collective reference. My use of the term follows theologian Kelly Brown Douglas' eloquent description in "Black Church Homophobia: What

To Do About It?" published online in the spring issue of the Yale Divinity School magazine *Reflections* in 2006:

> The Black Church community is not a monolithic reality. This Church is a disparate collective of churches that reflect the diversity of the Black community itself. These churches are diversified by origin, denomination, doctrine, worshiping culture, spiritual ethos, class, size, and other less obvious factors. They may be within white denominational structures or independent of them. They can reflect congregational, connectional, or episcopal polities. They can be urban, suburban, or rural. They range in size and structure from storefronts to mega-churches. Yet, as disparate as Black churches are, they share a common history and play a unique role in Black life, both of which attest to their collective identity as the Black Church. In short, Black churches emerged as a fundamental part of Black people's active resistance to dehumanizing white racist oppression, even as they have played a central role in Black people's struggle for life and freedom.
>
> With this in mind, and with the knowledge that a minority of black churches now represent progressive doctrinal approaches that slide on a spectrum from the less judgmental "gay friendly" worship environment to an inclusive "pro-gay" stance, I clarify that my use of "black church" is meant to encompass, generally, black-led, racially segregated Christian denominations and their institutional alliances, associations, unions, and hierarchies.

2. As I discussed in the previous chapter, scholars of Black Theology laid the groundwork for our current understandings of how the black church has always functioned as a political, physical, and spiritual sanctuary. Examples wrought from their collective analyses are bible verses that speak of slavery in neutral terms, with proverbs for the enslaved as well as the slave owner: Leviticus 25: 44–5, 53; Exodus 21:4, Deuteronomy 20:14, Ephesians sixth chapter, and Colossians third chapter. In African American literature we learn from ex-slave narrators and abolitionist propaganda that white ministers used these texts in sermons tailor-made for enslaved people. David

Walker's *Appeal* and Frederick Douglass's autobiographies and speeches famously take on this kind of "slaveholder Christianity" but many slave narratives reveal the ways in which the bible's stories of escape were interpreted as evidence that God is always on the side of the oppressed.

3. Famous examples of black leaders who interpreted Christianity's uses for resistance to slavery include Frederick Douglass, Denmark Vesey, Harriet Tubman, and Richard Allen.
4. Jeremiah Wright is the retired senior pastor of Trinity United Church of Christ in Chicago and former pastor of President Barack Obama. He is one of the architects of institutional Black Theology. Wright gained national attention in March 2008 when ABC News excerpted parts of his sermons that criticized the U.S. government for its imperialist wars and the country's history of systemic racism. One notorious aphorism, "Not 'God Bless America'; God *damn* America," headlined the news cycle for weeks. President Obama denounced the pastor's statements and eventually resigned his membership in the church.
5. For analyses of the social significance of spirituals and gospels: LeRoi Jones, *Blues People*; Dena J. Epstein, *Sinful Tunes and Spirituals*; and Arthur C. Jones, *Wade in the Water: The Wisdom of the Spirituals.*
6. Religion and political activism were entwined in the Civil Rights Movement. Political organizing took place in many church buildings and, at times, was spearheaded by clergymen. Prayer was a common component of demonstrations and acts of civil disobedience. Also, Martin Luther King Jr. speaks directly to Christian leaders as part of his moral argument for ending legal segregation in the 1963 essay "Letter from A Birmingham Jail."
7. For more history of adaptation and politics in African American sacred songs, see Bernice Reagon Johnson, *If You Don't Go, Don't Hinder Me: The African American Sacred Song Tradition*; and Bob Darden, *People Get Ready: A New History of Black Gospel Music.*
8. It is not my position that Christianity is the only religion that black people inherited in the United States or that it precedes oppositional consciousness. When the Protestant evangelical movement began to grow in the eighteenth century, Christianity swept across enslaved populations as well. It eventually became the dominant religious force but that is not to say that African religions were stamped out. Chapters Three and Four will explore some other influences on African American spirituality. For an historical look at predominately black

denominations in the United States, see Albert Raboteau, *Slave Religion*; Curtis and Sigler, *The New Black Gods*; and Anthony Pinn, *Varieties of African American Religious Experience.*

9. The Harlem Renaissance/New Negro Movement beheld the first generation of black writers whose aim was not to prove their humanity. This movement aimed to prove itself as a culture with diverse intellectual and artistic abilities, which also contributed greatly to American society and culture. The intellectuals at the head of the movement carefully selected, promoted, and created publication opportunities for the artists they deemed worthy to represent the best of the Negro race before white audiences and to serve as inspirational visionaries for the common black folk. The mentoring of the new black voices also involved discouraging against negative portrayals of black life, even if they were realistic. See A. B. Christina Schwartz, *Gay Voices of the Harlem Renaissance*; Faith Berry, *Langston Hughes: Before and Beyond Harlem*; and Wayne Cooper, *Claude McKay: Rebel Sojourner in the Harlem Renaissance.*
10. For details on Hughes' travel companions and domestic partners, see Faith Berry, *Langston Hughes: Before and Beyond Harlem.*
11. See A. B. Christa Schwartz, *Gay Voices of the Harlem Renaissance*, 83.
12. Schwartz, 7.
13. Christopher Vitale cites Thomas Wirth, Nugent's literary executor, as the source for this nugget about Hurston's bisexuality in "The Untimely Bruce Nugent," 25. For discussion of the prevalence of same-sex liaisons at that time or the impact of what is now considered "lesbian" or "gay" inflection in black literature of the 1920s to 1930s see Simon Dickel, *Black/Gay: The Harlem Renaissance, the Protest Era, and the Constructions of Black Gay Identity in the 1980s and '90s*; Gary Edward Holcomb, *Claude McKay, Code Name Sasha: Queer Black Marxism and the Harlem Renaissance*; and James Wilson, *Bulldaggers, Pansies, and Chocolate Babies: Performance, Race, and Sexuality in the Harlem Renaissance.*
14. See George Chauncey, *Gay New York: Gender, Urban Culture, and the Making of the Gay Male*; and Charles Kaiser, *Gay Metropolis: The Landmark History of Gay Life in America.*
15. Arnold Rampersad published Hughes' prefatory notes to *Montage of a Dream Deferred*, in which the poet eloquently describes how he hopes the ninety-one individual poems will be perceived as a single poem that functions, in voice and form, "like bebop . . . marked by

conflicting changes, sudden nuances, sharp and impudent interjections, [and] broken rhythms" in *The Collected Poems of Langston Hughes*, 387.

16. For further study, see the historical analyses authored by Jonathan Katz or John D'Emilio. Also, read Martin Meeker's cogent insights in "Behind the Mask of Respectability: Reconsidering the Mattachine Society and Male Homophile Practice, 1950s and 1960s" (*Journal of Homosexuality* 2001).
17. Van Vechten was a wealthy and famous music critic, novelist, and photographer. In 1962, he placed among his papers at Yale University's Beinecke Rare Books and Manuscript Library, a box that he asked to remain sealed until twenty-five years after his death. It contained nearly twenty scrapbooks that he had maintained from the 1930s to the 1950s in which he had accumulated gay rights advocacy paraphernalia, photos from underground clubs and drag balls, and news stories of gender passing revelations and gender reassignment surgeries. The scrapbooks premiered as part of Yale's 2004 library exhibit, "The Pink and The Blue: Lesbian and Gay Life at Yale and in Connecticut, 1642–2004" and continue to be held in the archives there. His intimate friendship with Hughes is documented in their thirty-nine years of correspondence, collected in *Remember Me to Harlem* (Knopf 2001).
18. Further, evidence of Delmar's soft masculinity: His nickname is Delly, which could evoke Dolly or Nelly (a gay or intra-community synonym for sissy).
19. Schwartz sums up Hughes' sexual ambiguity thusly:

    > A major impediment to an assessment of Hughes's sexual status is his successful shielding of his private life from public gaze. His correspondences evidences only scant references to sexual experience, and he also excluded fellow Renaissance writers from his private life. . . . A rare exception to this pattern of mystery and secrecy is Hughes's intimation of his first same-sex experience to a friend. [Arnold] Rampersad [a Hughes biographer] briefly mentions this disclosure yet fails to give a date and also does not specify his source. (69)

20. Cathy J. Cohen elaborates on the institutional limits of black community membership in *The Boundaries of Blackness*.
21. Hughes' depiction is one of the earliest examples of what has become

a common rendition of the male choir director as a feminized or sexually ambiguous figure in the African American imaginary. In addition to the writers discussed in this book, the highly successful popular novelist, E. Lynn Harris, situates homosexual romance in church choirs in his black gay serial, which began with *Invisible Life*. The gay/sexually ambiguous choir director also appears in black-cast films and plays including *Holiday Heart* (2000), *Let God Be the Judge* (2010), *First Sunday* (2008), and *Dirty Laundry* (2006).

22. Examples of the focus on gays in the Black Church include: Mashaun Simon, "Gay Choir Directors 'Don't Ask, Don't Tell' in Black Church," *The Grio* (December 2, 2010); an historical overview of the gay subculture in gospel choirs in "Gays and Gospel," *Windy City Times* (May 1, 2006); and Anthony Heilbut, *The Fan Who Knew Too Much: Aretha Franklin, the Rise of the Soap Opera, Children of the Gospel Church, and other Meditations*. Note: *Children* is a coded term in black gay culture, used to refer to gay people.
23. In a chapter titled "The Pulpit and the Pew," C. Eric Lincoln provides ample data that supports his view that "in spite of their importance in the life of the church, the offices of preacher and pastor of churches in the historic black churches remain a male preserve and are not generally available to women" (*The Black Church in the African American Experience* 275).
24. Punk has taken on other meanings, such as "weak" or "novice," and in the context of music, "punk rock" is an alternative to mainstream rock genres.
25. James Weldon Johnson describes the black sermonic performance in his book of verses inspired by it, titled *God's Trombones*:

> An electric current ran through the crowd. It was in a moment alive and quivering; and all the while the preacher held it in the palm of his hand. He was wonderful in the way he employed his conscious and unconscious art. He strode the pulpit up and down in what was actually a very rhythmic dance, and he brought into play the full gamut of his wonderful voice, a voice—what shall I say?—not of an organ or a trumpet, but rather of a trombone, the instrument possessing above all others the power to express the wide and varied range of emotions encompassed by the human voice—and with greater amplitude. (6–7)

26. It would be a disingenuous stretch to imply that men do not faint or respond with emotional exuberance in church; yet it is more commonly depicted in literature as a feminine reaction to the touch of the spirit. Poet Pat Parker illustrates it thusly: Daughter of Ham lies on a church floor / filled in orgasm with her Maker / a spent lover ignorant of a hard bed (55). And Nella Larsen's *Quicksand* narrates "the writhings and weepings of the feminine portion [of the congregation], which seemed to predominate" (141). Larsen's protagonist Helga Crane observes, "Behind her, before her, beside her, frenzied women gesticulated, screamed, wept, and tottered to the praying of the preacher. . . . The women dragged themselves upon their knees or crawled over the floor like reptiles, sobbing and pulling their hair and tearing off their clothing" (141–142).
27. Greenwich Village since the 1920s is known as a district where beatniks, bohemians, racial and sexual minorities found community among other socially alienated groups. The most expansive source for Greenwich Village as a site of sexual dissidence is George Chauncey, *Gay New York*. Chauncey provides a social history of the gay saloons, bathhouses, cafeterias, widely publicized dances and elaborate drag balls that were regularly held in Greenwich Village, Harlem, and Times Square. He argues that gay men carved out public and private space for themselves in parks, beaches, books, and on stage and that straight folk openly flocked to these events and spaces from the 1890s to the 1940s. The cultures went underground but continued to flourish, according to Chauncey, after laws against sodomy and cross-dressing were introduced in the 1930s. Hughes moved to Harlem in the 1920s and mentions drag balls in his memoir, *The Big Sea*. Also useful for this topic is the documentary *Before Stonewall*.

CHAPTER THREE

1. "The Outing" and *Go Tell It on the Mountain* appear in *James Baldwin: Early Novels and Stories* (1998), a compilation in the Literary Classics series distributed by Penguin Books. My citations from *Just Above My Head* are from the Dell paperback edition (1980).
2. David, when he was king, saw Bathsheba bathing and summoned her for sex. He was married to multiple women already; she was married, too, but he was the king. She could not deny him and was

impregnated. Her husband was in the king's army and was away in battle. David tried to cover it up by having Bathsheba seduce her husband so that he would think the baby his. This fails, so David had the husband killed in order to keep her for himself (2 Sam. 11:1–27). All of this takes place after the death of Jonathan.

3. For a roundup of critical interpretations of the threshing floor scene, see Barbara K. Olson, "Come-to-Jesus stuff in James Baldwin's *Go Tell It on the Mountain* and *The Amen Corner*." *African American Review* 31.2 (Summer 97).
4. There is an argument to be made about the ways in which eroticized suffering, bondage, and wounding, all of which are prominent themes in Christian and Jewish religious imagery, are also being engaged in Baldwin's work. My concern is with the struggle against internalized homophobia and the fear of God's rejection, and the rhetoric Baldwin constructs regarding this through the thoughts, emotions, and outcomes of his characters.
5. For an extensive explication and application of Burke's arguments about logology, see Michael Cobb, *God Hates Fags: The Rhetorics of Religious Violence*, 65–68.
6. For insight into spirituals as liberation theology, see Howard Thurman, *Deep River: An Interpretation of Negro Spirituals*; Bernice Johnson Reagon, *If You Don't Go, Don't Hinder Me: The African American Sacred Song Tradition*, and Arthur C. Jones, *Wade in the Water: The Wisdom of the Spirituals.*
7. In "The Outing," it states, "daily [Johnnie] recognized that he was black with sin, that the secrets of his heart were a stench in God's nostrils." This is a reference to the word "abomination" for which according to Strong's Hebrew and Greek dictionaries, there are eight Hebrew words and four Greek words (or some closely related word) in the KJV Bible. The connotations are either ethical or ritualistic. Two of the meanings include "filthy, unclean" and "to stink." In both of Baldwin's renderings of this character, John/Johnnie's abominable sins include his unfaithfulness to the teachings of the bible, his hatred of his father, and his homosexual desires.

CHAPTER FOUR

1. Judylyn Ryan undertakes a similar investigation, though she applies an African diasporic framework to argue, in *Spirituality as Ideology in*

Black Women's Film and Literature, that through art, black women act as theologian, theorist, and priestess.

2. According to the *Dictionary of Literary Biography*, Shockley published more than a dozen short stories in magazines and newspapers between 1950 and 1974, which were focused on anti-racist themes. It was not until she created the black feminist lesbian character that her writing drew her most visible critical attention. L. H. Stallings provides a roundup of negative reviews in the essay "Re-Reading Ann Allen Shockley through Queer Queen Bee Eyes" (full citation in Bibliography).
3. Rita Dandridge wrote in a 1984 review article that Reverend Black is a "dissembler and a parasite" (162). Dandridge also identifies the reverend's brightly colored wardrobe, worn with a clerical collar, as symbolic of the incongruous aspects of her identity. Tomeiko Ashford characterizes Reverend Black's transformation from itinerant revival preacher to settled, one-church pastor as a move from a "shallow, power-and sex-driven preacher to a well-rounded, loving partner and disclosed lesbian pastor" (293).
4. Ministers are role models of Christian sexual ethic. Public knowledge of a male preacher's heterosexual activity would not automatically undermine his authority unless it was adulterous or abusive. Even in those cases they are often forgiven. Homosexual activity is always already immoral and would discredit a male or female minister in conventional Protestant churches. See Betty J. Overton, "Black Women Preachers: A Literary View," *Southern Quarterly* 23.3 (Spring 1985): 58; see also Traci West, "A Space for Faith, Sexual Desire, and Ethical Black Ministerial Practices" in *Loving the Body* (edited by Pinn and Hopkins).
5. For more on the syncretization of African cosmologies and Christian beliefs, see historical perspectives in the work of Peter J. Paris, John Blassingame, Lawrence Levine, and John Mbiti.
6. Jacqueline Bobo summarizes the various angles of the men's criticism and discusses black women's complicated responses in "Black Women's Responses to the Color Purple" in *Jump Cut* 33 (February 1988).
7. The noisy sex occurs in the novel, while the porch scene occurs in Walker's adaptation for Steven Spielberg's movie version. I realize that they are not the same text; however, Walker is the author of the novel, screenplay, and of all the characters. Her vision of these

relationships is consistent. The screenplay, "Watch for me in the Sunset," is published in *The Same River Twice: Honoring the Difficult* (Scribner 1996) 91.

8. The categorization of Shug's sexuality is not required—that logic would ultimately undermine my claim to a queer analytics—to understand the character. I spend time reviewing terminology and models of nonmonogamous sexuality as a way to situate Walker's illustration within a broader cultural context and because the clarification of the function of a character's sexual expression is central to this project.
9. In Albert's house, Grady makes "goo-goo eyes at Squeak and Shug sorta tease him about it" (115) and in the passage in which Shug tells Celie about her affair with Germaine, she claims to be relieved that Grady finally "lit out after Mary Agnes" (249), which is Squeak's proper name.
10. For practitioners and ethnographers who discuss the importance of consent and open communication in polyamorous communities, see the work of Serena Anderlini-D'Onofrio, Elisabeth Sheff, and co-authors Dossie Easton and Janet Hardy.
11. L. H. Stallings introduced the use of the question mark in her explication of the Queen B(?) character as a way to signify and discuss the multiple uses of the trope and "to highlight the fluctuating position of this outlaw figure in African American culture" (170). The "B"-word in the phrase "Queen B(?)" can indicate bitch, bulldagger, or bee depending on context.
12. My assertion of a "Blues ministry" draws from the school of thought, primarily pursued in the 1970s, which asserts a theological essence of Blues music: James Cone, *The Spirituals and the Blues: An Interpretation* (New York: Seabury Press, 1972); Paul Oliver, *The Meaning of the Blues* (New York: Collier Books, 1966); William Ferris, *Blues from the Delta* (Garden City, NY: Anchor/Doubleday, 1979); Rod Gruver, "The Blues as Secular Religion," *Blues World* 29 (April 1970).
13. Celie narrates a church scene in which the preacher "take (Shug) condition for a text. He don't call no name but he don't have to. Everybody know who he mean" (43–44).
14. Phillips and Stewart define buffet flats as private parties, which featured an assortment of illegal activities, erotic shows, and sex acts (33).
15. Matthew 16:24; Mark 8:34; Luke 9:23.
16. Thank you, Darius Bost, for this particularly valuable critical insight.

CHAPTER FIVE

1. Depictions of interracial same-sex romance, especially those set in the 1970s and 1980s, are often wrought with tensions regarding racial solidarity and pride. Birtha's work on this topic was in conversation with many black women writers actively publishing at the time, including Pat Parker, Anne Allen Shockley, and Audre Lorde.
2. It is significant that Holiness/Pentecostal denominations were also scandalized by Jackson because they have a history of marginalization for some of the same reasons Jackson was being ostracized. Pentecostals were expelled from the black Baptist denomination at the turn of the twentieth century. Major factors for their expulsion from mainstream African American worship are the belief in glossolalia (the ability to speak an unknown language, presumed to be God's words spoken directly through the person via spiritual possession); as well as xenoglossy (also a gift of the Holy Spirit, which is the ability to speak in a foreign language without having previously learned it). They were also castigated for their belief in the laying of hands—the power to heal through physical touch—a practice that led to charges of paganism, heathenism and even heresy (Douglas Field, "Pentecostalism and all that Jazz: Tracing James Baldwin's Religion," 441).
3. Paul refers to Jesus as the "last Adam" in First Corinthians 15:45. "Second Adam" is a common—and contested—variation of this phrase. Paul's teachings also refer to Jesus as the "end of the law" in a manner that is interpreted to separate the Mosaic Law (Ten Commandments and book of Leviticus) from the teachings of Jesus (see Romans 10:3–5).
4. Shakers believe that Ann Lee (1736–1784) was the female counterpart to Jesus, meaning she was the second coming of Christ. She came to reveal that God is also feminine and that celibacy is preparation for God's holy kingdom. The religious instruction of the United Society of Believers in Christ's Second Appearing, their formal name, derives from "Mother Lee's" spiritual revelations.
5. I thank Charles Nero for sharing this insight regarding the queerness of asexuality and celibacy in a keynote address given at the Penn State University Celebration of Contemporary African American Literature on October 1, 2011. Nero expounds on this idea in his essay, "Queering The Souls of Black Folk: A Celebration of W.E.B. Du Bois. *Public Culture* 17.2 (Spring 2005): 255–276.

6. Jackson records her dissatisfaction with the Watervliet community's outreach to black people before creating the family in Philadelphia. Her missionary zeal was met with disapproval from the Shaker leadership and the Rebeccas' decision to exit was an act of rebellion. The black Shakers were initially an independent group, but Perot and Jackson were able to reconcile with the Watervliet family; and with reconciliation came economic support from the more established group (*Gifts of Power* 29–36).
7. Neo-slave narratives are modern or contemporary fictional works substantially concerned with depicting the experience or the effects of New World Slavery. They include historical novels set in the antebellum South and social or magical realist renditions set in later periods. The major unifying feature is that they represent slavery as an historical phenomenon that has lasting cultural meaning and enduring social consequences. *The Oxford Companion to African American Literature*, 533–534.
8. All citations for "In the Life" are from the anthology *Black Like Us: A Century of Lesbian, Gay and Bisexual African American Fiction*, 289–300.
9. Grace's femme aesthetic is established in earlier depictions of her night-on-the-town wear: silk dresses, fur stole, pearl necklace, long gloves, and so on.

CHAPTER SIX

1. Edwords' argument that modern secular and religious humanists ultimately share the same worldview and basic principles stems from the fact that both secular and religious humanists were among the signers of *Humanist Manifesto I* in 1933, *Humanist Manifesto II* in 1973, and *Humanist Manifesto III* in 2003. Their internal disagreements are not about the philosophy, but what it means in practice, and the definition of religion. Religious humanists, according to Edwords, define religion as any central life-guiding and life-organizing belief system. Their social lives, including rites of passage ceremonies, and educational, intellectual, and activist endeavors are framed by humanist thought. Conversely, secular humanists argue that religion is, universally, a theologically based worldview that atheists and agnostics, by definition, do not abide.
2. Donna Andreolle describes Earthseed as a "newfound Christianity" and Butler's rhetorical project as one that "reflects the validity

of Judeo-Christian values as the necessary ideological foundation of social order in the American foundation" ("Utopias of Old, Solutions for the New Millennium," *Utopia Studies* 2001); Jim Miller reads Olamina, somewhat contradictorily, as a Christ-figure who authors a religion yet which also "lacks pious self-sacrifice" ("Post-Apocalyptic Hoping," *Science Fiction Studies* 1998).

3. In an interview with Stephen Potts, Butler responds to critical misreadings: "I'm not too upset when they are factually wrong about some incident, which can happen to anybody, but I am when they are inaccurate about something sweeping. For example, somebody writing a review of *Parable of the Sower* said, 'Oh, the Earthseed religion is just warmed over Christianity,' and I thought this person could not have been troubled to read the Earthseed verses and just drew that conclusion from the title" ("We Keep Playing the Same Record." *Science Fiction Studies* 1996).
4. It is predicted that "they'll make a god of her" on the first page of *Talents*. In interviews, Butler had also revealed plans for additional titles in the series, which would extend the narrative into several generations beyond Olamina's death in an off-world (or off-Earth) setting. Unfortunately, Butler passed away before completing the series in 2006.
5. An antichrist is one whose beliefs are non-Christian and therefore considered heretical, as described in 1 John 2:18, 2:22, 4:3, and 2 John 7.
6. Aside from being a masculine name, Cory is Olamina's deceased stepmother's name; she states that she hopes her long-lost stepbrother may hear the name and interpret it as a signal that Olamina is alive.
7. Realness is also a barometer for a male-bodied person's performance of femininity. One has achieved true realness when the transition from "man" to "woman" is seamless in its presentation.
8. In *Female Masculinity*, Halberstam distinguishes between the roles and identities of drag kings, male impersonators, and drag butches. Not all male impersonators are lesbians but, in the case of drag kings and drag butches, a lesbian or dyke identity is central to their masculine aesthetic. Nonetheless, each category and purpose requires realness to be successful. Marlon Bailey, author of *Butch Queens Up in Pumps: Gender, Performance, and Ballroom Culture in Detroit* (University of Michigan 2013), has also done extensive work in realness in African American ballroom performance culture and its function as a survival strategy.

9. Although there is another definition of voyeurism as literary device, I limit my discussion to the psychoanalytic definition. These are the definitions supplied by the *Oxford English Dictionary* and *Diagnostic and Statistical Manual of Mental Disorders.* The novel creates the context for a medical paradigm with its sci-fi definition of her condition. I examine Butler's fictional medical diagnosis through the lens of sexuality studies and assert that Olamina's hyperempathy syndrome creates a *voyeuristic relationship* between her and anyone in her view who is experiencing any sexual sensation.
10. In *Discourse on Colonialism* (1955), Aime Cesaire challenges the "civilizing mission" of European colonization and identifies the ways in which Europeans objectified African cultures and people. In his famous formulation, "colonization = thingification" because, to construct their own sense of superiority, Europeans destroyed the history, cultures, and agency of non-Europeans. Otherwise, Europeans would have no justification for dominating the rest of the world. Cesaire further argues that colonialism caused the devolution of Europe as it progressively became savage in its treatment of colonized people. African American ex-slave narrators make similar assertions regarding the demoralization and dehumanization of white slave owners in their participation in a slavery-based society.
11. Phillips refers here to consensual sexual acts between trusting partners with established rules of engagement. I am interested here in the effects of Olamina's ability to absorb torturous pain and pleasure simultaneously as an aspect of her sexuality. My theory is based on the (bio)logical conclusion of the male partner's (rapist's) heterosexual encounter as it intersects with King's theory regarding the absorption and expenditure of pain from the black body (victim and empathizer): orgasm as tool of psychic and spiritual survival.
12. *Zami*, 100.
13. Butler mentions her pervasive disillusionment during the Reagan administration and the U.S. government's general malaise and apathy regarding global climate change in many of the interviews collected in *Conversations with Octavia Butler*. See 23, 128, 183, 200, 224.

CHAPTER SEVEN

1. Gomez published a short story collection, *Don't Explain*, in 1998. Her critical and personal essays have appeared in the *New York Village*

Voice, Essence, Callaloo, Black Scholar, and *Advocate*. To date, her works in progress include a comic novel, *Televised*, about black activists from the 1960s as they face middle age, and "Waiting for Giovanni" a play based on the life of James Baldwin. A second volume of *Gilda Stories* is also in the works; an excerpt appears in *Where We Sit: Black Writers Write Black Youth* (2011) edited by Victoria Brownworth.

2. In *Disidentifications: Queers of Color and the Performance of Politics*, Jose Esteban Munoz theorizes the disidentifying subject. He argues that in drag performances and comedy shows, minority subjects appropriate aspects of the oppressive dominant culture in ways that may appear self-negating but that are actually strategies of resistance and survival in a racist homophobic environment. I cite from his discussion in a chapter titled "Performing Disidentity: Disidentification as the Practice of Freedom," in which Munoz emphasizes the limits of such strategies in an emotionally and psychically dangerous environment.
3. Science fiction genres are traditionally xenophobic and tend to reinscribe narratives of colonization. See Octavia Butler's commentary on this trope in an interview with Stephen Potts entitled "We Keep Playing the Same Record" in *Science Fiction Studies* 23.3 (1996). The vampire tradition reflects European (and, later, white male American) anxieties regarding the seductive but contaminat-ed/-ing alien other who "looks like us but is not us." See Shannon Winnibst's essay "Vampires, Anxieties, and Dreams: Race and Sex in the Contemporary United States" for a roundup of critical perspectives on the topic. Also, sexual queerness is a normalized aspect of the vampire genre; mainly, the vampire is depicted as indiscriminate in choice of feeding/sexual partners. This is why Gomez's creation of a decidedly lesbian vampire sexuality is a departure from the random nature of earlier characterizations.
4. Vampires have the ability to "glamour" humans, which means to elicit blind obedience and/or to redact certain memories through mind control. Conventional wisdom interprets this attribute among the other superhuman powers vampires possess as a reflection of societal fear of colonization and loss of cultural identity.
5. Critics have noted that Kaplan theorizes a homoerotic desire when she argues that women writers desire women readers and invite those readers through sensual and erotic subtexts. I modify Kaplan's terminology to point out the overt expressions and depictions of same-sex

behavior. As I say further into the discussion, the ideal listener and lover is not just female in Gomez's novel, she is also lesbian.

6. The emphasis on loyalty to one's maker is a recent phenomenon in twentieth-century vampire literature. In *Dracula* (1897) Bram Stoker created the legend that his Dracula is the first vampire, made because he cursed God. His vampiric wives are at his command and he cared for them enough to show them how to survive. Recent authors, such as Ann Rice (*The Vampire Chronicles*) and Charlaine Harris (*The Southern Vampire Series*) emphasize this connectedness in a way that transformed the mythos so that one's relationship with one's maker is tantamount to blind faith. It is separate from the "glamouring" effect, which is a type of mind control. Octavia Butler also relies on this new mythological facet in *Fledgling* (2005). *Gilda Stories*, however, maintains the earlier tradition of connectedness without ownership.
7. This is not to suggest that women's activist organizations began in the 1960s. African American women have been organizing on their own behalf and on the behalf of universal freedom and citizenship in the United States since they were first enslaved.
8. See Linda Lumsden's research into the evolution of gender politics in the Black Panther Party as articulated in their weekly newspaper. "Good Mothers with Guns: Framing Black Womanhood in the *Black Panther*, 1968–1980," *Journalism and Mass Communications Quarterly* 86/4 (Winter 2009): 900–922.

Bibliography

Althaus-Reid, Marcella. *Indecent Theology: Theological Perversions in Sex, Gender and Politics*. London and New York: Routledge, 2000.

Anderlini-D'Onofrio, Serena. *Plural Loves: Designs for Bi and Poly Living*. Binghamton, NY: Haworth, 2004.

Andreolle, Donna. "Utopias of Old, Solutions for the New Millennium: A Comparative Study of Christian Fundamentalism" in M. K. Wren's *A Gift Upon the Shore* and Octavia Butler's *Parable of the Sower*." *Utopian Studies* 12.2 (2001): 114–124.

Andrews, William L. *To Tell A Free Story: The First Century of Afro-American Autobiography, 1760–1865*. Urbana and Chicago: University of Illinois Press, 1986.

Ashford, Tomeiko, R. "Marginal Black Feminist Religiosity: Ann Allen Shockley's Construction of the Divine Heroine in *Say Jesus and Come to Me*." *CLA Journal* 48.3 (March 2005): 290–307.

Baker-Fletcher, Karen. "The Erotic in Contemporary Black Women's Writings." In Pinn and Hopkins.

Bal, Mieke. *Lethal Love: Feminist Literary Readings of Biblical Love Stories.* Bloomington: Indiana University Press, 1987.

Baldwin, James. *Early Novels and Stories*. New York: Literary Classics of the United States, 1998.

———. *Giovanni's Room*. New York: Dell, 1956.

———. *Go Tell It on the Mountain*. New York: Doubleday, 1952.

———. *Just Above My Head*. New York: Dell, 1978.

———. *The Price of the Ticket: Collected Nonfiction 1948–1985*. New York: St. Martin's Press, 1985.

Barr, Marleen, ed. *Afro-Future Females: Black Writers Chart Science Fiction's Newest New-Wave Trajectory.* Columbus: Ohio State University Press, 2008.

Bassard, Katherine Clay. *Spiritual Interrogations: Culture, Gender & Community.* Princeton: Princeton University Press, 1999.

Beam, Joseph, ed. *In the Life: A Black Gay Anthology*. Boston: Alyson, 1986.

"Becky Birtha." *Contemporary Authors Online*. Accessed via Literature Resource Center at University of North Carolina Wilmington. Gale Cengage Learning, 2013.

Berlant, Lauren. "Race, Gender, and Nation in *The Color Purple*." *Critical Inquiry* Vol. 14, No. 4 (Summer 1988): 831–859.

Bernard, Emily, ed. *Remember Me to Harlem: The Letters of Langston Hughes and Carl Van Vechten, 1925–1964*. New York: Knopf, 2001.

Berry, Faith. "Breaking Silence: The Meaning of Biographical Truth." Appendix A. *Langston Hughes: Before and Beyond Harlem.* New York and Canada: Citadel Press, 1992, 359–367.

Birtha, Becky. *The Forbidden Poems*. Seattle: Seal Press, 1991.

———. *For Nights Like This One: Stories of Loving Women*. Palo Alto: Frog In the Well, 1983.

———. "In the Life." *Black Like Us: A Century of Gay, Lesbian and Bisexual African American Fiction,* edited by Devon W. Carbado et al. San Francisco: Cleis Press, 2002.

———. *Lover's Choice.* Seattle: Seal Press, 1987.

Blassingame, John Wesley. *The Slave Community: Plantation Life in the Antebellum South*. New York: Oxford University, 1972.

Bridgforth, Sharon. *love/conjure blues.* Washington, DC: RedBone Press, 2004.

Bould, Mark. "The Ships Landed Long Ago: Afrofuturism and Black SF." *Science Fiction Studies* 34.2 (2007): 177–186.

Brodie, Thomas L. *The Crucial Bridge: The Elijah-Elisha Narrative as Interpretive Synthesis of Genesis-Kings and a Literary Model for the Gospels*. Collegeville, MN: Liturgical Press, 2000.

Brown, Elaine. *A Taste of Power: A Black Woman's Story.* New York: Random House, 1992.

Brown, Laurinda. *Fire and Brimstone.* Bowie, MD: Strebor Books, 2002.

Burke, Kenneth. *The Rhetoric of Religion: Studies in Logology*. Boston: Beacon Press, 1961.

Butler, Judith. *Excitable Speech: A Politics of the Performative*. New York: Routledge, 1997.

Butler, Octavia. *Parable of the Sower*. New York: Grand Central, 1993.

———. *Parable of the Talents*. New York: Warner Books, 1998.

Calhoun-Brown, Allison. "No Respecter of Persons? Religion, Churches and Gender Issues in the African American Community." *Women and Politics* 20.3 (Summer 1999): 27–44.

Call, Lewis. "Structures of Desire: Erotic Power in the Speculative Fiction of Octavia Butler and Samuel Delany." *Rethinking History* 9.2/3 (June/September 2005): 275–296.

Campbell, James. *Talking at the Gates: A Life of James Baldwin*. New York: Penguin Group, 1991.

Cannon, Katie G. "Sexing Black Women: Liberation for the Prisonhouse of Anatomical Authority." In Pinn and Hopkins.

Clarke, Cheryl. *The Days of Good Looks: The Prose and Poetry of Cheryl Clarke 1980–2005*. New York: Carroll & Graf, 2006.

Cobb, Michael. *God Hates Fags: The Rhetorics of Religious Violence*. New York: New York University Press, 2006.

———. "Pulptic Publicity: James Baldwin and the Queer Uses of Religious Words." *Journal of Gay and Lesbian Studies* 7.2 (2001): 285–312.

Cohen, Cathy J. *The Boundaries of Blackness: AIDS and the Breakdown of Black Politics*. Chicago: University of Chicago Press, 1999.

———. "Deviance as Resistance: A New Research Agenda for the Study of Black Politics." *Du Bois Review* 1.1 (2004): 27–45.

———. "Punks, Bulldaggers, and Welfare Queens: The Radical Potential of Queer Politics?" *Gay & Lesbian Quarterly: A Journal of Lesbian and Gay Studies*, Vol. 3, No. 4 (May 1997): 437–465.

Cole, Johnetta Betsch, and Beverly Guy-Sheftall. *Gender Talk: The Struggle for Women's Equality in African-American Communities*. New York: Ballantine, 2003.

Coleman, James W. *Faithful Vision: Treatments of the Sacred, Spiritual, and Supernatural in Twentieth-Century African American Fiction*. Baton Rouge: Louisiana State University Press, 2006.

Conrad, Linda. "Religion and Social Change: The Fiction of Flannery O'Conner and Alice Walker." *Social Alternatives* 7.3 (1988): 21–25.

Constantine-Simms, Delroy, ed. *The Greatest Taboo: Homosexuality in Black Communities*. New York: Alyson, 2001.

Cooper-Lewter, Nicholas C. *Soul Theology: The Heart of American Black Culture.* San Francisco: Harper & Row, 1986.

Crow, Charlotte. "The Cult of Beauty: The Aesthetic Movement 1860–1900." *History Today* March 24, 2011. www.historytoday.com

Curtis, Claire P. "Theorizing Fear: Octavia Butler and the Realist Utopia." *Utopian Studies* 19.3 (2008): 411–431.

Dandridge, Rita B. "Review: Shockley, The Iconoclast." *Callaloo* 22 (Autumn 1984): 160–164.

Davis, Angela Y. *Blues Legacies and Black Feminism: Gertrude "Ma" Rainey, Bessie Smith, and Billie Holiday*. New York: Pantheon Books, 1998.

De La Croix, St. Sukie. *Chicago Whispers: A History of LGBT Chicago before Stonewall*. Madison: University of Wisconsin, 2012.

Delany, Samuel. *Tales of Neveryon.* Middletown, CT: Wesleyan University, 1993.

Dery, Mark. "Black to the Future: Interviews with Samuel R. Delany, Greg Tate, and Tricia Rose." In *Flame Wars: The Discourse of Cyberculture*, edited by Dery. Durham, NC: Duke University, 1994.

Dias, Stephan Lee. "Don't Turn Your Back On Me." In Beam.

Douglas, Kelly Brown. *Sexuality and the Black Church: A Womanist Perspective*. Maryknoll, NY: Orbis Books, 2003.

Douglas-Chin, Richard J. *Preacher Woman Sings the Blues: The Autobiographies of Nineteenth-Century African American Evangelists.* Columbia: University of Missouri Press, 2001.

Dyson, Michael Eric. *Race Rules: Navigating the Color Line*. New York: Random House, 1996.

Easton, Dossie, and Janet Hardy. *The Ethical Slut: A Practical Guide to Polyamory, Open Relationships, and Other Adventures*. Berkeley, CA: Celestial Arts, 2009.

Edelman, Lee. *Homographesis: Essays in Gay Literary and Cultural Theory*. New York: Routledge, 1994.

Edwords, Fred. "What is Humanism?" *American Humanist Association*. www.americanhumanist.org

Field, Douglas. "Pentecostalism and All That Jazz: Tracing James Baldwin's Religion." *Literature & Theology* 22.4 (December 2008): 436–457.

Francis, Consuela, ed. *Conversations with Octavia Butler*. Jackson: University Press of Mississippi, 2010.

Frontain, Raymond-Jean. "Baldwin's 'The Outing' and the Sacral Quality of Male Love."*Journal of the Short Story in English* 30 (Spring 1998). www.jsse.revues.org/73

———. Editor. *Reclaiming the Sacred: The Bible in Gay and Lesbian Culture* 2nd edition. Binghamton, NY: Harrington Park Press, 2003.

Gates, Henry Louis Jr., and Nellie McKay, eds. *Norton Anthology of African American Literature* 2nd edition. New York: Norton, 2004.

Gilkes, Cheryl Townsend. "'A Connection to All That Is': *The Color Purple* as Subversive and Critical Ethnography." *Embracing the Spirit: Womanist Perspectives on Hope, Salvation and Transformation,* edited by Emilie M. Townes. Maryknoll, NY: Orbis Books, 1997.

Goldberg, Michael Lewis. *Definition: Queer Theory*. Department of Interdisciplinary Arts & Sciences, University of Washington Bothell. n.p., n.d.

Goldman, Ruth. "Who Is that Queer Queer? Exploring Norms around Sexuality, Race, and Class in Queer Theory." In *Queer Cultures*, edited by Deborah Carlin. Upper Saddle River, NJ: Pearson, 2004.

Gomez, Jewelle. *The Gilda Stories and Bones & Ash*. Quality Paperback Book Club Edition, Bookspan, 2001.

———. Rev. of *Celebrating Hotchclaw*, by Ann Allen Shockley. *Lambda Book Report* (Spring 2006): 10.

Goss, Robert. "Queer Theologies as Transgressive Metaphors: New Paradigms for Hybrid Sexual Theologies." *Theology & Sexuality* 10 (March 1999): 43–54.

"Grandmama's Pride." *Kirkus Reviews* 73.22 (11/15/2005). www.kirkusreviews.com

Griffin, Horace L. *Their Own Received Them Not: African American Gays and Lesbians in Black Churches*. Cleveland, OH: Pilgrim, 2006.

Halberstam, Judith. "Between Butches." In Munt.

———. *Female Masculinity.* Durham and London: Duke University Press, 1998.

Hall, Stuart. "Cultural Identity and Diaspora." *Colonial Discourse and Post-Colonial Theory: A Reader*, edited by Patrick Williams and Chrisman. London: Harvester Wheatsheaf, 1994, 392–401.

Hampton, Gregory J. "Vampires and Utopia: Reading Racial and Gender Politics in the Fiction of Octavia Butler." *CLA Journal* 52.1 (September 2008): 74–91.

Hankinson, Stacie Lynn. "From Monotheism to Pantheism: Liberation from Patriarchy in Alice Walker's *The Color Purple*." *Midwest Quarterly* Vol. 38, No. 3 (Spring 1997): 320–328.

Hardy, Clarence E. *James Baldwin's God: Sex, Hope, and Crisis in Black Holiness Culture*. Knoxville: University of Tennessee, 2000.

Haritaworn, Jin, Chin-ju Lin and Christian Kleese. "Poly/logue: A Critical Introduction to Polyamory." *Sexualities* Vol. 9, No. 5 (December 2006): 515–529.

Harraway, Donna. *Simians, Cyborgs, and Women: The Reinvention of Nature.* New York: Routledge, 1991.

Harris, Craig G. "Cut Off from Among Their People." In Beam.

Harris, E. Lynn. *Invisible Life.* New York: Anchor Books, 1994.

Harris, Trudier. *Black Women in the Fiction of James Baldwin.* Knoxville: University of Tennessee Press, 1985.

Hemphill, Essex, ed. *Brother to Brother: New Writings by Black Gay Men.* Boston: Alyson, 1991.

Henderson, Mae Gwendolyn. "Speaking in Tongues: Dialogics, Dialectics, and the Black Woman Writer's Literary Tradition." In *African American Literary Theory: A Reader*, edited by Winston Napier. New York: New York University, 2000.

Hinson, Glenn. *Fire in My Bones: Transcendence and the Holy Spirit in African American Gospel.* Philadelphia: University of Pennsylvania Press, 2000.

hooks, bell. *Talking Back: Thinking Feminist, Thinking Black.* Boston: South End Press, 1989.

———. *Yearning: Race: Gender, and Cultural Politics.* Boston: South End Press, 1990.

Hopkins, Dwight N. *Introducing Black Theology of Liberation.* Maryknoll, NY: Orbis Books, 1999.

Hughes, Langston. "Blessed Assurance." In *Black Like Us: A Century of Lesbian, Gay and Bisexual African American Fiction*, edited by Devon W. Carbado, Dwight A. McBride, and Donald Weise. San Francisco: Cleis Press, 2002.

———. *The Collected Works of Langston Hughes Volume 6: Gospel Plays, Operas, and Later Dramatics,* edited by Leslie Sanders. Columbia: University of Missouri, 2004.

Hull, Akasha Gloria. *Soul Talk: The New Spirituality of African American Women.* Rochester,VT: Inner Traditions International, 2001.

Humez, Jean M. "In Search of Harriet Tubman's Spiritual Autobiography." *NWSA Journal* 5.2 (Summer 1993): 162–182.

———. "Introduction." In *Gifts of Power: The Writings of Rebecca Jackson, Black Visionary, Shaker Eldress*, edited by Humez. Amherst: University of Massachusetts, 1981.

Hunt, V. "A Conversation with Randall Kenan." *African American Review* 29.3 (Fall 1995): 411–420.

Hurston, Zora Neale. *Their Eyes Were Watching God.* New York: Harper & Row, 1937.

Jabir, Jahari. "Preachers and Punks, Sissies and Saints: Constructions of Black Religious Masculinity in the Climactic Moment of Black Worship." In *Summary Report of the Second National Conference of the African American Roundtable: Souls A'Fire 2.* Project of the Center for Lesbian and Gay Studies in Religion and Ministry at Pacific School of Religion: June 23–25, 2005, Chicago, Illinois.

Jackson, Rebecca Cox. *Gifts of Power: The Writings of Rebecca Jackson, Black Visionary, Shaker Eldress*, edited by Jean McMahon Humez. Amherst: University of Massachusetts, 1981.

Jacobs, Harriet. *Incidents in the Life of a Slave Girl.* New York: Oxford University, 1988.

"James S. Tinney." *Lesbian, Gay, Bisexual and Transgender Religious Archives.* www.lgbtran.org

"Jewel Gomez." *Encyclopedia of Contemporary LGBTQ Literature of the United States.* Santa Barbara, CA: Greenwood Press, 2009.

Johnson, E. Patrick. *Appropriating Blackness: Performance and the Politics of Authenticity.* Durham: Duke University Press, 2002.

———. "Feeling the Spirit in the Dark." In *The Greatest Taboo: Homosexuality in Black Communities,* edited by Delroy Constantine-Simms. Los Angeles and New York: Alyson Books, 2000.

Johnson, Judith. "Women and Vampires: Nightmare or Utopia?" *Kenyon Review* 15 (Winter 1993): 72–80.

Jordan, June. "A New Politics of Sexuality." *Progressive* 55.7 (July 1991): 12–14.

Kaganoff, Penny. Rev. of *The Forbidden Poems. Publishers Weekly* 238.6 (1991): 77.

Kanner, Melinda. "Toward a Semiotics of Butch." *The Gay & Lesbian Review* (March/April 2002): 27–29.

Kaplan, Karla. *Erotics of Talk: Women's Writing and Feminist Paradigms.* New York and Oxford: Oxford University Press, 1996.

King, Debra Walker. *African Americans and the Culture of Pain.* Charlottesville: University of Virginia Press, 2008.

Kirk-Duggan, Cheryl A. "Salome's Veiled Dance and David's Full Monty: A Womanist Reading on the Black Erotic in Blues, Rap, R&B, and Gospel Blues." In *Loving the Body: Black Religious Studies and the Erotic*, edited by Anthony Pinn and Dwight Hopkins. New York: Palgrave McMillan, 2004.

Kurtz, Paul. In *Defense of Secular Humanism*. Buffalo, NY: Prometheus Books, 1983.

Larsen, Nella. *The Complete Fiction of Nella Larsen: Passing, Quicksand and the Stories.* New York: Anchor Books, 2001.

Lauret, Maria. *Alice Walker*. Modern Novelists Series, edited by Norman Page. New York: St. Martin's Press, 2000.

Lawal, Babatunde. "The Living Dead: Art and Immortality among the Yoruba of Nigeria." *Africa: Journal of the International African Institute* 47.1 (1977): 50–61.

Levine, Lawrence W. *Black Culture and Black Consciousness: Afro-American Folk Thought from Slavery to Freedom*. New York: Oxford University, 1987.

Lincoln, C. Eric, and Lawrence H. Mamiya. *The Black Church in the African-American Experience.* Durham and London: Duke University Press, 1990.

Lorde, Audre. *Sister/Outsider*. Freedom, CA: Crossing Press, 1984.

———. *Zami: A New Spelling of My Name*. Freedom, CA: Crossing Press, 1982.

Loughlin, Gerard. "What Is Queer? Theology after Identity." *Theology and Sexuality* 14.2 (2008): 143–152.

"love/conjure blues." *New Dramatists: Dedicated to the Playwrights*. Studio Holling & Q Collective. N.d. www.newdramatists.org

Mahalia Jackson: The Power and the Glory. Produced by Sheftel Taylor Productions. DVD. Santa Monica, CA: Xenon Pictures, 2002.

Majors, Richard, and Janet Mancini Billson. *Cool Pose: The Dilemmas of Black Manhood in America*. New York: Simon & Schuster, 1992.

Maltz, Robin. "Real Butch: The Performance/Performativity of Male Impersonation, Drag Kings, Passing as Male, and Stone Butch Realness." *Journal of Gender Studies* 7.3 (1998): 273–286.

Mbiti, John. *New Testament Eschatology in an African Background*. New York: Oxford University, 1971.

McBride, Dwight. "Can the Queen Speak? Racial Essentialism, Sexuality and the Problem of Authority." *Callaloo* 21.2 (1998): 363–379.

McDowell, Deborah E. *The Changing Same: Black Women's Literature, Criticism, and Theory*. Bloomington: Indiana University, 1995.

McNeir, D. Kevin. "OUT at CHM: Gays and Gospel." *Windy City Media Group.* May 1, 2006. www.windycitymediagroup.com

Meeker, Martin. "Behind the Mask of Respectability: Reconsidering the Mattachine Society and Male Homophile Practice, 1950s and 1960s." *Journal of the History of Sexuality* 10.1 (January 2001): 78–116.

Meese, Elizabeth, A. *(Sem)Erotics: Theorizing Lesbian: Writing*. New York and London: New York University Press, 1992.

Mehaffy, Marilyn, and AnaLouise Keating with Octavia Butler. "Radio Imagination: Octavia Butler on the Poetics of Narrative Embodiment." *MELUS* 26.1 (Spring 2001): 45–76.

Melancon, Trimiko C. "Toward an Aesthetic of Transgression: Ann Allen Shockley's *Loving Her* and the Politics of Same-Gender Loving." *African American Review* 42.3–4 (Fall/Winter 2008): 643–657.

Metzl, Jonathan M. "From Scopophilia to Survivor: A Brief History of Voyeurism." *Textual Practice* 18.3 (2004): 415–434.

Miller, Jim. "Post-Apocalyptic Hoping: Octavia Butler's Dystopian/Utopian Vision." *Science Fiction Studies* 25.2 (1998): 336–360. *Academic Search Premier*. EBSCO.

Miyakawa, Felicia M. "'Jazz at Night and Classics in the Morning': Musical Double-Consciousness in Short Fiction by Langston Hughes." *Popular Music* 24.2 (2005): 273–278.

Moody, Joycelyn. *Sentimental Confessions: Spiritual Narratives of Nineteenth-Century African American Women.* Athens and London: University of Georgia Press, 2001.

Morrison, Toni. "Rootedness: The Ancestor as Foundation." *Black Women Writers (1950–1980) A Critical Evaluation*, edited by Mari Evans. New York: Anchor/Doubleday, 1984, 339–345.

———. *Sula.* Vintage International Edition. Introduction by Morrison. New York: Vintage Books, 2002.

Mullen, Harryette. "African Signs and Spirit Writing" in Napier, 623–642.

Munoz, Jose Esteban. *Disidentifications: Queers of Color and the Performance of Politics*. Minneapolis: University of Minnesota Press, 1999.

Munt, Sally R., ed. *Butch/femme: Inside Lesbian Gender.* London and Washington: Cassell, 1998.

Napier, Winston, ed. *African American Literary Theory: A Reader*. New York and London: New York University Press, 2000.

Nero, Charles. Rev. of *Gay Rebel of the Harlem Renaissance: Selections from the Work of Richard Bruce Nugent*, edited by Thomas H. Wirth. In *Journal of the History of Sexuality* 12.4 (October 2003): 672–676.

———. "Toward a Black Gay Aesthetic: Signifying in Black Gay Literature." In Hemphill.

Newton, Huey P. *The Huey P. Newton Reader,* edited by David Hilliard and Donald Weise. New York: Seven Stories Press, 2002.

Nilges, Mathias. "'We Need the Stars': Change, Community, and the

Absent Father in Octavia Butler's *Parable of the Sower* and *Parable of the Talents*." *Callaloo* 32.4 (2009): 1332–1352.

Nugent, Richard Bruce. *Gay Rebel of the Harlem Renaissance: Selections from the Work of Richard Bruce Nugent*, edited by Thomas Wirth. Durham, NC: Duke University, 2002.

O'Brien, John. "Alice Walker: An Interview." *Alice Walker: Critical Perspectives Past and Present.* Amistad Literary Series, edited by Henry Louis Gates Jr., and K. A. Appiah. New York: Amistad Press, 1993.

Paris, Peter J. *The Spirituality of African Peoples: The Search for a Common Moral Discourse*. Minneapolis, MN: Fortress Press, 1995.

Parker, Pat. *Movement in Black: The Collected Poetry of Pat Parker 1961–1978*. Ithaca, NY: Firebrand Books, 1978.

Phillips, Anita. *A Defense of Masochism*. New York: St. Martin's Press, 1998.

Phillips, Jerry. "The Intuition of the Future: Utopia and Catastrophe in Octavia Butler's *Parable of the Sower*." In *Novel: A Forum on Fiction* 35.2/3 (2002): 299–311.

Phillips, Layli, and Marla R. Stewart. "Nontraditional, Nonconforming, and Transgressive Gender Expression and Relationship Modalities in Black Communities." In *Black Sexualities: Probing Powers, Passions, Practices, and Policies*, edited by Juan Battle and Sandra L. Barnes. New Brunswick, NJ: Rutgers University, 2010.

Pinn, Anthony. "Anybody There? Some Reflections on African American Humanism." *Religious Humanism Journal* Vol. 31, No. 3 (1997). The Unitarian Universalist Humanist Association. www.huumanists.org/publications [sic]

———. *The End of God-Talk: An African American Humanist Theology*. New York: Oxford University, 2012.

Pinn, Anthony B., and Dwight N. Hopkins, eds. *Loving the Black Body: Black Religious Studies and the Erotic*. New York: Palgrave Macmillan, 2004.

Potts, Stephen W., and Octavia E. Butler. "We Keep Playing the Same Record: A Conversation with Octavia Butler." *Science Fiction Studies* 23.3 (November 1996): 331–338.

Quashie, Kevin Everod. *Black Women, Identity, and Cultural Theory: (un)becoming the subject*. New Brunswick, NJ: Rutgers University, 2004.

Rahming, Melvin B. "Reading Spirit: Cosmological Considerations in Garfield's *Linton's Voodoomation: A Book of Foretelling*." *Caribbean Vistas*

Journal: Critiques of Caribbean Arts and Cultures 1.1 (April 2013). www.caribbeanvistas.wordpress.com

———. "Theorizing Spirit: The Critical Challenge of Elizabeth Nunez's *When Rocks Dance* and *Beyond the Limbo Silence*." *Studies in the Literary Imagination* 37.2 (Fall 2004).

Ramirez, Catherine S. "Cyborg Feminism: The Science Fiction of Octavia E. Butler and Gloria Anzaldua." In *Reload: Rethinking Women + Cyberculture*, edited by Mary Flanagan and Austin Booth. Cambridge (MA) and London: Massachusetts Institute of Technology Press, 2002, 374–402.

Rampersad, Arnold. Forward. *Gentleman Jigger*. By Richard Bruce Nugent. Philadelphia: De Capo Press, 2002.

———. Introduction. *The Big Sea.* By Langston Hughes. New York: Hill and Wang, 1993.

———. *The Life of Langston Hughes Volume II: 1941–1967 I Dream A World*. Second Edition. New York: Oxford University Press, 2002.

Rawls, Tonyia M. "Yes, Jesus Loves Me: The Liberating Power of Spiritual Acceptance for Black Lesbian, Gay, Bisexual, and Transgender Christians." *Black Sexualities: Probing Powers, Passions, Practices, and Policies*, edited by Juan Battle and Sandra L. Barnes. New Brunswick, NJ: Rutgers University Press, 2010.

Razak, Arisika. "Her Blue Body: A Pagan Reading of Alice Walker Womanism." *Feminist Theology* 18.1 (2009): 92–116.

Reid-Pharr, Robert. "A Child's Life." *Black Gay Man: Essays*, edited by Reid-Pharr and Samuel Delaney. New York: New York University Press, 2001.

Romanet, Jerome. "Revisiting Madeleine and 'The Outing': James Baldwin's Revision of Gide's Sexual Politics." *MELUS* 22.1 (Spring 1997): 3–14.

Roof, Judith. *A Lure of Knowledge: Lesbian Sexuality and Theory*. New York: Columbia University Press, 1991.

Russell, Danielle. "Homeward Bound: Transformative Spaces in *The Color Purple*." In *Dialogue: Alice Walker's* The Color Purple. New York: Rodopi, 2009.

Ryan, Judylyn. *Spirituality as Ideology in Black Women's Literature and Film.* Charlottesville and London: University of Virginia Press, 2005.

Sanders, Leslie. Edited and Introduction. *The Collected Works of Langston Hughes Volume 6: Gospel Plays, Operas, and Later Dramatics*. Columbia: University of Missouri, 2004.

Scott, Lynn Orilla. *James Baldwin's Later Fiction: Witness to the Journey*. East Lansing: Michigan State University Press, 2002.

Sekou, Osagyefo Uhuru. "Queering Democracy and Christianity." *Feminist Wire* (July 7, 2011). www.thefeministwire.com

Sheff, Elisabeth. "Polyamorous Women, Sexual Subjectivity and Power." *Journal of Contemporary Ethnography* Vol. 34, No. 3 (June 2005): 251–283.

Shockley, Ann Allen. *Say Jesus and Come to Me.* Tallahassee, FL: Naid Press, 1987.

Silberman, Seth Clark. "'Youse Awful Queer, Chappie': Reading Black Queer Vernacular in Black Literatures of the Americas, 1903–1967. Diss. University of Maryland, 2005.

Simawe, Saadi A., ed. *Black Orpheus: Music in African American Fiction from the Harlem Renaissance to Toni Morrison.* New York: Garland, 2000.

Simcikova, Karla. *To Live Fully, Here and Now: The Healing Vision in the Works of Alice Walker*. Lanham, MD: Lexington Books, 2007.

Smith, Barbara, ed. *Home Girls: A Black Feminist Anthology*. New Brunswick and London: Rutgers University Press, 1983.

———. *The Truth that Never Hurts: Writings on Race, Gender, and Freedom.* New Brunswick and London: Rutgers University Press, 1998.

Smith, Max C. "By the Year 2000." In Beam.

Smitherman, Geneva. *Talkin that Talk: Language, Culture, and Education in African America*. London and New York: Routledge, 2000.

Smyth, Cherry. "Excerpts from Lesbians Talk Queer Notions." In *Queer Cultures*, edited by Deborah Carlin. Upper Saddle River, NJ: Pearson, 2004.

Sneed, Roger A. "Like Fire Shut up in Our Bones: Religion and Spirituality in Black Gay Literature." *Black Theology* 6.2 (May 2008): 241–261.

Spencer, Jon Michael. *Protest & Praise: Sacred Music of Black Religion*. Minneapolis, MN: Fortress Press, 1990.

Spillers, Hortense. "Imaginative Encounters." In Barr 3–5.

Stallings, L. H. *Mutha Is Half a Word: Intersections of Folklore, Vernacular, Myth, and Queerness in Black Female Culture.* Columbus: Ohio State Press, 2007.

———. "Re-Reading Ann Allen Shockley through Queer Queen B Eyes." *Obsidian III: Literature in the African Diaspora* 4.2 (Fall/Winter 2002–2003): 61–89.

Standley, Fred L., and Louis H. Pratt, eds. *Conversations with James Baldwin.* Jackson: University of Mississippi, 1989.

Stillman, Peter G. "Dystopian Critiques, Utopian Possibilities and Human Purposes in Octavia Bulter's Parables." *Utopian Studies* 14.1 (2003): 15–35.

Storr, Merl. "Epistemologies of the Fence." *Bisexuality: A Critical Reader.* New York: Routledge, 1999.

Streeter, Caroline. "Was Your Mama Mulatto? Notes toward a Theory of Racialized Sexuality in Gayl Jones's Corregidora and Julie Dash's Daughters of the Dust." *Callaloo* 27.3 (2004): 768–787.

Sweasey, Peter. *From Queer to Eternity: Spirituality in the Lives of Lesbian, Gay & Bisexual People.* London: Cassell, 1997.

Thomas, Sheree R., ed. *Dark Matter: A Century of Speculative Fiction from the African Diaspora.* New York: Warner Books, 2000.

Tinney, James S. "Why A Gay Black Church?" In Beam.

Valkeakari, Tuire. *Religious Idiom and the African American Novel, 1952–1998.* Gainesville: University of Florida, 2007.

Vogel, Shane. "Closing Time and the Queer Poetics of Harlem Nightlife." *Criticism* 48.3 (Summer 2006): 397–425.

Walker, Alice. *Anything We Love Can Be Saved: A Writer's Activism.* New York: Ballantine Books, 1997.

———. *By the Light of my Father's Smile.* New York: Random House, 1998.

———. *The Color Purple.* New York: Harcourt, 1982.

———. *Living By the Word: Selected Writings 1973–1987.* San Diego, CA: Harcourt Brace Jovanovich, 1988.

———. *Possessing the Secret of Joy.* Orlando, FL: Harcourt Brace Jovanovich, 1992.

———. *The Same River Twice: Honoring the Difficult.* New York: Scribner, 1996.

Wallace, Michelle. *Black Macho and the Myth of the Superwoman.* Brooklyn, NY: Verso Classics, 1999.

Washington, Robert E. *The Ideologies of African American Literature: From the Harlem Renaissance to the Black Nationalist Revolt.* Lanham, MD: Rowman & Littlefield, 2001.

Wasserman, Jerry. "Queen Bee, King Bee: *The Color Purple* and the Blues." *Canadian Review of American Studies* Vol. 30, No. 3 (2000): 301–316.

Webster, Lisa. "Gay Black Church: An Interview with Bishop Yvette Flunder." *Religion Dispatches* (September 30, 2010). www.religiondispatches.org

Weir-Soley, Donna Aza. *Eroticism, Spirituality, and Resistance in Black Women's Writings*. Gainesville: University Press of Florida, 2009.

Wekker, Gloria. "Mati-ism and Black Lesbianism: Two Idealtypical Expressions of Female Homosexuality in Black Communities of the Diaspora." *Journal of Lesbian Studies* Vol. 1, No. 1 (1996): 11–24.

Wilmore, Gayraud, ed. *African American Religious Studies: An Interdisciplinary Anthology*. Durham, NC: University Press of Duke, 1989.

Winnibst, Shannon. "Vampires, Anxieties, and Dreams: Race and Sex in Contemporary United States." *Hypatia* 18.3 (Summer 2003): 1–20.

Index